SOCIAL SCIENCE PERSPECTIVES ON CITIZENSHIP EDUCATION

SOCIAL SCIENCE PERSPECTIVES ON CITIZENSHIP EDUCATION

RICHARD E. GROSS
THOMAS L. DYNNESON
Editors

Teachers College, Columbia University
New York and London

Published by Teachers College Press, 1234 Amsterdam Avenue
New York, NY 10027

Library of Congress Cataloging-in-Publication Data

Social science perspectives on citizenship education / Richard E.
    Gross, Thomas L. Dynneson, editors.
        p.   cm.
    Includes bibliographical references and index.
    ISBN 0-8077-3052-1 (alk. paper) : $40.95. — ISBN 0-8077-3051-3
(alk. paper) : $20.95
    1. Civics—Study and teaching.   2. Social sciences—Study and
teaching.   I. Gross, Richard E.   II. Dynneson, Thomas L.
H62.S722   1990
320.4—dc20   90-46620

ISBN 0-8077-3052-1
ISBN 0-8077-3051-3

Printed on acid-free paper

Manufactured in the United States of America

98 97 96 95 94 93 92 91   8 7 6 5 4 3 2 1

Contents

Introduction

Today, throughout our nation, there exists a deep concern over "good citizenship"—whatever that may mean. As one peruses the lists of scholarly references that follow each chapter of this volume, and which contain many works from the last decade, there is clear evidence of the broad spectrum of individuals and organizations who desire substantial improvement in citizenship. Often, from parents and teachers to legislative bodies and national commissions, we find grievances, pleas, and prescriptions calling for the rebirth of vital sociocivic qualities in our youth. This situation reflects, in part, what our own initial research in this area has revealed: that in recent years, citizenship education has not really been taken seriously by the schools and/or has been promoted by ineffective means. This condition has existed in spite of the substantial lip service that is commonly given to citizenship education by teachers and administrators.

An immediate challenge presents itself to anyone trying to attend to the claims, arguments, and remedies offered concerning civic education. Clearly citizenship has numerous meanings and facets, so many in fact that it seems to defy definition. This problem is magnified, for example, when one compares the overall goals of schooling with those stated for citizenship education. This duplication is even more evident when one examines the typical aims listed for the social studies curriculum. The implications of this situation and the need to gain agreement on a more precise understanding of citizenship education are examined in the first chapter of this volume.

For almost a decade, the editors of this volume and the authors of Chapter 1 have been carrying on research and writing concerning various phases of citizenship education. Our attempts have included making definitional suggestions designed to improve the focus of citizenship education in a manageable sociocivics arena, as well as exploring the possibility of organizing civic education and learning procedures in terms of the maturing developmental needs and tasks of children and youth. We are also seeking to ascertain current attitudes of teachers, administrators, parents, and students about various phases of citizenship and civic education. Our Citizenship Development Study Project looks forward to eventually helping resolve some of the issues now compounding attempts to improve citizenship education.

Early in our examination of the field, we came to the conclusion that a somewhat more precise definition of citizenship education was in order. Also, we felt that such education might best concentrate on the sociocivic knowledge, competencies, and attitudes that can be provided particularly by the social science disciplines and history, which are the normal mainsprings of citizenship education in the schools. While history is not among the social sciences, at least in the accepted view as to their basic objective approaches, in the schools history is the major carrier of sociocivic learning. Philosophy is also not a social science, but the humanistic studies throw valuable light on the area of citizenship and its rights and responsibilities. Out of these subjects come particularly important facts, values, and skills that contribute to the development of an understanding, humane, and committed citizen.

We decided to approach specialists in these academic fields to help us with our inquiries, and this provided the genesis of this volume. Each chapter examines a single disciplinary area and includes treatment of the following:

- A review of the definitional issues according to each social science area,
- An exploration of the concepts and ideologies of citizenship pertaining to each discipline,
- A descriptive narrative of background issues and trends of citizenship within each area of specialization,
- A review of critical issues and problems associated with citizenship in each subject field,
- The development of a set of recommendations designed to improve the conditions of citizenship in the United States and similar free nations.

While each author's approach is individualized, taken together, we anticipate that these analyses and presentations will provide guidance to curriculum planners, teachers, textbook authors, and others concerned with citizenship education. Each chapter suggests emphases and selections that should characterize these subjects and the social studies in the schools. This should help insure a sound focus as well as indicate prime content for more vital and effective programs of civic education for the youth of free nations. Such programs will contribute to the seven major goals of citizenship education, which we identify in the manifesto at the conclusion of Chapter 1.

In the first chapter, we draw on the research findings of our Citizenship Development Study Project. We discuss the definition of citizenship education, the dilemma of different interpretations, and overlapping and contrary goals as well as the severe challenges to civic education in our culture and environment. We then summarize some of the more striking findings of our initial examinations of the attitudes concerning and the conditions of citizenship education in the schools of the four states that we sampled initially. The chapter concludes with suggestions for the revitalization of citizenship education.

In Chapter 2, Robert B. Woyach of the Mershon Center at Ohio State University treats the subject from the perspective of political science. In Chapter 3, Kerry J. Kennedy of the University College of Southern Queensland, Australia views the contributions of history. In Chapter 4, Ronald A. Banaszak of the Foundation for Teaching Economics examines economic literacy and citizenship. In Chapter 5, Nicholas Helburn of the University of Colorado looks at the role of geography. In Chapter 6, Philip Wexler, Raymond R. Grosshans, Qiao Hong Zhang, and Byoung-Uk Kim of the University of Rochester examine the cultural elements related to sociology. In Chapter 7, Allan Brandhorst of the University of North Carolina examines the contexts and processes related to social psychology. In Chapter 8, John H. Chilcott of the University of Arizona explores the anthropological insights. In Chapter 9, H. Michael Hartoonian of the Wisconsin Department of Public Instruction examines citizenship and philosophy. In Chapter 10, Andrew F. Smith, President of the American Forum for Global Education, presents the emerging international perspectives of citizenship. We wish to thank each of these scholars for their thoughtful contributions in underscoring what their disciplines offer to education for democratic citizenship. We are also indebted to President Duane M. Leach of the University of Texas of the Permian Basin, for his support of this effort, as well as to Editors Ron Galbraith and Nina George of Teachers College Press, Columbia University.

We are now in the second era of major concerns about citizenship education that have characterized this nation over the past 40 years following the end of World War II. Just previous to that era the Educational Policies Commission, the National Education Association, and the American Association of School Administrators sponsored a valuable case book in civic education, entitled *Learning the Ways of Democ-*

racy (1940), resulting from visits to 90 American schools. The movement culminated in a volume published by the National Council for the Social Studies (1967), *Promising Practices in Civic Education*, a report from a team of educators that examined 83 schools in 27 states. Sandwiched between these publications was a profusion of civic education projects and reports. Some of these were substantial and included valuable programs and insights concerning the improvement of citizenship education that remain quite pertinent. Included, among others, were the Citizenship Education Project of Teachers College, Columbia University; the Detroit Citizenship Study; the Kansas Study of Education for Citizenship; the Cambridge Civic Education Project; and the Stanford Social Education Investigation. A number of the excellent programs and approaches that characterized these efforts, as well as those described in other reports of the period, found adoption in schools across the nation. Some of these have been maintained, but many have been lost.

Today a new generation of teachers, often without adequate knowledge of the applicable and well-designed approaches of the past, is highly concerned over good citizenship. These teachers also face a considerable challenge in that the concept of good citizenship that has evolved seems to be highly individualistic and subjective, just at a time that calls for citizenship obligation and involvement. It should be understood that new times and conditions frequently call for new strategies. So, while we may well need to rediscover valuable past practices that still hold virtue, there are also new directions and timely methods that are now in order. New and old approaches all need to be explored and evaluated. Both the tried and the emerging elements of education for democratic citizenship will be found in the pages of this book. We anticipate that crucial signposts for the current era of civic concern will emerge from these presentations.

Democracies need citizens who not only understand sociocivic issues, but who have the requisite skills for their analysis. Equally important is a sense of personal efficacy in the resolution of sociocivic problems, as well as the desire and willingness to participate in societal improvement and progress. If there is one lesson that emerges clearly from the history of ancient Athens and extends to the present struggles to maintain and extend democracy in many countries throughout the world, it is this: Citizens are not free because they live in free nations; rather, nations become and remain free because their citizens believe and act as free citizens must.

Richard E. Gross
Thomas L. Dynneson

1 The Educational Perspective

Citizenship Education in American Society

THOMAS L. DYNNESON
RICHARD E. GROSS

Citizenship values and behaviors often are considered derivatives of an individual's society and culture. The American experience has generated citizenship values and behaviors that are "American." These values and behaviors grew out of the Judeo–Christian ethic and mainstream European influences, which were modified by geographic and social requirements associated with colonization and early settlement experiences. The ideological and philosophical currents that influenced Europe also found a receptive environment in the New World.

After two centuries of democratic experience, the concept of citizenship continues to change and evolve, because American society is constantly attempting to redefine the essence of its existence in light of a democratic ideology. In a recent book, Allan Bloom (1987) has charged that cultural relativism has replaced our basic belief in the ideals of the founders of this country, and that cultural pluralism, or the philosophy of openness, ultimately must reject basic prescriptions for moral and ethical conduct. Should this state of affairs be true, will it mean that citizenship education no longer has a place in American education? We hope that teachers as a group will continue to support citizenship education, including the values and principles associated with democracy, as an important goal of public education, along with the concomitant traditional values of family and community.

Citizenship training in American education continues to be based upon the yearning for a better society, a society that requires a commitment to educate youth to support the democratic way of life, which is based on specific and identifiable moral and ethical behaviors. According to Bloom (1987), "Democratic education, whether it admits it or not, wants and needs to produce men and women who have the tastes, knowledge, and character supportive of a democratic regime" (p. 26). To survive, democracies must be built on sound moral and ethical principles, including those of fair play, moral conduct, and the rejection of extremism except in the defense of democracy.

THE CITIZEN, CITIZENSHIP AND CITIZENSHIP EDUCATION IN A DEMOCRATIC SOCIETY

The first democracy emerged in Athens under Solon in the sixth century B.C. and flowered under Pericles in the fifth century B.C. Democracy arose in response to tyranny and the privileges granted to clans and aristocratic families with large land holdings (Smith, 1955). Later democratic values and principles re-emerged in Europe in response to the rule of monarchs and the growing power of the urban middle classes. During the Enlightenment, citizenship was expanded to include the artisans, tradespeople, and working classes, which mainly had been excluded from the affairs of state. In addition, political philosophers including Locke, Montesquieu, and Rousseau contributed to new democratic principles related to the civil liberties of the citizen, to limiting or diffusing the power of government (creating checks and balances), and to the idea of the will of the people as the ultimate sovereign of the state. These principles became important foundations upon which the new republic in America could be built (Butts, 1955).

In America, educating the people for citizenship was advanced by Hamilton and Jefferson as a means of assuring the establishment and continuation of the republic; therefore, citizenship in the democratic society tended to place an important and heavy burden on educational processes. In time, the public school system in America was given the mission of educating students for political literacy, including fundamental subject areas and skills related to the political system and the promulgation of democratic values. According to Broudy (1972), the democratic citizen has a moral duty that goes beyond that of citizens in other political systems: "In a society presumably committed to democracy, the citizen has the duty (not merely the privilege) to make decisions in accordance with his concern for the public good" (pp. 160–161).

American Citizenship

The related ideas of citizen and citizenship are fundamental concepts to our understanding of the role and function of citizenship education in American society. According to the Fourteenth Amendment to the U.S. Constitution, "All persons born or naturalized in the United States, and subject to the jurisdiction thereof, are citizens of the United States and of the States wherein they reside." In addition to legalistic descriptions such as this, there are more descriptive ones that attempt to specify the role of the citizen in society. In reaching back to the roots of democratic citizenship, Butts (1980) cites ancient Aristotelian ideology that seems to describe the nature and role of the democratic citizen or the citizen of the republican and constitutional form of government. According to this conception, all citizens are seen as officeholders of the state:

> All citizens hold the "office of citizen." There are two kinds of office. One has a fixed term and is determined in length. These are held by the government officials who are elected or appointed to a specific office for specific functions. The other "office of citizen" is of indeterminate or continuous duration and applies to the duties and responsibilities that all citizens have in their capacities as rulers, deciders, and judgers in the legislative assemblies and court of the commonwealth. [p. 28]

Citizenship, on the other hand, describes the tenets of membership in a defined body, and more. The description of citizenship usually includes a legalistic descriptive definition and a set of requirements, as in the following:

> *Citizenship* One's status as a person who is entitled to all the rights and privileges guaranteed and protected by the Constitution of the United States. Citizenship is conferred by Congress. Since the Civil Rights Act of 1866, all persons born or naturalized in the United States are citizens of the United States. [Chandler, Enslen, & Renstrom, 1985, pp. 392–393]

Further, according to Gould and Kolb (1964), in *A Dictionary of the Social Sciences*, "Citizenship may be defined as a state of relationship existing between a natural person and a political society, known as a state, by which the former owes allegiance and the latter protection" (p. 88).

After interviewing a large number of citizens from every part of the United States, Bellah (1985), writing in *Habits of the Heart*, identified three types of understanding related to politics and citizenship, each reflecting a variety of meanings that may not be compatible with one another. The first type he identifies as "a matter of making operative the moral consensus of the community, reached through free face-to-face discussion." The second understanding he describes as a general type of citizenship in which "politics means the pursuit of differing interests according to agreed-upon rules." The third understanding he describes as "'the politics of the nation,' which exalts politics into the realm of statesmanship in which the high affairs of national life transcend particular interests" (pp. 200–201).

Also, inferentially associated with citizenship are the cultural descriptions of citizenship that are based on sets of behaviors and relationships that one acquires from a member of a social or cultural body. Anthropologists deal with citizenship from a somewhat different perspective than do political scientists. In the following excerpt, De Vos and Romanucci-Ross (1975) address citizenship from within the context of ethnic identity: "In a complex society, the body to which an individual gives his greatest commitment depends on whether he is oriented primarily to the past, the present, or the future. With a present orientation, one's primary loyalty is directed toward his country" (p. 18). The authors go on to describe other conditions in which ethnic identity is more important than state or national identity, conditions that possibly could lead to the breakdown of the state.

Good Citizenship

Good citizenship is a commonly used term, especially within the citizenship education literature; however, it is seldom described in operational terms. As a consequence, there seems to be a characteristic amount of confusion and disagreement related to the cultural perception of the "good citizen." We therefore include here an operational description of the "good citizen" that we derived from our survey studies on student perceptions related to citizenship (Dynneson, Gross, & Nickel, 1989). A "good citizen" is one who "cares about the welfare of others, is moral and ethical in his dealing with others, is able to challenge and critically question ideas, proposals and suggestions, and, in light of existing circumstances, is able to make good choices based upon good judgement" (p. 74).

Citizenship Education

Citizenship education has long been the basic societal means whereby each new generation of youth is expected to acquire the knowledge, skills, and values needed to maintain and perpetuate the republic. The nature of citizenship education includes more than a description of a system of governance or the description of institutional relationships. It consists of a set of complex formal and informal educational processes that attempt to instill appropriate knowledge, skills, values, and behaviors in youth who are destined to become citizens of the American republic. These processes are partially ingrained in educational programs that are designed by the schools to help youth acquire an understanding of their citizenship roles as members of American society.

In 1985, we conducted a survey of social studies instructors in which they were asked to show their level of agreement with a particular definition of citizenship education. The following statement received a 70-percent affirmation from those responding participants:

> While an important and central element of the social studies, citizenship education is a responsibility of the entire school. It includes the means by which individuals are prepared to gain the knowledge, skills, and values that enable them to understand, examine, decide and participate in public affairs and in forwarding the well-being of other individuals and of their society. [Dynneson, Gross, & Nickel, 1988, p. 8]

In this chapter we will attempt to focus on the educational implications of citizenship in American society, including some of the social dilemmas that affect individuals' expression of citizenship and the processes of citizenship development, a review of instructional orientations and approaches that are aimed at promoting citizenship education, and some recommendations regarding the revitalization of citizenship education, leaving the study of specific legalistic process of citizenship to other sources (e.g., see the *Guide to American Law*, Vol. 2, 1985).

In addition to preparing youth for American citizenship, citizenship education can serve several scholarly functions, including that of a barometer for measuring the extent to which a given society will go to preserve responsible action by citizens in relation to the perceived cultural values associated with the idea of the common good. In addition, citizenship education can serve as a kind of preventative action against the recognizable forces that work against the cohesion of the society or state. Finally, citizenship education can inspire those social, political, and/or economic movements that become identified as desirable goals in a quest for a higher level of values which may lead to a higher order of existence within a given society or state. In other words, the study of citizenship education can be used as a study of society or of the state. The results of citizenship education studies may prove useful in the assessment of the current conditions within a society, and can also be used as a means of predicting trends and directions in terms of the vitality of a society or state.

THE DILEMMA OF CITIZENSHIP EDUCATION: DISCONTINUITIES WITHIN CULTURE, HOME, AND SCHOOL

The processes of citizenship education must become educationally effective, in order to overcome an array of societal problems that threaten to undermine the development of democratic values and behaviors in American society. It seems that the advance of democratic citizenship is plagued by a growing number of individuals and groups who demonstrate a range of behaviors that are considered counterproductive to the normal development of good citizenship. Because of the freedom that exists in democratic societies, counterproductive behavior, including less threatening forms of social deviance, must be tolerated. Citizenship processes are disrupted when positive citizenship behaviors are blocked by the growing strength of counterproductive behaviors. In his day, Socrates was equally concerned about this issue in Athenian society. He believed if the citizens of Athens would "examine their lives honestly that they would put less value on money, honor, and reputation and would put more value on wisdom, truth, and improvement of the soul" (Troxell, 1968, p. 71). In our times, there seem to be many more counterproductive behaviors at work to undermine the processes of citizenship education; however, a closer historical examination suggests that every society, whether democratic or not, must of necessity wrestle with various antisocial forces that undermine citizenship development (Butts, 1955). What one considers subversive depends on one's perspective. In totalitarian states, for example, antisocial or anticitizenship elements may include those who espouse democratic reforms.

Counterproductive behaviors or social discontinuities are often mild forms of social deviance that affect citizenship and its expected development. Discontinuities in citizenship are often due to apathy about citizenship, or to behavioral practices that are inappropriate for the general good of society. The problem is compounded when large segments of the population exhibit such attitudes and behaviors, or when they become a form of popular expression, promoted through music, drama, and other arts. Citizenship education processes have a difficult time overcoming the consequences of such cultural phenomena, whereby it simply becomes popular or fashionable for youth to reject the established traditional values of citizenship. In addition, families who are apathetic about citizenship may rear children who do not or will not participate in the affairs of the community, society, or state.

Cultural Dilemmas

The United States represents the type of cultural pluralism that produces complex adaptations to basic societal needs, including the need to develop a unified social order. William M. Newman refers to cultural pluralism as a force that both unites and divides a society: "Pluralism and assimilation remain useful concepts if they are viewed, not as absolutes, but reciprocal aspects of group relationships. Like social change and social order, group conflict and group consensus, pluralism and assimilation may be viewed as twin aspects of the social structure" (quoted in Greeley, 1977, p. 64).

This country has always consisted of diverse groups of people who were allowed to maintain their own cultural values, attitudes, customs, and traditions. From one generation to the next, each new group's customs and traditions have tended to weaken, as its members have become assimilated into the society. Where there is unrestrained and uncontrolled immigration, however, it may pose a real threat to the cohesion of the state, especially when the integrating institutions of the state (including the schools) are not able to cope adequately with these cultural conditions and therefore are not able to fulfill a citizenship education mission (Barrera, 1988). As a result, pluralism may contribute to the development of a divergent and disintegrated society.

Ehlers (1977) refers to the conditions of pluralism in democracy as a form of social ferment that is brought about by conditions of political interaction among groups: "To see democracy in action is to see hundreds of zealous minorities clamoring for power, each sure of its own truth and righteousness" (p. 1). Consequently, national leaders have had to work constantly to attain and maintain a degree of social unity that would override group interests. With the rise of urbanism (especially after the Civil War) and its concomitant effects on population density and cultural diversity, the problems of unity have been intensified as groups have competed with one another for social, political, or economic advantage. Some of the changes brought about by conflicting group values and attitudes have led to mixed effects for the republic; as a result, national leaders have attempted to manage the more negative consequences through various institutional means, including education (Butts, 1989).

Cultural accommodation is critically important to societies that are made up of groups with different cultural backgrounds. In recent years a number of conflicts have threatened certain countries with dissolution, including Canada and the Soviet Union. Lebanon and Northern Ireland, too, have experienced long-running religious conflicts that have destabilized their social, economic, and political development. The United States has been relatively successful in regard to accommodating differences, but much of this may be credited to the emergence of a universal system of public education. This system has continually been scrutinized and criticized by educational reformers. The current criticism includes the suggestion that schools should become extensively reorganized and perhaps privatized, in order to improve educational standards. There is danger in making such changes without consideration for the effects they will have on the processes of social accommodation and the integration of society's cultural groups (Butts, 1989).

The current crisis expressed through cultural conflicts reported in the United States and around the world can be considered as a warning signal, suggesting that cultural assimilation and accommodation have not worked well in the twentieth century. The next generation of American citizens will have to find the means of dealing with the forces of disintegration that result from those differences originating within the value system and which are used to regulate the social relationships within our society. Citizenship education might be used to help youth confront those issues that result from cultural differences, and thereby seek resolutions that would lead to a greater degree of social integration and cohesion.

At the same time, the cultural values and attitudes of various groups undoubtedly will influence the conditions and the effects of citizenship education. These values seem to make an important contribution to the development of one's perspective on life, or one's concept of reality, and on the formation of the social relationships that are characteristic of society. Differences between societies often are due to the different ways in which they respond to nature, needs, and technology. Customs, traditions, and rituals reflect the adaptations that society has accepted in order to respond to the demands of life. For example, children born into hunting and gathering societies are influenced mainly by the family, tribe, or clan; while children born into urban industrial societies are influenced by the family and various levels of complex social patterns that form the structure of society. Even more complex are societies in which the dominant social pattern includes pluralistic populations.

Because of the great diversity within American society and the practical need for a unified society, we feel that some emphasis should be placed on reaching a fairly broad social consensus within society based upon the following areas:

1. A shared or common language,
2. A shared or common economic philosophy,
3. A shared or common political ideology,
4. A shared or common set of moral and ethical principles.

While emphasizing the positive aspect of pluralism as a means of enriching the quality of a unique American culture, we must also realize that emerging conditions in American society regarding unequal economic opportunities, political disinterest, lack of civic participation, and deviant values can thoroughly undermine the unity needed to maintain a vital democratic society.

Pluralistic societies in which different groups compete for social, economic, and political advantage can lead to prejudiced attitudes. Historical biases by which some groups are considered biologically and/or socially inferior choke off the process of citizenship development, not just for those who suffer from the effects of an inferior status caused by prejudice and poverty, but for the entire group.

Since poverty tends to heighten the risks of survival, some people are forced to seek alternative and mainly antisocial means of meeting basic needs. In addition, they come to perceive themselves as less than adequate in measuring up to the standards of society. Poverty-stricken individuals also have less interest in or need for the social, economic, and political affirmations of the community or state, making participation in public affairs less likely. As an essential element of survival, democratic societies must monitor the economic status of their citizens; develop wide-ranging policies that are designed to maintain and expand the middle class; and, at the same time, address the specific needs of the poor, the alienated, and the disheartened.

A maladjusted citizenry can help to establish a pattern of antisocial behaviors that are difficult to alter. As McGee (1975) writes,

> There are circumstances in which the nature of society can generate definite pressures upon individuals or social groups which lead them to nonconforming behavior; that is, there are circumstances in which nonconformity is a reasonable and entirely normal response to the demands of society. [p. 206]

> "Deviation" is a characteristic of neither acts nor persons. It is a label which gets applied to some people as a result of a long social transaction. [p. 206]

> We can understand some deviant behavior, then, by observing that
> it is expressed by those who have managed to grow up outside the
> normal commitment process, who never have become implicated in
> the web of standard relationships, commitments, and conventions.
> [p. 217]

Some children are reared under conditions of isolation and neglect,
in which family or group values reflect attitudes that are contrary to the
prevailing norms of conduct. As a result, the social environment contributes to the establishment of a deviant form of citizenship. Most
commonly, a maladjusted form of citizenship reflects self-indulgent behaviors in which extreme forms of racial and ethnic prejudice, drug
abuse, and underground and illegal actions are expressed. In addition,
there is a profound distrust and rejection of the institutions of society,
so these individuals instead seek causes and associations that work to
undermine the status quo or the standards that support the current
social infrastructure of society.

Increasingly, the civic influences of the family, the local community, and the traditional culture are being modified by the impact of the
media. The needs, desires, values, and practices of both young persons
and adults are being shaped particularly by television, movies, and both
the recording and publishing industries. While there are contradictory
reports regarding the effects of television, we worry that millions of
children and youth no longer benefit from adult models in the extended
family and are spending as much or more time before television sets
than in school and that numerous of the media offerings project dubious characteristics and antisocial practices as normal, if not even good.
Unprincipled desires for economic gain, coupled with hedonistic and
narcissistic attitudes, exemplified by the purveyors of these negative
values, provide one of the greatest challenges to those who would maintain the important traditional citizenship attitudes and values of American society.

Personal and Social Dilemmas

Personal and formal relationships are important social influences
that help to shape democratic citizenship, especially in infancy and
adolescence. Normally the most important sources for these influences
are family relationships. They can provide the foundation for the formation of positive, neutral, and negative citizenship behaviors and beliefs.
Other relationships that contribute importantly to all aspects of early

citizenship development are those with close friends and those between students and teachers (Dynneson et al., 1989).

Thus, those who nurture and instruct children seem to have a significant influence on their citizenship development. Each child lives in a somewhat unique social world, and the values and behaviors that are learned in these settings are influenced by the dominant values that are maintained by the empowered individuals in them, such as parents, teachers, administrators, siblings, grandparents, day-care workers, domineering friends, and so forth (Hess & Torney, 1970). The social setting thus serves as the stage upon which the citizenship drama is acted out on a daily basis. Children acquire their perceptions of appropriate citizenship from the immediate social environment and those who influence the nature of the social relationships that will be formed and will operate within the social setting.

The level of participation in the affairs of the local community and state suggest that large numbers of children are reared in apathetic or citizenship-neutral families, by which we mean that they seldom participate in the affairs of the community and are generally uninformed and/ or unconcerned about the larger social community, state, nation, and world. While citizenship development does take place within these families, the development is mainly limited to family affairs and family relationships. Should this pattern of child rearing be repeated from generation to generation, large segments of society would tend to refrain from participation in public affairs.

Citizenship education may be able to help overcome some of the consequences of uninvolved families by promoting instructional programs that emphasize community participation, sharing, cooperating, and working on group projects related to the classroom and the community. While it is common practice for all citizens to fail occasionally in their civic responsibilities, the offspring of nonparticipating families rarely participate in community affairs, which is a form of deprivation for the individual as well as for the community, state, and society.

Positive citizenship influences also can be thwarted by harmful social experiences that occur in connection with the formation of critical personal and formal relationships during childhood and adolescence. These relationships occur within the family, the school, the neighborhood, and the community. The development of a positive citizenship perspective may be affected as a result of secondary social disruptions such as divorce, death of a parent, poverty, various forms of neglect, and a multitude of problems that interrupt normal family life (Dawson & Prewitt, 1969). Difficulties in these areas can result in the retardation of normal citizenship development. The individual may never quite be able to respond to the expectations of community and society and may develop a poor self-concept and experience a form of self-rejection, as reflected in a lack of interest in the affairs of the community. In some cases, self-rejection leads to deviant social behavior.

School Dilemmas

In order to provide effective instructional programs for citizenship, educators in a pluralistic democratic society must consider and plan for those influences that are attributed to the social setting in which the child is reared, including the home and school. The social setting—a product of the family, neighborhood, school and community—provides the environment in which child rearing occurs. This setting has an indirect but important influence on citizenship development. The general social setting also serves as a repository of social customs, traditions, and beliefs that contribute to the shaping of citizenship (Dawson & Prewitt, 1969). The school is an important child-rearing institution, and the environment of the school contributes to the students' understanding of the realities of society outside of the family.

School experiences can work either for or against a positive citizenship development. Harmful school experiences can negate children's desire to become involved in classroom activities, to the extent that they withdraw and isolate themselves. In effect, harmful school experiences can lead to the rejection of classroom values, in favor of alternative and antisocial ones. In a real sense, the classroom represents a miniature community in which citizenship skills are expressed, developed, and practiced. The need for a positive atmosphere in which democratic citizenship values and attitudes can be experienced requires that teachers refrain from the more traditional authoritarian classroom operations that are often characteristic of school settings.

To advance the cause of citizenship education, defining the role and responsibility of the teacher in citizenship education processes must become a priority for the schools, but school authorities have an equally important role to play in creating an appropriate environment in which democratic values and principles dominate the school setting. For example, excessively authoritarian practices may maintain a serious barrier to citizenship development in the schools. Even where these are tempered by a wide range of democratic experiences for students, such as selecting student representatives and having some voice in the decisions that affect student affairs in the schools, such measures are simply not adequate to overcome the totalitarian experiences that persist. Unfortunately, few schools are organized to prioritize or promote citizenship development as a practical and routine experience for students, and far too few classrooms reflect the democratic principles that actually can be learned there (Dawson & Prewitt, 1969).

THE ACQUISITION OF CITIZENSHIP: SETTINGS, AGENTS, AND PROCESSES

In a recent research study (Dynneson et al., 1989) we began by asking, "How do children acquire their citizenship values and behaviors in American society?" This question led to some initial field studies in which students were given some survey questions and then were interviewed about their responses. As a consequence of these field trials, we constructed a questionnaire that was administered to four groups of students in four states. One of the questions pertained to the sources of citizenship influence. Students ranked the following categories: parents, friends, siblings, religious leaders, media, extended family members, guardians, teachers, school administrators, extracurricular activities, other students, and coaches. The results showed that these students believed that the most important sources of citizenship education in their lives had been their parents, their friends, and their teachers. This provides some insights into the setting, agents, and processes—or conditions—under which citizenship education occurs in American society.

The agents of citizenship development include those persons who help to shape our youth in this area, whether or not the results are appropriate in terms of the criteria or societal standards of good citizenship. These agents include a variety of persons with whom young people come into contact or close association during one of the critical periods or stages of citizenship development. The results of these associations, when combined with individual attributes, with other relationships, and with experiences and social conditions created within a cultural environment, are citizenship characteristics that are, on the one hand, unique and individualistic and, on the other hand, the outcome of a more or less standardized or normalized social experience from within the culture. These patterns of social behavior then become the individual's expression of citizenship or membership in a community.

The agents of citizenship development are therefore considered especially important to an understanding of individual citizenship. The importance of these agents is closely related to the processes of political socialization that take place within American society. By examining some critical factors that are related to various social environments or places, including some important personal and formal relationships that are developed there, a clearer understanding may be obtained regarding the citizenship development process.

Citizenship Development
Within the Cultural Setting

The qualities of the "good" citizen are defined by the dominant cultural setting, which includes the values that are generally shared by most members of that culture (Dawson & Prewitt, 1969). Cultures consist of shared cognitive and social behaviors, including language, religion, world view, symbol systems, customs, and traditions and/or ideologies.

Pluralistic societies contain a variety of subgroups whose subculture values, language, customs, traditions, symbol systems and outlook differ from one group to another. However, these differences are not so great that they cannot be accommodated to the general framework of the society, provided that the overall societal framework is sufficiently inclusive to tolerate broad subgroup differences. Under the U.S. Constitution, the United States was required to construct a very broad and general societal framework in order to convince the wide-ranging groups within the colonies to join the new republic. The problem for pluralistic societies is to be able to continually emphasize the benefits of cohesion over separation. Therefore, pluralistic societies must strengthen all aspects of integration and cohesion in order to survive. Education, especially citizenship education, can play an important role in forming a set of shared values that can be used to help tie individual groups together within the pluralistic society. Cohesion and integration never can be fully attained because of a variety of changing conditions and perceptions, but an adequate cohesion may be possible as long as each new generation recognizes the benefits of togetherness over separatism. (The Civil War exemplifies the breakdown of accommodation when differences become greater than the desire to oblige cultures, systems, or groups.)

The source of moral conduct from within various cultural groups may be derived from religious teachings that address and define basic social relationships. For example, the ten commandments of the Judeo–Christian tradition, in addition to outlining the moral rules of conduct for its members, have also served as the moral basis for Christian individuals and groups within the state. Therefore, cultural groups are often identified by customs, traditions, symbols, signs, emblems, and even a world view that is derived from religious sources.

Since the founding of the republic and the acceptance of the principle of separation of church and state, the state has been required to develop and substitute secular standards of citizenship conduct for the original religious standards of conduct (Butts, 1950). In other words, the rules of citizenship conduct must be derived from secular or democratic principles, doctrines, laws, and most of all, court decisions, in place of the religious moral teachings of a national church; furthermore, this secular authority has to take precedence over all other sources of moral authority, in order to unite its diverse peoples. This has led some writers (e.g., Bloom, 1987) to lament the condition in American society in which secular cultural relativism seems to have eroded the moral fiber of American society.

Our student survey (Dynneson et al., 1989), mentioned earlier, also contained a question about the influence of religious leaders on citizenship development in the United States. The students indicated that the influence of religious leaders varied somewhat by region, with groups in Arkansas, Minnesota, and Texas indicating a moderate influence and the group in California indicating a lower influence.

The existence of subcultures raises questions about the individual's sense of citizenship identity. Ideally, each subculture, regardless of cultural identity, would support and participate in the broader aspects of democratic ideology and citizenship. As an important aspect of citizenship, each cultural group would keep its cultural identity in an appropriate balance with the whole of society, as framed by democratic principles, processes, and values.

Citizenship Development Within the Community Setting

Community and neighborhood are important social environments for citizenship development, ones that will be somewhat different for every child. Each community has an identity that is based on geographic, economic, political, and social factors that are synthesized into a community environment. This affects the individual's perception of the broader social world, through the process of transferring the known to the unknown. The dominant values of the community also help to define and to determine some important values and attitudes that will be carried throughout life. For example, community values may have an influence on both the public and personal decisions that the individual will be required to make over time.

The criteria and standards for the idealized citizen also would be qualified by community values and standards. Since the advent of the industrial revolution and the concurrent urban revolution, social reformers often have blamed the breakdown of family and community life on the industrial and economic influences that drew rural populations out of small rural communities and environments, thereafter, making it necessary for the schools to provide the sense of family and community that the urban setting has failed to provide (Butts, 1989).

Citizenship Development
Within the Family Setting

While the family has been and continues to be a major agent of citizenship development, in recent years the ties between parent and child appear to be breaking down. On the surface, the child seems to be falling under the influence of those outside the family. Preschool and day-care centers are replacing the working mother in the very early years of child rearing (Bronfenbrenner, 1986). A high divorce rate, combined with nontraditional social relationships, also have contributed to changes in family life. In reality, however, parents continue to be the single most important source of citizenship development for the majority of children born in the United States (Dynneson et al., 1989).

Parents and home experiences are the initial and most important sources for citizenship development during the early years of life. Mothers and/or fathers have the primary nurturing responsibility for the child, and this condition alone guarantees an important citizenship development role for them. The family is a critical source of cultural continuity in American society and will undoubtedly endure for generations, helping to assure that cultural traditions will be passed on from one generation to the next, well into the foreseeable future.

Parents most likely will remain the most important modifying agent of citizenship development during the critical child-rearing years. McGee (1975) comments as follows on the ongoing and pervasive role of the family in society: "It is the function of the family to produce new members of the society and to equip them with the information, skills, norms, and understandings which will permit them to function effectively as adults upon reaching maturity, however that is defined locally" (p. 119).

The environment, the home, and family are constant factors that seem to affect citizenship development during the entire formative years of life. The home environment is established by the parents in order to provide children with basic needs, including shelter, food, and clothing.

The personalities of the parents and the nature of their relationship, including their values and attitudes toward children and child rearing, greatly affect children's experiences. Children are most dependent on their parents and are full-time participants in the affairs of their homes, while at the same time living as subordinates to their parents (Dawson & Prewitt, 1969).

The relationship between parents and their children is fundamentally important to children's understanding of societal roles and expectations. In addition, parental attitudes toward the school, neighborhood, and community provide children with attitudes that will greatly influence children's citizenship in terms of both self-identity and political identity (Dawson & Prewitt, 1969).

Citizenship Development
Within the Personal Setting

Individual differences are important contributors to each person's citizenship. Personality differences, as well as the experiences of each individual, are combined conditions that can lead to positive, negative, or neutral citizenship values and behaviors. To a great extent, citizenship development depends on the composition and direction of the individual's life. Even when family ties are strong and positive, negative tendencies often dominate individual citizenship behavior. The existence of individual differences tends to suggest that, in spite of positive shared experiences, good citizenship development is not guaranteed. Clearly it is a process that is to some degree different for every child. The way in which each individual responds to social relationships and to community affairs may be as much a product of personality as it is a product of education. Similarly, the expression of citizenship may be as much the expression of personality as an expression of political education. At the same time, positive experiences with citizenship development can help control the negative side of individual citizenship by modifying and replacing destructive behaviors with more socially acceptable citizenship behaviors.

Citizenship Development
Within the School Setting

As the child matures, parental and family influences seem to slowly weaken, while friends, peers, workers, and teachers tend to increase their influence over the child's citizenship. The teacher becomes an especially important agent of citizenship development in the early years of the child's life (Dynneson et al., 1989). Commenting more generally on the role of the teacher, Dewey (in Battle & Shannon, 1968) wrote, "The problem of pupils is found in subject matter; the problem of teachers is what the minds of pupils are doing with this subject matter" (p. 13).

Teachers are in an ideal position to detect and possibly correct defective citizenship traits. Because teachers' citizenship responsibility extends beyond detection into the domain of correction, they are expected to play a dual role that is critical to the development of student citizenship. This includes (1) a modeling role in which teachers represent a model democratic citizen as reflected in both conduct and relationships with students and (2) a diagnostic and treatment role for malignant forms of behavior that are inappropriate and harmful for the development of the ideal democratic citizen.

Elementary-age children are especially influenced by their teachers. These children spend a great deal of time with teachers and are quite dependent on them during the elementary school years. Elementary teachers are especially influential in the areas of citizenship knowledge, skills, and values. While their influence may diminish during the secondary school years, they, and the school, remain an important source of citizenship knowledge and skills, even as friends and peers grow in their influence on citizenship values.

The classroom setting is the place where important formal peer groups confront the child and where close personal friendships are formed. Close friends seemingly are an even more influential agent of citizenship development than teachers during the adolescent years, peaking in importance as students become young adults. These critical social relationships may have a lifelong influence on children's formation of a social perspective. Peers, on the other hand, are influential but not nearly as influential as close personal friends or even teachers (Dynneson et al., 1989).

During the secondary school years, the sources of citizenship values are complicated by sexual maturation and the needs associated with an individual's preadult social identity. During adolescence the peer group becomes a significant aspect of the individual's changing concept of citizenship. Among teenagers, in a society undergoing the value conflicts of our do-your-own-thing and self-centered era, the direction of some peer group influences can provide serious challenges to the maintenance of good citizenship. By recognizing the importance that close personal friends have in citizenship development, adult society has the opportunity to direct these relationships into avenues of constructive citizenship formation.

The classroom provides all the elements of a social community. Children's first encounter with a formally organized and highly structured social setting usually occurs at the time they enter the schools. Formal schools have been around for a relatively long period of time and were created, in part, to teach those elements of culture considered too important to be left to chance. Early American visionaries, including Jefferson, Madison, and Mann, wanted the school to become a source of shared experience, a common community of like ideals that every citizen knew and valued. The nature of this common community and experience was to be democratic. The teacher's concern for citizenship within the classroom setting is a critical factor in the establishment of an appropriate classroom environment. Without a concern for citizenship education, classrooms probably will not provide the type of social environment that will promote democratic citizenship (Dawson & Prewitt, 1969).

Citizenship education in the schools is often associated with the content, skills, and values that are taught in connection with American history and government. While these instructional programs are an important aspect of citizenship education, they are more readily identified within a special orientation known as "civic learning" (Butts, 1980). At the same time, there are leading advocates of citizenship education who tend to equate civic learning with citizenship education. Our survey work has suggested that students do not identify citizenship education with political education as much as they associate it with social and moral considerations (Dynneson, Gross, & Nickel, 1989, 1990). In spite of these differences, it is important to consider the programmatic, curricular, or instructional aspects of the schools when attempting to analyze citizenship education.

While the entire school has citizenship obligations and opportunities, the social studies are commonly accepted as being an important content source for citizenship development. Social studies teachers have a vast realm of skills, knowledge, and attitudes to draw upon in formulating their units and decisions. The knowledge areas and disciplines that service the social studies contain the content resources needed to address almost all aspects of the historical, social, political, and economic foundations related to American citizenship (Dawson & Prewitt, 1969). The social studies, assisted by the humanities, provide the commonwealth knowledge resources from which citizenship education content can be selected and organized for instruction.

A Six-stage Citizenship Development Process

Citizenship development consists of the social and cultural processes that contribute to children's acquisition of citizenship perceptions, values, and behaviors. A few years ago we completed work on a citizenship development theory that identified the most important phases of the citizenship development process as characterized by American society (Dynneson & Gross, 1987). The process contains six stages of citizenship development that are based on the important social relationships that emerge out of the formal and informal effects of American societal settings, structures, and requirements (see Figure 1.1). We took the position that children experience a series of important relationships that shape their citizenship conceptions during the formative years of growth from birth to early adulthood. These relationships begin with the mother and are expanded to include the father, relatives, siblings, playmates and peers, teachers, religious leaders, school officials, and others who nurture, supervise, or associate—in close and constant contact, in terms of social distance—with children.

Citizenship development is therefore considered unique to each society, depending on the social and educational requirements that regulate the social life related to child rearing. Out of these relationships, children are expected to learn the appropriate behaviors and attitudes

FIGURE 1.1.   The Six Stages of Citizenship Development

Stage One: Biological Citizenship: Infant Dependency and Maternal Shaping—Birth through Three Years of Age

Stage Two: Family Citizenship: Expanding Kinship Influences—Four and Five Years of Age

Stage Three: Formative Social Citizenship: The Initiation of Nonbiological Dependencies—Six through Nine Years of Age

Stage Four: Stratified Social Citizenship: The Development of Social Categories and Group Membership Behaviors—Ten through Twelve Years of Age

Stage Five: Chronological Age Group Citizenship: Horizontal Social Relationships Within and Between Groups—Thirteen through Fifteen Years of Age

Stage Six: Complex Social Citizenship: A Search for Accommodation and Adult Identity—Sixteen Years of Age to Adulthood

---

Source: Dynneson, Thomas L., & Richard E. Gross. An Eclectic Approach to Citizenship: Development Stages. *The Social Studies,* Vol. 76, pp. 23–27 (January/February 1985). Reprinted with permission of the Helen Dwight Reid Educational Foundation. Published by Heldref Publications, 4000 Albemarle St., NW, Washington, D.C. 20016. © 1985.

that, among other things, shape their citizenship values and behaviors. In regard to American society, we have concluded that "there are six stages of citizenship development in which social relationships contribute to the formation of the individual's perspective of his overall relationship with community and society" (Dynneson & Gross, 1987, p. 1). Each stage marks a transitional point in the lives of children reared in American society. This six-stage theory of citizenship development is undergoing scrutiny through various field research projects sponsored by the Citizenship Development Study Project.

While all six of our developmental stages are unique to the social and cultural conditions of American society, stages one and two take place primarily in the home setting and also in the community setting, but stages three through six take place in the home, community, and school settings. The agents of citizenship development for stage one are primarily the mother, along with the rest of the family; while the primary agents for stage two include the family, extended family, and the neighborhood. Stages three through six identify teachers, friends, and peer group members as important agents of citizenship development. Consequently, the role of the school in citizenship development is of great importance as the agent of the community, society, and the state and, second only to the family and close personal friends, teachers are prominent agents of citizenship development.

CITIZENSHIP EDUCATION: ORIENTATIONS, PROJECTS, AND INSTRUCTIONAL APPROACHES

Citizenship education, like the curriculum of the schools, seems to take place at two levels of experience for the student, the formal and informal. The formal level of citizenship education begins in the elementary schools as the students study various aspects of the community and, in time, move on to study about various aspects of the workings of American government. In the secondary schools, students study more specialized subjects related to civics and government. During these years students are expected more or less to master the fundamentals of government, including its structures, organizations, operations, and processes.

The informal aspects of citizenship education occur as a consequence of the conditions created by the social setting of the schools. This setting is dominated by the practices, attitudes, and inclinations of the teachers, administrators, staff members, and peer groups who operate within this setting. As a result of social interactions that take place within the school, students learn many of the basics of the practical realities of citizenship in a group and institutional environment. The school experience becomes an additional aspect or feature of citizenship development, just as the family, neighborhood, and community became aspects of citizenship development prior to the school experience. Therefore, the schools make a significant contribution to citizenship development, thereby making citizenship education an even more important aspect of planned citizenship development.

In this section we discuss three important themes that contribute to the current direction of citizenship education within American schools. The first subsection, in which we have attempted to delineate the differences between two major citizenship education traditions which include civic learning and sociocivic learning, describes the overarching instructional orientations. The second subsection includes a cursory review of citizenship projects that are currently promoting citizenship education in the school and in society. The third subsection contains descriptions of an array of instructional approaches that we and other scholars have identified as a consequence of our study of the social studies literature.

Overarching Instructional Orientations

The curricular programs of the schools seem to consist of two fundamentally different instructional orientations, one that focuses on civic learning and another that focuses on sociocivic-learning orientation. We identified these orientations as a result of literature searches and recent survey work regarding the status of citizenship education in the schools (Dynneson & Gross, 1983).

The civic-learning orientation emphasizes political learning as a part of the formal school curriculum. This orientation has its roots in the social studies curriculum, as those formally taught concepts, skills, and values relate to learning about the American system of government. The sociocivic-learning orientation focuses on the social, political, and economic aspects of citizenship; it includes the concerns that have been expressed in the study of political socialization (Newmann, 1977; Gross & Zeleny, 1958). This orientation contains a concern for the consequences of cultural and social relationships, the influence of citizenship development at various stages of maturation, the perceptions of "good" citizenship within the social setting, the moral and ethical considerations of citizenship, and the social and cultural influences that impact on political decisions.

This aforementioned orientation is vital for the achievement of the goals of civic education. Society has many expectations; but youth can respond favorably or unfavorably to them, depending upon the nature of the relationships among curriculum, teacher, and student. Research shows that only when the relationships become tension-relieving and goal-achieving for youth may they be expected to respond positively to the teacher and the curriculum. Conversely, youths tend to respond negatively when the relationships block tension-relieving opportunities. The implications of this hypothesis are profound when applied to the problem of educating for democratic citizenship. They mean that "the curriculum (including the teacher) and youth must be so correlated that the needs of society and youth are satisfied in one unified living process" (Gross & Zeleny, 1958, p. 4).

Civic Learning. In recent years, a small group of educators has made an impressive attempt to revitalize civic learning within the school curriculum. This effort has been spearheaded by the eminent scholar, R. Freeman Butts, and some of his close associates in education and political science. In 1980, Butts, while pressing for this revitalization, also attempted to confine it. What he calls "civic learning" may be seen as an academic or discipline-centered approach to the teaching of political content, process, skills, and values associated with the U.S. Constitution and the American system of government. As Butts (1980) puts it,

> Learning in this sense is a corpus of knowledge and scholarship that informs and challenges the highest reaches of the intellectual, moral, and creative talents of humankind. Thus, a revival of civic learning must be based upon the major disciplines of knowledge and research. [p. 121]

He goes on to state:

> Learning also means the different processes whereby individuals acquire knowledge, values, and skills at different ages and stages of their development and in all the contexts of modern life. This civic learning includes all those skills and experiences relating to the political processes and the moral judgments that underlie the political system. Civic learning embraces the fundamental values of the political community, a realistic and scholarly knowledge of the working of political institutions and processes, and the skills of political behavior required for effective participation in a democracy. [pp. 121–122]

Butts's support for the civics-learning approach reflects a general preference to political education over social education, when it comes to citizenship education. He observes that,

> Whether the approach is through history or civics, law-related education, public issues, or student participation, there is more hope for civic education in the programs that stress the political concepts underlying our democratic constitutional order. [Butts, 1989, p. 218]

As for values education and moral education, he asserts,

> They mix up personal values with civic values. Although personal and social values are interrelated, moral or ethical values as often defined in school curriculums trail off into diffuse, naive, unsophisticated terms that carry little guidance beyond the obvious or the trite. [p. 220]

He sees all-inclusive approaches to citizenship education as problematic:

> It is also troublesome to see included within the rubric of citizenship education such activities as values clarification, personal development, prosocial behavior modification, school community education, work-study plans, or consumer education. Such an all-inclusive approach to civic education is likely to lead to yet another laundry list of competencies, values, or behaviors, each of which may have some intrinsic usefulness for some educational purpose, but which provide no coherent or consistent intellectual framework by which to judge what civic education is or ought to be. [p. 215]

Therefore, Butts's preference is more or less limited to political education:

> I believe that civic education should be focused upon education in relation to the political system. It should not try to encompass all urgent social, economic, or intellectual problems. Yet it must be broad enough to go beyond sheer information to include the political values and concepts, as well as political knowledge and political participation. [Butts, 1980, pp. 122–123]

In his analysis of Butts's work, Jones (1989) suggests that the civic-learning approach is aimed at two mandates: the teaching of history and the teaching of the U.S. Constitution. Critics of the civic-learning orientation, as the sole means of educating students for citizenship, object to this orientation on the grounds that civic learning only deals with half of the problem related to citizenship education. For example, Dawson and Prewitt (1969) argue that,

> At best, attending a class in American government leads to incremental increases in a student's level of political information, his sense of political effectiveness, his feeling of patriotism, or his propensity to be a political participant. This study [by H. Murray Williams] is consistent with materials presented earlier; the American high school student is rarely socialized with respect to many political attributes by this stage in his life cycle. Civics courses have little influence. [p. 151]

While the civic-learning orientation seems to make good sense and allows for a clearer approach to citizenship education, its weaknesses relate to a lack of emphasis on the citizenship consequences of social influences, social relationships, and social interactions. To some extent, civic learning represents the traditional government approach that has long served as one of the "big three" of the social studies curriculum— history, government, and geography. Another problem may be found in the effectiveness of this approach with students, since our survey results (Dynneson et al., 1989) seem to suggest that this approach does not have a strong appeal for students. This may be due to the extent to which political education is taught without including the social conditions out of which political structures and systems arise.

According to our survey studies (Dynneson et al., 1989, 1990), the civic-learning orientation seems to be perceived by students as a not very appealing means of dealing with citizenship activities in the schools. This was noted in the way students perceived or described a "good" citizen. While civic learning seems to be based on sound philosophical insights, the civic-learning orientation may have too great a dependence on political content at the expense of other emphases, including social aspects, and a lack of concern for the personal needs of students at various stages of development.

Sociocivic Learning. Compared with the highly politically centered and formalized civic-learning orientation, the sociocivic-learning orientation is more vernacular. It attempts to deal with citizenship education in the marketplace of everyday life. It is a practical experience type of political education, in which citizenship education attempts to go beyond the formalisms of political knowledge to include the transactions of everyday life. There exists a respectable body of literature in political science that deals with political socialization, describing, among other things, citizenship development issues and related processes associated with how we acquire our citizenship values and behaviors. The main focus of political socialization is the influences and processes whereby a child acquires political understandings, skills, values, and attitudes (Dawson & Prewitt, 1969; Greenberg, 1970; Renshon, 1977). These subjects are less likely to be emphasized in the civic-learning orientation.

The sociocivic-learning orientation, as we have described it, also centers mainly on integrated social and educational influences and processes, including those that are produced by the social environment; by the conditions in which the child is reared; by educational systems imposed upon the child as a result of formal actions, laws, regulations, or impositions of government; by those influences that affect important values, expectations, and by important social relationships from within the social and educational setting. It also takes into account the influences of formally organized educational experiences related to the operations and curricular programs of the schools, including a variety of instructional approaches. (We discuss these later.)

Our recent survey (Dynneson et al., 1989), in which we probed student perceptions of the qualities of a good citizen, included the following list of characteristics:

1. Knowledge of current events;
2. Participation in community or school affairs;
3. Acceptance of an assigned responsibility;
4. Concern for the welfare of others;
5. Moral and ethical behavior;
6. Acceptance of authority of those in supervisory roles;
7. Ability to question ideas;
8. Ability to make wise decisions;
9. Knowledge of government; and
10. Patriotism.

We then sorted these characteristics according to student perceptions of what is and what is not a "good" citizen.

> In the *what is not* category, students were in agreement that participation in community and school affairs and knowledge of government were not important as characteristics or qualities of a good citizen. In the *what is* category, students were in agreement that a concern for the welfare of others and the ability to make wise decisions were the most important qualities of a good citizen. In addition, students in all

four groups identified four items as related to the characteristics of a good citizen. According to these student perceptions, *a good citizen is a person who cares about the welfare of others, is moral and ethical in his dealing with others, is able to challenge and critically question ideas, proposals, and suggestions, and in light of existing circumstances, is able to make good choices based upon good judgement.* [p. 74]

In keeping with our interpretation of the sociocivic-learning orientation, the schools should make an attempt to compensate and accommodate the vernacular social influences (as just described) that contribute to the children's citizenship development, by incorporating these elements into the study of government. This should be done such that students can come to relate the everyday concerns that dominate their daily lives with the abstractions of political theory, the structure and organization of government, the processes and practices of government, and the principles and values of democracy. In other words, we are suggesting that the study of government must become as familiar to them as is their home, school, neighborhood, and community.

By combining the civic-learning orientation with the sociocivic-learning orientation, a more effective citizenship educational curriculum may result, one that is more balanced and wholistic than those currently being proposed for the revitalization of citizenship education. The drive to revitalize civic education tends to exemplify the more limited civic-learning orientation of citizenship education as seen in most of the following projects.

Citizenship Projects

Citizenship education is the focus of several projects that are aimed at improving or revitalizing various aspects of civic learning. At a recent meeting of the National Council for the Social Studies in St. Louis, Missouri, a presentation was made on behalf of four of these projects. They included the Close Up Foundation, the Foundation for Teaching Economics, the CIVITAS Project (cosponsored by the Foundation for Teaching Economics and the Council for the Advancement of Citizenship), and the Constitutional Rights Foundation.

Since 1971, the Close Up Foundation, a nonprofit educational foundation, has brought thousands of high school students to Washington, D.C., in order to provide them with an opportunity to study their government from inside the national capital. In addition to the Washington experience, the Close Up Foundation attempts to encourage participation in a variety of civic learning activities, including state and local programs and a Citizen Bee competition for students (Close Up Foundation, 1987).

The Foundation for Teaching Economics (FTE), in cooperation with the Constitutional Rights Foundation (CRF), is in the process of developing new civics materials for students in Grades 8 and 9. This project is attempting to merge content from economics and civics, as a means of providing a new approach to the study of civics. It is described in a publication entitled *Our Democracy: How America Works* (FTE & CRF, n.d.).

The third project, CIVITAS, is cosponsored by the Center for Civic Education, under the direction of Charles Quigley, and the Council for the Advancement of Citizenship (CAC), under the direction of Diane U. Eisenberg. Both directors serve as codirectors of the CIVITAS Project (CAC, 1988). Several affiliated organizations have contributed to the CIVITAS Project, and a number of important educators and scholars have served on its Framework Development Committee. For example, Earnest Boyer chaired the National Review Council, which included the executive directors of many important educational and citizenship service types of organizations that make up the CAC membership. An initial draft of the framework for CIVITAS was circulated among various committee members for review, outlining a basic civic-learning approach to citizenship education for the schools. It included issues and topics related to the function, structure, and organization of government; types of government and comparative government; the law and legal systems; politics and government related to the United States, including basic democratic principles and a relatively strong emphasis on the Constitution; the structure of government, including federalism; the rights and responsibilities of the American citizen; and a strong emphasis on the need for citizenship participation (*CIVITAS: A Framework for Civic Education*, 1989).

The fourth project, the Constitutional Rights Foundation, is a nonprofit organization that has contributed to the advancement of citizenship education for over 25 years. While focusing its efforts within a regional area, the CRF is well known for its Youth Community Service programs, which have existed since 1961. In 1984 this organization began a special project in cooperation with the Los Angeles Unified School District, in order to engage Los Angeles students in youth service programs aimed at "developing leadership skills related to becoming responsible citizens" (CRF, 1988).

The growing concern about citizenship seems to be reflected in the

growing number of projects related to some aspect of citizenship education. These diverse and varied efforts are coming together under the
auspices of the Council for the Advancement of Citizenship, which, in
addition to promoting citizenship in American society, also serves as a
clearinghouse for the various organizations that are interested in citizenship issues in American society.

Instructional Approaches

In 1983, we began analyzing instructional approaches to citizenship education, based on a review of 20 years of social studies literature
(Dynneson & Gross, 1983). We tentatively identified eight such approaches that are used within the schools (see Figure 1.2). These became the basis for a series of studies and research reports that assessed
the current status of citizenship education within the social studies.

The first study in this series was aimed at assessing the perceptions
of college and university social studies methods instructors (members
of the National Council for the Social Studies/College and University
Faculty Assembly) regarding, among other things, the importance of
these eight approaches as preparation for individuals who would become social studies teachers (Dynneson et al., 1988). The second and
third reports in the series were based on a survey of four student groups
who were about to graduate from their respective high schools in Arkansas, California, Minnesota, and Texas, in 1987. This study and the re-
sultant two reports surveyed student perceptions of how each of the
eight approaches affected their understanding of citizenship (Dynneson
et al., 1989, 1990).

All of these studies were of an exploratory nature and were designed to provide the groundwork for another round of scientific survey
studies and possible experimental research that we plan to conduct in
the 1990s. The eight instructional approaches are important in that they
seem to be the most obvious means for dealing with democratic citizenship concerns within the curriculum of the schools.

Our more recent research draws on the work of Fred M. Newmann
who in 1977 also identified a list of eight citizenship education approaches. By combining additional lists of approaches, we have attempted to develop a set of 12 approaches that seem to reflect the status
of citizenship instruction in the schools. In addition, we have attempted
to isolate four core approaches that seem to be the dominant means, at
present, for delivering citizenship education to students (see Figure 1.3).

By comparing Newmann's list with ours, we have found some interesting similarities that suggest that there is a common core of four

**FIGURE 1.2.   Dynneson and Gross's Eight Approaches for Citizenship
Instruction**

1. Citizenship as Persuasion,
    Socialization and Indoctrination.
    This approach is based on the
    assumption that children need to
    be taught the perceived norms and
    values of their society and culture.

2. Citizenship as Contemporary
    Issues and Current Events. This
    approach is based on the
    assumption that in order to
    become effective and concerned
    citizens, students must participate
    in studying the contemporary
    issues of their times.

3. Citizenship as the Study of
    American History, Civics,
    Geography and Related Social
    Sciences. The underlying
    assumption of this approach is
    that students will become "good
    citizens" through the
    accumulation of factual
    information pertaining to the
    setting, history, process of
    government, and the American
    economic system.

4. Citizenship as Civic Participation
    and Civic Action. This approach
    is based on the assumption that
    "good citizens" are capable of
    participating directly in the affairs
    of adult society.

5. Citizenship as Scientific Thinking.
    The basic underlying assumption
    of this approach is that students
    should be trained in certain
    intellectual processes and
    procedures in order to help them
    assume the responsibilities of
    effective citizenship.

6. Citizenship as a Jurisprudence
    (legalistic) Process. This approach
    is based on the assumption that
    traditional constitutional and
    legalistic processes hold the key to
    successful citizenship in a
    democratic society.

7. Citizenship as Humanistic
    Development (concern for the total
    welfare of the student). This
    approach is based on the
    assumption that citizenship rests
    on the growth and development of
    healthy and well-adjusted
    children.

8. Citizenship as Preparation for
    Global Interdependence. This
    approach reflects the growing
    concerns about nationally
    centered programs that tend to
    neglect the growing world-wide
    needs, links, and responsibilities
    of humankind.

Source: Dynneson, Thomas L., & Richard E. Gross. Citizenship Education and the Social Studies: Which Is Which? *The Social Studies,* Vol. 73, pp. 229–234 (September/October 1983). Reprinted with permission of the Helen Dwight Reid Educational Foundation. Published by Heldref Publications, 4000 Albemarle St., N.W., Washington, D.C. © 1983.

FIGURE 1.3.   Newmann's Eight Approaches for Citizenship Instruction

1. *Disciplines approach*
   emphasizes the teaching of history, civics and government

2. *Law-related education approach*
   became a product of the Law-Related Education Act of 1976

3. *Social problems and public issues approach*
   focuses on issues and problems such as war and peace and the problems of American society

4. *Critical thinking and decision-making approach*
   attempts to help students develop cognitive thinking skills related to decision making

5. *Values clarification approach*
   attempts to help students clarify the influences that shape values and attitudes

6. *Moral development approach*
   incorporates the stages of Lawrence Kohlberg's theory on cognitive moral development in order to help students confront moral dilemmas

7. *Student participation in community involvement approach*
   encourages students to become involved in worthy community projects

8. *Institutional school reform approach*
   attempts to create more of a democratic environment within the schools in order to provide opportunities for students to develop and demonstrate civic skills.

Source: Adapted from Newmann, Fred. Alternative Approaches to Citizenship Education: A Search for Authenticity. In *Education for Responsible Citizenship: The Report of the National Task Force on Citizenship Education* (pp. 175–187). Used with permission of the Institute for Development of Educational Activities, Inc. (IDEA), and cosponsored by The Danforth Foundation and the Institute and the Charles F. Kettering Foundation. Published by McGraw-Hill (1977) with all rights reverting to IDEA.

instructional approaches in the social studies: the academic-disciplines approach, the jurisprudence or legal-political approach, the critical-thinking approach, and the citizenship-as-civic-participation or civic-action approach. In addition, there are eight related or subordinate approaches contained in both lists. These include the social-problems or public-issues approach, the values approach, the moral-development approach, the institutional school-reform approach, the persuasion (socialization and indoctrination) approach, the contemporary-issues approach, the humanistic approach, and the preparation-for-global-interdependence approach.

By combining the approaches from the two lists, then, a comprehensive list of 12 instructional approaches for citizenship education can be compiled, which combine both the social and political concerns of society. These are shown in Figure 1.4. They open up new research horizons that may allow for a more comprehensive perspective on citizenship development within the social studies curriculum. This list of 12 may not be entirely inclusive, and some approaches may need to be combined with others or eliminated altogether. The 4 instructional approaches we have placed at the core are currently at the heart of citizenship education, while the 8 subordinate approaches may be in the process of becoming core approaches or of fading away.

It should be noted here that, during his tenure at the University of Wisconsin-Madison, Newmann's research interests included a concern for the direction and status of citizenship education in the schools. In 1975, he published a book entitled *Education for Citizenship Action*, in which he outlined his concerns and attitudes about citizenship education in the schools. In a section called "Pitfalls of Citizenship Education," he noted the failures of the various instructional approaches in dealing with real-life concerns and problems of students. He argued that meaningful civic participation was preferable to the inept programs that were (and still are) in place in the schools. As he put it, "Considered as a whole, these dimensions of citizenship education are plagued by an orientation that, in subtle ways, tends to communicate unworkable notions of citizenship participation" (p. 6).

Newmann's (1975) concerns are insightful and reasonable, but they point out the difficulties that education encounters in meeting its citizenship education responsibilities. It is a dilemma in which the schools are placed in a most difficult position. Newmann raises several interesting questions, particularly about the role and status of students attending our compulsory schools. Most societies, whether primitive or civilized, allow time for the socialization process to do its preparatory work. During this time students are in a kind of "limbo" state in which full membership in society is neither granted nor withheld. It is a time when students are given instruction in the basic domains of the knowledge, skills, and values of society. In other words, students are quasi-participants in the affairs of the adult world.

Therefore, the issue before us is to determine to what extent youth,

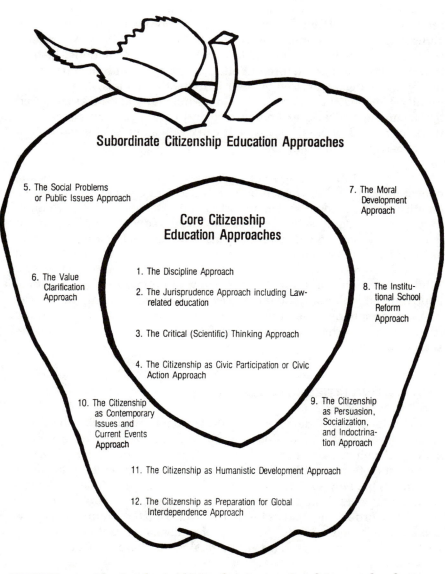

Subordinate Citizenship Education Approaches

5. The Social Problems
   or Public Issues Approach

7. The Moral
   Development
   Approach

**Core Citizenship
Education Approaches**

6. The Value
   Clarification
   Approach

1. The Discipline Approach

2. The Jurisprudence Approach including Law-
   related education

3. The Critical (Scientific) Thinking Approach

4. The Citizenship as Civic Participation or Civic
   Action Approach

8. The Institu-
   tional School
   Reform
   Approach

10. The Citizenship
    as Contemporary
    Issues and
    Current Events
    Approach

9. The Citizenship
   as Persuasion,
   Socialization,
   and Indoctrina-
   tion Approach

11. The Citizenship as Humanistic Development Approach

12. The Citizenship as Preparation for Global
    Interdependence Approach

**FIGURE 1.4.   The Synthesized List of 12 Instructional Approaches for
Citizenship Education in the Social Studies**

in a democratic society, should be entitled or encouraged to participate and exercise adult rights, and therefore to be held accountable for adult responsibilities. Those who support Newmann's (1975) position regarding the level of student participation in society should be required to address the level of student responsibility for their actions. At present, students are not held accountable as adults for their actions; instead they are given time to mature in both their physical and mental capacities, while being supervised by their parents, the schools, and the community. The idea of total immersion in participatory action, as espoused by Newmann and also as emphasized in the CIVITAS framework, may work for a few students, but may not work well at all for the majority of students (Dynneson et al., 1990).

At this point, it is important to suggest that, in the minds of some educators, citizenship education is so broad and contains so many orientations and approaches that almost anything taught in the curriculum might be considered some form of citizenship education. Therefore, it is important that some general consensus be reached among educators as to which of the two orientations and which of the many instructional approaches are most important to the education of American youth. While some educators support a narrow orientation toward political education and others would include everything taught within the curriculum of the schools, there is a need to search for some common ground for citizenship education, emerging from both philosophical and research sources.

REVITALIZING CITIZENSHIP EDUCATION

The ideology of democracy and the social needs of a pluralistic society have combined in this country to form the basis for a unique society. Revolutionary leaders were challenged by the need to form a unified society shaped by the social, economic, and political needs of the time. This new society was established on the principles of democracy, which were designed to encourage the common people to change the social order that had refused them citizenship status. This new society was based on a new concept of citizenship, rooted in a democratic creed in which each free individual would have an equal voice in societal affairs.

The public schools were envisioned, by Jefferson and Mann in particular, as the institutions that would educate the common people for their citizenship responsibilities. Education per se—including the ability to read, write, and do basic computations—was seen as the means for preparing the children of the new republic for citizenship. Democratic values would be acquired through a basic knowledge of the U.S. Constitution. It was Jefferson who first articulated the inextricable tie that was to be formed between education and the politics that would characterize our society, when he wrote, "If a nation expects to be ignorant and free in a state of civilization, it expects what never was and never will be" (Cremin, 1965, p. 5).

In time, the status and direction of citizenship education in the schools became an important indicator of the health and vitality of American society as a democratic entity. The role, purpose, and importance of citizenship education in changing curriculum programs may thereby serve as a barometer that signals change in the social environment of the nation and the nation's ability to maintain a continued commitment to the development of a democratic society.

The development of a public school system played an unusually important role as a socializing agent and as a means of building social unity. The schools were expected to integrate the nation's diverse cultures and to help recent immigrant youth to find their way into the mainstream of American society. After decades of working with diverse cultural groups, the most successful accomplishment of the schools has been to achieve some degree of linguistic unity. Less successful has been the achievement of social values that reflect a unified cultural perspective. At present, the schools continue to be held responsible for many aspects of citizenship development. These include the educational expectations for individuals living in a democratic society, especially in regard to knowledge about American heritage, American government, free enterprise, and the balance that must exist between individuals' democratic rights and responsibilities (Butts, 1989; National Commission on Excellence in Education, 1983).

Today, there are still thoughtful people who are convinced that pluralistic societies can survive if they are able to maintain a commitment to a higher ideology, one that accommodates multiple social perspectives and values. The democratic ideology provides the basis upon which a culturally pluralistic state can exist. Democratic values, principles, and processes serve as the uniting ideology that bonds the diverse segments of society. This same ideology serves as the basis for resolving cultural conflicts that are bound to exist between cultural groups. Conflict-resolution and consensus-building strategies can be taught by the schools as a means to help youth learn to deal with the cultural pressures that exist in complex societies. Educational leaders should encourage an open examination of existing social problems, including current social, economic, and political problems. Citizens can be taught rational processes that can be used to resolve emotionally charged conflicts and thereby maintain the balanced perspective that is needed if just solutions are to be found. As public institutions, schools need to play a more important role in helping youth learn values, principles, processes, and skills that are needed to resolve complex societal problems.

Schools that serve the needs of a democratic society are burdened with both formal and informal expectations. Typically the schools are organized around specific educational goals and an established program of instruction. In addition, schools in a democracy are expected to address the needs of citizenship that go beyond the stated educational goals and curriculum outlines. As Dewey (1916) commented, "A democracy is more than a form of government; it is primarily a form of associated living, of conjoint communicated experience" (p. 101).

Reason tells us that citizenship goals and standards must become omnipresent through the entire educational process and experience, if we are to preserve our democratic heritage. While many educators may prefer to avoid stating citizenship goals and standards, time may be running out for the schools to fulfill their responsibilities as builders of social unity. We therefore believe that citizenship goals and standards must be stated and prioritized by the schools, before it is too late.

A Manifesto for the Schools

Earlier in this chapter, we discussed some special aspects of citizenship development and some of the means whereby the schools attempt to provide citizenship instruction to students within the social studies curriculum. While numerous instructional approaches for citizenship education were identified through an extensive review of the social studies literature, they did not originate from a unified rationale. Education, and the social studies in particular, might benefit by the development of a specific set of goals and standards that could originate from a unified theory and rationale and thereby serve as the basis for a standard citizenship education in the schools. The following list of goals and standards is offered as a possible basis for such efforts.

1. Schools should educate their students to achieve a level of social awareness sufficient to insure the development and continuation of a just society. The schools would develop this level of awareness related to a wide range of social problems such as poverty, prejudice, ignorance, disease, pollution, overpopulation, illegal immigration, alcohol and drug abuse, crime, conflict, and war.

2. Schools should encourage students to participate in the social, political, and economic affairs of government. The schools are to be held responsible for helping each individual become familiar with the systems that have been created to operate the government. This knowledge allows the citizen to help solve personal and public problems.

3. Schools should enable their students to acquire a level of literacy necessary for their participation in the affairs of the community, state, nation, and world. The schools must work to elevate students to a satisfactory level of literacy so that they can contribute to the welfare of the nation as well as to maximize their own potential as members of the community at large.

4. Students should be taught to evaluate critically information that relates to important issues that affect the community. The schools must help students develop their analytical and critical thinking skills, in order that they may deal appropriately with the volumes of information that exist within the public domain. Each individual must be trained to apply reasoned processes related to both public and private social, economic, and political concerns.

5. Schools should educate their students to contribute to the economic well-being of the community, by providing labor, skills, talent, goods, or services that will be of benefit to the community. The schools are responsible for providing the knowledge, skills, and attitudes that will help each student become a productive and contributing citizen. While not every individual possesses the same intelligence, energy, creative thought, or artistic inclination, all citizens should be encouraged to contribute to society according to the best of their ability.

6. Schools should develop in their students those interpersonal skills that will help them build positive social relationships, in order to get along with others. The schools are expected to help each student develop interpersonal skills by providing the appropriate social opportunities in which each individual can share and contribute to the goals of a group. These goals and standards are especially important because, in democratic systems, social actions are primarily group actions; therefore, the individual must learn to work with and through groups and organizations.

7. Schools should teach students to understand, adopt, and support the ethical principles of democracy. The schools are expected to promote democratic principles and values by providing and creating opportunities for students to use democratic processes in the solution of school-related issues, conflicts, and problems. The schools must cease to be authoritarian communities and establish a social environment in which the concepts of mutual respect, individual worth, and the dignity of each person are espoused. Because democratic ethics are the impor-

tant standards used by citizens to evaluate the conduct of others in society, these ethics must prevail within the school environment.

A Call for Educational Leadership

Educators can contribute to the advancement of a strengthened democratic citizenship by recognizing and responding to the needs of society. Thomas Jefferson envisioned a school system that was designed to intervene in the life of the public, in order to help unify the nation. He realized that, without an important and potent intervening educational system, democracy could never become a reality. The school, next to the family, is the single most important source of citizenship development; however, in recent years it often seems to have lost its sense of mission, if not its commitment to the citizenship task.

While there are many important issues and tasks facing educators, school leaders must do more to advance the cause of democracy. Educators must provide a new quality of leadership, committed to citizenship education for all youth. Democratic citizenship can be advanced when educational leaders—teams of talented teachers and administrators— take the following actions:

1. Prioritize educational goals by placing desired democratic citizenship outcomes ahead of or at least equal to the fundamental processes of reading, writing, and arithmetic.

2. Re-examine the school curriculum frameworks and materials through such techniques as content analysis, with an eye toward enhancing the democratic appeal of educational programs by identifying the prime and unique contributions that each subfield makes to citizenship education.

3. Reconsider the nature, placement, and organization of current citizenship content, as a means of providing a reorganized sequence of continuous K–12 citizenship education experiences for students.

4. Study ways in which citizenship education can be enhanced as an important aspect of teacher education programs.

5. Sponsor community-wide forums in which parents, teachers, and community leaders can begin dialogues on the ways and means of strengthening citizenship education in the home, school, and community; and establish cooperative school/community programs that provide citizenship participation opportunities for parents and students.

6. Identify and promote effective teaching strategies and activities that are appropriate as democratic experiences for students, such as including students in making important changes regarding the school environment.

7. Develop experimental model citizenship programs that can be tested in pilot programs throughout the nation, and establish a communication network that will link those experimental programs together, in order to share results.

CONCLUSION

Since the earliest days of the republic, the schools, in the eyes of society, have held important sociocivic responsibilities. Their role has been especially important during the decades of heavy immigration into the United States. The schools—the major institution of socialization for American youth—have been expected to help each succeeding generation to develop the shared civic attitudes and competencies valued by the society. As workshops of democratic citizenship, the schools frequently have succeeded, but they also have often failed to meet the citizenship needs of youth and society. While they have implanted many patriotic ideas, they have failed to provide instruction in and functional models of democratic processes. American teachers and schools frequently have been seriously wanting; they have failed especially to provide the kind of learning experiences that promote the understandings and skills of democratic citizenship. This failure goes beyond irresponsibility, as the schools have actually contributed to the building of anti-egalitarian attitudes on the part of pupils. The unfortunate result is that young people often tend to look at what is espoused as the essence of the American way as but hypocritical statements of adult society, institutions, and government, made by those who say they believe one thing and behave in opposite ways.

In order to succeed, our educational system must have a sense of mission and a commitment to the establishment of a democratic society, a just society that is fortified by democratic laws and institutions. In their programs and approaches, schools should mirror desired civic qualities. The schools, more than any other social institution, will determine the extent to which democratic goals can be achieved. When educational leaders lose sight of their democratic responsibilities, the nation is in danger of losing its vision and direction.

While the nation may be at a low point regarding the status of citizenship education in the schools, it is not too late to revitalize the nation's commitment to citizenship education and to the democratic way of life. The schools, however, must come to accept their democratic mission as a serious and important obligation and trust to the nation. The people ultimately must determine the nature of the good and just society and decide on the values that will prevail. We hope that the decision will be to continue to support and strengthen the values that form the foundation of the democratic way of life. To some extent, this decision is in the hands of educators.

REFERENCES

Barrera, M. (1988). *Beyond Aztlan: Ethnic autonomy in comparative perspective.* New York: Praeger.

Battle, J. A., & Shannon, R. L. (Eds.). (1968). *The new idea in education.* New York: Harper & Row.

Bellah, R. N. (1985). *Habits of the heart: Individualism and commitment in American life.* New York: Harper & Row.

Bloom, A. (1987). *The closing of the American mind.* New York: Simon & Schuster.

Bronfenbrenner, U. (1986). Alienation and the four worlds of childhood. *Phi Delta Kappan, 67,* 430–436.

Broudy, H. S. (1972). *The real world of the public schools.* New York: Harcourt Brace Jovanovich.

Butts, R. F. (1950). *The American tradition in religion and education.* Boston: Beacon Press.

Butts, R. F. (1955). *A cultural history of western education.* New York: McGraw-Hill.

Butts, R. F. (1980). *The revival of civic learning: A rationale for citizenship education in American schools.* Bloomington, IN: Phi Delta Kappa Educational Foundation.

Butts, R. F. (1989). *The civic mission in educational reform: Perspectives for the public and the profession.* Stanford, CA: Hoover Institution Press.

Chandler, R. C., Enslen, R. A., & Renstrom, P. G. (1985). *The constitutional law dictionary: Vol. 1: Individual rights.* Oxford, England: ABC-CLIO.

CIVITAS: A Framework for Civil Education. (1989). Unpublished draft manuscript.

Close Up Foundation. (1987). *The Close Up Program: A citizenship experience in Washington, D.C.* Washington, DC: Author.

Constitutional Rights Foundation. (1988). *Annual report.* Los Angeles: Author.

Council for the Advancement of Citizenship. (1988, Fall). *CAC: Citizenship Education News, 7,* 1–15.

Cremin, L. A. (1965). *The genius of American education.* New York: Vintage.

Dawson, R. E., & Prewitt, K. (1969). *Political socialization.* Boston: Little, Brown.

De Vos, G., & Romanucci-Ross, L. (1975). *Ethnic identity: Cultural continuities and change.* Palo Alto, CA: Mayfield.

Dewey, J. (1916). *Democracy and education.* New York: Macmillan.

Dewey, J. (1968). The function of the teacher. In J. A. Battle & R. L. Shannon (Eds.), *The new idea in education* (pp. 13–15). New York: Harper & Row.

Dynneson, T. L., & Gross, R. E. (1983). Citizenship education and the social studies: Which is which? *The Social Studies, 73,* 229–234.

Dynneson, T. L., & Gross, R. E. (1987). *The citizenship development framework: A six stage socio/cultural theory.* Odessa, TX: The Citizenship Development Study Project.

Dynneson, T. L., Gross, R. E., & Nickel, J. A. (1988). *An exploratory survey of CUFA members' opinions and practices pertaining to citizenship education in the social studies, 1985–86.* Stanford, CA: Center for Educational Research at Stanford.

Dynneson, T. L., Gross, R. E., & Nickel, J. A. (1989). *An exploratory survey of four groups of 1987 graduating seniors' perceptions pertaining to (1) the qualities of a good citizen, (2) the sources of citizenship influence, and (3) the contributions of social studies courses and programs of study to citizenship development.* Stanford, CA: Center for Educational Research at Stanford.

Dynneson, T. L., Gross, R. E., & Nickel, J. A. (1990). *An exploratory survey of four groups of 1987 graduating seniors' perceptions pertaining to (4) student preferred citizenship approaches, (5) teacher preferred citizenship approaches, (6) citizenship approaches and elementary students, and (7) citizenship approaches and secondary students.* Stanford, CA: Center for Educational Research at Stanford.

Ehlers, H. (1977). *Crucial issues in education.* New York: Holt, Rinehart and Winston.

Foundation for Teaching Economics, and the Constitutional Rights Foundation. *Our democracy: How America works.* (n.d.). San Francisco: Author.

Gould, J., & Kolb, W. L. (Eds.). (1964). *A dictionary of the social sciences.* New York: Free Press.

Greeley, A. M. (1977). Pluralism in America. In H. Ehlers (Ed.), *Crucial issues in education,* pp. 61–67. New York: Holt, Rinehart & Winston.

Greenberg, E. S. (Ed.). (1970). *Political socialization.* New York: Atherton Press.

Gross, R. E., & Zeleny, L. D. (1958). *Educating citizens for democracy.* New York: Oxford University Press.

Guide to American law: Everyone's legal encyclopedia (Vols. 1–12). (1985). New York: West.

Hess, R. D., & Torney, J. V. (1970). The development of political attitudes in children. In E. S. Greenberg (Ed.), *Political socialization* (pp. 64–82). New York: Atherton Press.

Jones, A. H. (1989, Summer). Civic education: Alan Jones reviews R. Freeman Butts; Butts reviews Richard Pratte. *Educational Studies, 20,* 129–134.

McGee, R. (1975). *Points of departure: Basic concepts in sociology.* Hinsdale, IL: Dryden Press.

National Commission on Excellence in Education. (1983). *A nation at risk: The imperative for educational reform.* Washington, DC: U.S. Government Printing Office.

Newmann, F. M. (1975). *Education for citizenship action.* Berkeley: McCutchan.

Newmann, F. M. (1977). Alternative approaches to citizenship education: A search for authenticity. In *Education for Responsible Citizenship: The Report of the National Task Force on Citizenship Education* (pp. 175–187). New York: McGraw-Hill.

Renshon, S. A. (1977). *Handbook of political socialization*. New York: Free Press.

Smith, W. A. (1955). *Ancient education*. New York: Philosophical Library.

Troxell, L. (1968). On Socrates, who warned us of the danger of becoming misanthropists (haters of men) and misologists (haters of ideas). In J. A. Battle & R. L. Shannon (Eds.), *The new idea in education* (pp. 71–74). New York: Harper & Row.

2 The Political Perspective

Civic Participation and the Public Good

ROBERT B. WOYACH

If a casual observer were to open a college textbook on American government or introductory politics, that person might easily assume that political scientists paid little attention to citizenship. Beyond short descriptions of the legal bases for gaining and losing citizenship, the term would not appear in the book.

That casual impression would, of course, be mistaken. Citizenship is a core concern of political science. In the same introductory textbook, the observer would find chapters on civil rights, public opinion, voting, political participation, political parties, and interest groups. Those chapters describe the practice of citizenship in a representative democracy. A chapter on political philosophy would explore the appropriate nature of citizenship from various perspectives. Even political scientists who study international politics have become interested in citizenship as it relates to the international system.

This chapter draws on the philosophical and empirical research of political scientists to answer three broad questions. First, what are the dominant approaches to citizenship in American political science? Second, how have our views of citizenship changed over the past three decades, and what is the status of citizenship today? Finally, are there things educators can do to encourage citizen participation in the future?

MAINSTREAM APPROACHES TO CITIZENSHIP

Over the past 30 years, mainstream political scientists in the United States have held a remarkably consistent notion of the concept of citizenship. Within democratic political systems, citizenship involves a complex combination of claims against the community (including protection, political rights, and respect) and assumed responsibilities to the community (including loyalty, obedience to laws, respect for officials, self-control in public matters, and participation in the political life of the community) (Lane, 1972). The dimension of citizenship that has been of primary importance and interest to political scientists has been the responsibility to participate. Citizenship involves more than the rights of passive subjects living in a particular area. It involves more than acts of symbolic support for the civic community. Citizenship involves active participation in politics, that is, in the governance of the community (Thompson, 1970; Verba, 1969).

But what does participation in politics mean? What do citizens do in representative democracies such as the United States, in which elected officials are responsible for debating and making public policy? How much citizen participation is appropriate? Political scientists have agreed far less about the answers to these questions than they have about the basic concept of citizenship.

The Forms of Citizen Participation

Over the last 30 years, a number of empirical political scientists have explored the different ways in which citizens can participate in the political system and the extent to which different segments of the population actually do participate. In summarizing this research, Milbrath and Goel (1977, pp. 10–16) identify five distinct modes or forms of participation. They can be described as:

1. Voting and patriotic support (voters)
2. Campaign and party work (electoral gladiators)
3. Communicating opinions to political elites (watchdogs)
4. Participating in protest activities (protesters)
5. Organizing community groups on political issues (organizers)

With the exception of voting, individuals who routinely participate in one mode of activity rarely if ever participate in the others. Only about 11 percent of all Americans are likely to participate in all four of the more normative modes of activity; voting, campaign work, communicating opinions to political elites, and organizing community groups (Verba & Nie, 1972).

Voters.   Democratic theorists have typically regarded voting as the cornerstone of citizenship. Whether it be an election for town council, the state legislature, local judges, the national congress, or the president of the United States, voting has been seen as the most basic way through which citizens try to influence the political life of the community. Voting is also the most common form of civic participation.

Recent research, however, casts a very different light on voting as a mode of citizen participation. Most voters do not believe their vote has any meaningful impact on public policy (Milbrath & Goel, 1977). They vote out of a sense of duty and as a sign of support. In short, in behavioral terms voting is a form of patriotic support similar to paying taxes, flying the flag, respecting the police, or signing up for the draft. Most voters do not see their vote as an act that will influence the political life of the community.

Electoral Gladiators.   Only about 15 percent of the American public participates actively in political campaigns and political parties. These electoral gladiators campaign formally for candidates, belong to political clubs, try to persuade others how to vote, run for office, attend political rallies, and donate money to political parties and campaigns. In contrast to voters, electoral gladiators see themselves as highly influential citizen activists. They help determine who runs for office and thus who makes public policy. While electoral gladiators almost always vote, the typical voter—even if she never misses an election—is highly unlikely to become a campaign or party activist.

Watchdogs.   All political theories of citizenship give some attention to citizen participation between elections. Traditionally this dimension of citizenship has been seen in terms of a watchdog function (monitoring the performance of elected officials) and an interest-articulation function (voicing opinions to those officials).

Empirical research supports the idea that watchdogs represent a distinct form of citizen participation. In a multiyear study, Milbrath (1968) found a cluster of people who kept informed about politics, sent messages of support or protest to public officials, engaged in political discussions with others, informed others about politics, wrote letters to the editor, and communicated their opinions on issues to public officials. Watchdogs tended not to get involved in party politics; they did not campaign for particular candidates. Indeed, they tended to be more critical of government than electoral gladiators. Watchdogs also tended to be more highly educated, better informed, and more politically motivated than the average citizen. Milbrath found that, while most voters felt a responsibility to perform these watchdog functions, a sense of verbal inadequacy kept them from doing so.

Protesters. While watchdogs tend to be critical of government, they are decidedly different from protesters. Protesters engage in such activities as joining in street demonstrations, attending protest meetings, refusing to obey unjust laws, and even rioting in order to draw attention to perceived injustices. Until the civil rights and anti-Vietnam War movements put this mode of citizenship onto the public agenda, it had been relatively neglected by scholars. Up until the late 1970s, public opinion polls indicated that most Americans did not regard protest activities as legitimate forms of citizen participation (Citrin, 1981). Even now, fewer than 5 percent of white Americans and 19 percent of blacks could see themselves participating in some kind of protest activity (Milbrath, 1968). A large majority of Americans still see rioting as an illegitimate political activity.

Community Organizers and Single-issue Activists. This dimension of citizen participation remains the least well conceptualized, perhaps because it fits least well within political theories of representative democracy (Cobb & Elder, 1972). Yet a study by Verba, Nie, and Kim (1971) found this mode of participation—characterized by such activities as forming a group to deal with a social problem, getting an existing group to deal with a social problem, belonging to organizations concerned about particular issues, and contacting public officials about a particular issue—in all seven of the countries surveyed. (The countries included Austria, the Netherlands, India, Japan, Nigeria, and Yugoslavia, as well as the United States.) About 20 percent of all Americans tend to become involved in these types of activities at some point in their lives. These individuals routinely vote, but they rarely if ever become electoral gladiators, even though they share with them a high psychological involvement in community matters.

Elitist Versus Populist Perspectives

Despite widespread adherence to a democratic (i.e., participatory) ideal of citizenship, empirical studies describing the American political system clearly show that politics in the United States is essentially elitist (Bauer, Pool, & Dexter, 1972; Dahl, 1961; Lane, 1972; Milbrath, 1968; Milbrath & Goel, 1977; Rosenau, 1974). Whether it be local, state, or national politics, only a small elite directly influences the political agenda or public policy on a regular basis. The American political elite is only vaguely defined. One does not need to be part of the social or economic elite to be part of the political elite, although levels of political participation tend to be related to socioeconomic status.

This empirical description of American political practice is widely accepted. Less widely accepted is the assumption that an elitist system is either valid or necessary. Two starkly different ideologies of citizenship arise from this conflict. On the one hand are those who believe that representative government works best with less citizen participation. These analysts can be labeled "elitists." On the other hand are those who believe that democratic systems should have high levels of citizen participation; these are the "populists."

Elitism and populism have usually been treated as distinct and radically opposed categories. It may be more useful, however, to see them as the opposite ends of a complex continuum of opinion. The points at which different theorists or researchers can be placed on that continuum depend on their views of the "average citizen."

Elitist Assumptions About Citizen Incompetence.   Since World War II, no more than 68 percent of the American electorate has voted in any one presidential election (Burnham, 1982). As few as 25 percent vote in many local elections (Henry, 1984). Even smaller proportions of people engage in the more intensive modes of citizen participation. Public opinion polls show that most Americans lack a detailed understanding of current political issues and government; opinions on particular issues are extremely unstable. The average citizen is actually less committed to democratic ideology than most members of the elite (McClosky & Saller, 1984). In response to questions about specific situations, many do not support basic constitutional rights (Dye & Zeigler, 1978). In contrast to political elites, the average citizen can be described as less calculating and "more strongly influenced by inertia, habit, unexamined loyalties, personal attachments, emotions and transient impulses" (Dahl, 1961, pp. 90–91).

Political analysts on the elitist end of the spectrum interpret these data on participation and public opinion as evidence that the average citizen is too apathetic, too ill informed, too unthinking, and too antidemocratic to play an active role in political life. In his 1963 study of modern politics, Dahl concluded that most people are not "political animals" by nature, and therefore an elitist system may be inevitable. On the basis of interviews with blue-collar workers in a Connecticut city, Lane (1972) argued that elites must help average citizens understand their interests vis-à-vis particular issues. Dye and Zeigler (1978) take a clearly elitist position, arguing that democracy only works *because* the masses rarely become involved in politics. Greater participation by the masses could lead to "mobocracy," not democracy.

To elitists, mass participation can be particularly dangerous when the issue requires specialized knowledge, as in the areas of science and technology, economics, and foreign policy. Issues such as acid rain, the use of biotechnology, and monetary or foreign trade policy are simply too complex for the average citizen to comprehend. The pendulumlike swings in American attitudes toward foreign affairs that Almond (1961) has documented are used to demonstrate that, as a world leader, the United States can ill afford to let its foreign policy be strongly influenced—let alone governed by—an ill-informed and emotional citizenry.

Not surprisingly, elitists tend to see voting as the most legitimate form of citizen participation. Even with respect to voting, however, Dye and Zeigler (1978) have argued that low levels of participation can be desirable. People only become activated, they argue, when things are going poorly. Thus low voter participation reflects a healthy satisfaction with the status quo. Even those elitists who argue that high levels of voting are important, however, tend to ignore other modes of participation (e.g., Burnham, 1982). They fear that nonparticipation in elections reflects an unhealthy alienation from the political system. However, their implicit preference is to protect elected officials from the whims of public opinion between elections.

Populist Attitudes About Participation and Learning.   The most fundamental belief of populists, whether stated or not, is that individual citizens are the best judges of their own interests (Thompson, 1970). Thus the search for the public good—whether that be defined as the greatest good for the greatest number, or the greatest good for the community as a whole—can only be successful if citizen participation is maximized. But is the average citizen really the best judge of his interests? The empirical research cited by elitists would seem to cast doubt on that assumption.

Populists respond to the image of the incompetent citizen by raising two questions. First, while the data show that the average citizen is ill informed and relatively incompetent, do they necessarily imply that an elite can represent mass interests any better? Elitist systems, in other words, may adequately represent elite interests, but they may not represent the interests of the average person. They are even less likely to represent the interests of minorities, who face inequities or injustices within the political system.

Second, while the data show that today's citizens are less competent than is desirable, need we infer that citizens cannot become interested and competent? Indeed, the citizen today may be caught in a no-win situation. Within representative systems, citizen participation often has little or no impact on public policy. As a result, citizens participate very little. It is the low level of participation that causes low levels of knowledge and political skill. If citizens' actions had more impact, greater participation would be encouraged and the average citizen would become better informed, more competent, and more confident. With increasing knowledge, competence, and confidence, people would participate even more (Barber, 1984; Pateman, 1970; Thompson, 1970).

Because populists value the expansion of opportunities for citizen participation and learning, they tend to focus on citizenship, between elections (Raskin, 1986). Such modes of participation as community organizing involve people intimately and directly in public policy making. As such, they provide the most intense and valuable learning experiences. They also represent the most likely ways to expand participatory horizons: As citizens work toward parochial (neighborhood or local) goals, they see the need for appropriate policies in wider arenas (the state, nation, or world) as well (Alger, 1978).

THE CRISIS OF CITIZENSHIP
AND SHIFTING ATTITUDES TOWARD PARTICIPATION

Since the 1950s, there has been a none-too-subtle shift in American political scientists' views of citizen participation. This shift, affecting both elitists and populists, emerged during the 1960s and 1970s as a result of political trends and new interpretations of data on participation and attitudes.

From Privatism to Community Power

The decade of the 1950s can in many respects be characterized as a decade of privatism. The vast majority of Americans seemed too wrapped up in their private affairs to be concerned with public life or political issues. Not surprisingly, the 1950s were a high point of elitist ideas among political scientists. Although the empirical studies of the time, such as those of Banfield (1961), Dahl (1961), and Lane (1972), revealed unexpectedly low levels of political participation, most analysts saw this as a sign that citizens were satisfied with the political system. Active participation may have been, as Gabriel Almond (1980) put it, an "ideal, but passivity, trust in government, and deference to authority" (p. 16) were more conducive to political stability. (Excellent analyses of this period are contained in Almond, 1980; and Pateman, 1980.)

John Kennedy's 1961 inaugural challenge to "ask what you can do for your country" foreshadowed fundamental changes in the ideal and the practice of citizenship. Three key processes gave rise to the change. First, the civil rights movement shattered the belief that nonparticipation reflected satisfaction with the political system. Black Americans took to the streets, first in nonviolent demonstrations and later in violent riots, because they had no other effective voice. Second, while the Great Society programs of the Johnson Administration tried to address some long-neglected social ills, they also concentrated power in the hands of experts and bureaucrats in Washington. Rather than empowering people, they further removed government from them. Finally, the Vietnam War demonstrated to many white middle-class Americans just how far removed the government had become from the average American. Vietnam, followed by the Watergate scandals, shook Americans' faith in the political system.

Political movements of both the left and right responded to the events of the 1960s and early 1970s by calling for a return to community power. The neoconservative movement rejected big government because it undermined the integrity of local values and key social structures— such as the neighborhood—that had traditionally mediated between government and people (Berger & Berger, 1983; Berger & Neuhaus, 1977). Despite their concern for democratic accountability, however, the neoconservatives have not been advocates of popular participation. They blamed the excesses of the 1960s on increased participation coupled with unreasonable expectations (Huntington, 1975; Medcalf & Dolbeare, 1985; Nisbet, 1972). They rejected government intervention in favor of a return to the privatism of the 1950s. Government would not solve problems; private philanthropy would.

For those groups that grew out of the radical New Left of the 1960s, the Great Society represented a failed approach to populism. National government could not empower people, however well intentioned its policies. Writers like Charles Reich (1970), Jack Newfield and Jeff Greenfield (1972), and Jeremy Rifkin (1977) encouraged average citizens to take charge of their lives through neighborhood coalitions and other forms of direct democracy (Boyte, 1980; Medcalf & Dolbeare, 1985).

The Rise of Political Alienation

The surge of interest in decentralization during the early 1970s presented a reverse image of the actual trends in citizen participation during the next decade. The 1970s saw the average citizen become increasingly less interested in public life. Opinion polls pointed to a decline both in people's faith in government and in their ability to influence government. In short, Americans were becoming increasingly alienated politically.

Political analysts have looked for the causes of political alienation in many places, including the highly visible political scandals of the last decade, the decline of political parties, social alienation, and the very logic and structure of representative democracy. Two of the most critical roots, however, may be the apparent complexity of political problems and the apparent inability of local, state, and national political institutions to solve them.

Even in the 1950s, political scientists like David Apter (1964) had noted that science and technology were creating both a new potential for human society and a new obstacle to citizen participation. Knowledge gains in the physical sciences have generated complex new issues, such as genetic engineering and space exploration. They have radically complicated the debate over others, like environmental protection. The advance of the social sciences has probably had an even more profound impact. The social sciences have added immensely to our understanding of the complexity of social problems. Social scientists have underscored the naïveté of looking for simple solutions or "quick fixes." The complexity and the technical knowledge involved in many contemporary issues place enormous demands on people who hope to participate intelligently in public debate and decision making. They also create new criteria for legitimacy which inhibit or limit the participation of the average citizen.

The lack of simple, "quick fixes" to complex problems has probably also contributed to the perception that political institutions have become unresponsive to citizens' needs. The new challenges we have placed before government have also come at a time when declining American hegemony in the world and growing global interdependence have decreased the ability of American political institutions to dictate solutions to political and economic problems. During the 1970s, a failed war in Vietnam, increasing trade deficits, energy shortages, and "stagflation" all seemed to demonstrate that America had lost control of its destiny. Even for those who were comfortable with the end of American hegemony, the intrusion of global issues and forces seemed to move power another huge step away from the individual citizen.

In a sense, political alienation reflects a diffuse awareness that both citizenship and government have become more difficult and less effective in a complex, global age. However, while the causes of alienation may be diffuse and hard to prove, the manifestations of alienation are all too concrete. They range from declining voter participation to the specter of a new mass politics.

Disappearing Voters.   Behaviorally, the increase in political alienation has been most apparent in voting trends. American voting rates are
low by international standards. That has not, however, always been the
case. During most of the nineteenth century, the vast majority of the
potential American electorate—that is those people with the right to
register—voted in presidential elections. In three presidential elections
during the 1880s, over 86 percent of this potential electorate in the
northern and western states voted. More than 71 percent of this potential electorate voted in off-year congressional elections during the same
decade (Burnham, 1982). This former U.S. participation rate is about
equal to that of other democratic countries today.

During the early twentieth century, participation in American elections declined precipitously, reaching an all-time low during the 1920s.
After a brief upsurge during the Great Depression, the secular trend
toward declining participation began again. In 1980, despite a relatively
clear-cut choice between candidates, and subsequent rhetoric about a
Reagan "landslide," only 51 percent of the potential American electorate
even bothered to vote; in the 1982 congressional elections, the figure
was only 37 percent (Saffell, 1984).

Declining electoral participation in the United States has more than
one cause. To some extent, changes in voter turnout over the past century have reflected successive expansions of the electorate. However, the
long-term trend cannot be explained simply on this basis. Women
gained voting rights in the 1920s, and electoral participation fell because the new women voters were less likely to vote than men. Since the
1920s, however, voting rates for women have risen, but overall electoral
participation has fallen (Burnham, 1982).

Nor can declining electoral participation be interpreted primarily
as a reflection of a general satisfaction with the status quo. Nonvoters
tend to come from the lower-income, less educated groups, not from the
more satisfied upper and middle classes. Even among the middle class,
nonvoting stems primarily from a belief that political participation has
little or no impact on public policy and thus is not worth the effort
(Brady, 1978). In short, the long-term trend toward declining voter participation reflects an increase in political alienation.

Single-Issue Politics.   Individuals who are dissatisfied with the political system can choose to abstain from participation, or they can seek
alternative ways of participating which provide the impact or satisfaction missing in more normative modes. If these alternative modes of
participation undermine the cohesion of the political community or
democratic norms, they may ultimately be as dysfunctional as nonpar-

ticipation. People who feel powerless within the political system often try to enhance their sense of control through support of special-interest or single-issue groups. The increasing prominence of these groups since the 1960s has been an important characteristic of American politics.

The rise of groups advocating everything from a nuclear freeze to anti-abortion laws is seen by most elitists as a particularly aberrant form of citizenship. Special-interest groups are viewed as distorting the legislative process because they cannot afford to engage in the kind of compromise behavior essential to legislative politics (Berry, 1977). They divide rather than unite communities and lead to a paralysis of government (Medcalf & Dolbeare, 1985; Peters, 1983).

Even populists argue that single-interest and special-interest groups distort the political process. While these groups involve people in politics, they do not involve them in a political process that most populists regard as optimal. They typically do not invite their members to participate in political discussion, judgment, or reasoned decision making. They do not involve them in the search for the public good. Rather, they provide members with a particular image of a problem and a ready-made response to it. They encourage them to block off the search for the public good, in order to present a united front in the legislative process. Thus special-interest and single-issue groups only divide communities, without enhancing people's political skills or sophistication. They do not really empower people to participate responsibly in a democratic political process (Barber, 1984).

Mass Politics.   Individuals who perceive that they are powerless and adrift within the political community may also be far more easily mobilized by political demagogues who promise fulfillment and belonging but promote antidemocratic policies. From this perspective, the success of certain highly authoritarian and charismatic religious cults can be seen as a particularly troubling indicator of political alienation in contemporary American society.

The threat of political demagogues is heightened by the potential power of the mass media and the mass audiences they have created. A number of analysts, both elitists and populists, have criticized television's impact in particular. In presidential campaigns, for example, television has encouraged a trend toward image politics (Novak, 1974). Television cannot handle complex debates or issues. It does best when projecting simple, graphic images. In campaigns, this has encouraged candidates to neglect issues and to project what turn out to be hollow but attractive images of themselves, their values, and their policies.

In the hands of a political demagogue, image-based media might

well mobilize an alienated citizenry in quite irrational political movements. Thus modern communications and popular alienation may have
the potential to realize elitists' most profound fear—the tyranny of an
irrational mass public. (The classic statement of this argument is contained in Ortega y Gasset, 1957.) While research on the impact of the
media indicates that they do not have much direct effect on popular
attitudes under normal circumstances (Dye & Zeigler, 1978), the potential for abuse in a highly alienated population may be much greater.

Responding to Political Alienation

Political alienation threatens any political system. It distances a
person from the political community or group. Since alienated individuals feel that they have no impact on the political system, they also have
no sense of identity with or ownership over its policies. As a result,
alienated individuals may fail to comply with the most basic norms and
rules of the society. They may stop paying taxes and obeying laws. They
may fail to cooperate with energy conservation programs or draft laws.
At best, a society characterized by widespread alienation lacks the glue
necessary to respond collectively to external or internal threats. At
worst, it lacks the glue necessary to ensure the orderly conduct of everyday activities.

Thus it is not surprising that both elitists and populists have sought
responses to the growing political alienation in America. It is equally
predictable that they would look in very different places.

Revitalizing American Political Parties.   For elitists in particular, the
search for a response to alienation has led primarily to a look at those
institutions that in one way or another mediate between the average
citizen and government. Of particular interest has been the debate over
the revitalization and reform of political parties.

In a representative democracy, political parties are the single most
important agents for mobilizing electoral participation. They provide a
personal link between the average citizen and elected officials. Parties
funnel information to voters. In places where there is a healthy competition among parties, they facilitate the expression of different values,
needs, and ideas in the political arena. In the United States in particular, the political parties play a critical role because, in contrast to many
other Western democracies, our society is relatively unstructured (Burnham, 1982). Historically it has been the political parties, or the political
machines in urban areas, that have mobilized the economically disad-
vantaged and brought them into the political process. Thus it may be

no accident that political alienation has increased at the same time that party identification has declined.

Strategies for revitalizing the political party system in the United States vary widely. In general, voting tends to be highest in communities that have greater ethnic or economic differences. It is also higher in communities that have maintained partisan local elections and in which a partisan mayor plays a key role in local government (Henry, 1984). In this light, one of the most important reforms might be to encourage greater competition between parties. Burnham (1982), for example, criticizes the post–War trend toward bipartisanship as inimical to a healthy party system. The similar trend toward nonpartisan local elections earlier in the century may also have dampened competition among parties.

A more fundamental approach to revitalizing American parties is to open the parties themselves up to greater popular participation and control. The efforts to reform the Democratic Party along these lines during the early 1970s, however, had decidedly mixed results. A number of people who would otherwise probably not have become involved as electoral gladiators—especially minority-group members, women, and young people—were brought into the process. However, the reforms generally failed to produce new visions, effective coalitions, or even electable candidates. As a result, by 1980 the more established party elites were able to regain much of their control over the party (Shafer, 1983).

The most radical response to the lack of party competition, and to the weakness of party identification among lower socioeconomic groups, would be to encourage class-based political parties such as those found throughout Europe. However, this would probably require significant electoral reforms. In the United States, single-member election districts encourage a two-party system in which both parties must appeal to middle-class voters if they hope to succeed. Likewise, the dominance of capitalist ideology, which ascribes socioeconomic status primarily to personal actions, is as strong among the lower classes as the upper. This dominant ideology militates against the mobilization of people along class lines.

Even if American political parties could be reformed, many populists argue that such changes do not get at the roots of alienation—the system of representative government itself.

Creating New Forms of Participation. From a populist point of view, it is not the complexity of political issues or even the limited power of government that inhibits political participation. Rather, alienation results from the pervasive belief that the state has become autonomous from society (Nordlinger, 1981). Citizens, even those who participate, are not seen as succeeding in shaping the public agenda or determining public policy. As a result, citizenship has become a series of empty, symbolic gestures. Only by breaking out of the restrictions that representative democracy places on citizenship can alienation be reduced.

Populist theorist Benjamin Barber (1984), for example, has articulated a new vision of what he calls "strong democracy." Barber argues that citizens must be empowered to "choose with deliberation and act with responsibility" (p. 126). He outlines institutional changes that would allow average citizens to participate in the process of defining and discussing the public agenda, selecting courses of action, and even implementing public policy. These institutions would be flexible enough to allow citizens to participate at times and on issues of their own choosing. They would engage citizens in a political process designed to identify the public good, not simply to provide an avenue for attaining private interests. His specific reforms include a national system of neighborhood assemblies, a national referendum and initiative process, and universal citizen service.

Barber's (1984) image of a new citizen-centered politics seems to fly in the face of empirical research on citizen competence. It certainly suffers from a lack of real-world experience that could prove its viability. Nonetheless, similar ideas have even been advocated with respect to international issues and problem solving (Alger, 1977; Chittick, 1982).

The Reagan Revolution and the Return to Privatism

In certain respects, the Reagan revolution of the 1980s established an entirely new set of conditions for citizenship in the United States. Since the Bush Administration has maintained the general spirit of those changes, they represent an important benchmark for the political discussion of citizenship. Yet it is less clear that the changes wrought by the Reagan Administration have served either to reduce alienation or to strengthen citizenship fundamentally.

The Reagan Administration's New Federalism clearly encouraged a decentralization of power in many areas of social programming. For better or worse, state governments became responsible for funding social programs and thus were empowered to establish their own social agendas (Lees & Turner, 1988). In other words, Reagan's policies tried to relocate political agenda setting and policy making in the social realm to a governmental arena that was more accessible to the average citizen.

These policies, however, did not succeed in renewing local political vitality. The New Federalism proved more effective a tool for budget reduction than for political decentralization. Even to the extent that it succeeded in decentralizing power, the chief beneficiaries were state governments, which have traditionally been as elitist as the federal government. Finally, while the Reagan Administration did encourage localism through its on volunteerism as the most appropriate response to social ills, this, too, was essentially an elitist reform. While voluntary groups can serve as the incubators of political participation, participation in voluntary groups is itself a middle- and upper-class phenomenon. In short, the Reagan revolution was not meant to create conditions for a revitalized citizenship in populist terms.

In some respects the Reagan Administration did launch a new era in citizenship. It clearly restored a degree of loyalty to and good feeling about the nation. In effect, however, the Reagan reforms and rhetoric encouraged a return to the privatism of the 1950s. Whether the problem of political alienation can be solved by absolving citizens from the need to participate in public affairs is not at all clear. As the Bush Administration began, distrust of government among Americans remained high and the decline in electoral participation continued.

RECOMMENDATIONS FOR STRENGTHENING CITIZENSHIP

During the last two decades, many political analysts have concluded that political alienation represents a real and growing problem in the United States. They have not agreed, however, either about the roots of alienation or about the best response to it. Indeed, elitists and populists alike have become increasingly skeptical that citizenship can be strengthened.

For their part, elitists face an inherent contradiction between their image of a workable political system and the goal of reducing alienation. Political alienation can probably only be reduced through fundamental reforms of the political system (Burnham, 1982). Since alienation reflects a sense of powerlessness, those reforms probably must in some way enhance citizen efficacy. However, such reforms violate basic elitist beliefs about how democracy in the modern world must be structured to work effectively.

Populists also have little reason to be confident. Experiences with institutions that do empower people have not been without their frustrations (Crenson, 1983; Mansbridge, 1980). Citizen participation requires an appropriate attitudinal foundation. Not all people are interested in political participation, nor are they willing to participate in democratic

dialogue and learning. Many of those who do participate are more interested in private gain than in the public good. In short, people socialized
within an elitist political system do not necessarily develop the attitudes
required for healthy citizenship.

This section looks at the role that citizenship education can play in
laying a new foundation for citizenship. It outlines five distinct changes
in the way we approach politics, government, citizenship, and the civic
community, which are essential for a healthier citizenship. These are not
detailed suggestions for how to accomplish these attitudinal changes.
They are targets of opportunity, each one clearly affected by the ways in
which we educate young people for citizenship.

Attitudes Toward Politics

In the United States the term *politics* has come to be equated with
special interests, unethical deal making, and the compromise of basic
values. The routine denigration of politics may well make political alienation inevitable.

People in groups require politics. Politics allows free people living
in groups to create shared goals, to come to common understandings of
needs, and to pool their resources to accomplish shared images of the
future. Politics is not a process reserved to government; it is a part of
everyday life. Without politics a group cannot make decisions. Unless it
accepts authoritarian rule, it cannot act as a group. Groups and communities that cannot decide or act ultimately die.

The denigration of politics cannot lead to an apolitical society. It
does, however, deprive a group or community of a *legitimate* process for
defining the public good. As people withdraw from the disdainful world
of politics, public policy formation becomes a technical activity, con-
trolled by a narrow, tainted group of people. These bureaucrats, auto-
crats, or politicians are left to "do politics" while the rest go about the
allegedly more legitimate and more honest work of achieving personal
goals.

Educators, particularly in the social studies, can play an important
role in reasserting that politics is a healthy and intrinsic part of social
life. By having students look at political processes in their daily lives,
they can begin to see politics as an essential and potentially healthy
dimension of community life. This is not the same as pretending that
there are no mean-spirited, self-interested, or evil people in the world.
However, only if we see politics as an essential and healthy process can
we see unethical politics as an aberration that can and should be re-
sisted through a healthy citizenship.

Attitudes Toward Government
As the Focus of the Civic Community

Since the 1930s, American political culture has increasingly seen government as the institution within which the public agenda is set and responses to public needs and opportunities are implemented. The tendency to see government as the center of civic life is natural. In a representative democracy it is the only institution whose key figures are chosen by a broad electorate expressly for the purpose of making public policy. However, the more we have made government the surrogate for the civic community, the more politically alienated the society has become. In this sense, conservatives who criticize the tendency to look to government to solve all problems and rectify all injustices may be correct.

Reforming elitist institutions in order to encourage greater participation can only succeed up to a point. Representative government is not designed to engage large portions of the citizenry in the process of setting public agendas, making decisions, or implementing public policies. Merely opening up elitist institutions to broader participation may only encourage special-interest politics. Organized interest groups are better positioned to capture institutions like political parties and to use new opportunities to lobby legislatures than the disorganized body of citizens.

The schools cannot create a new political culture. Educators concerned about citizenship can, however, encourage their students to think about the civic community in ways that legitimize and empower nongovernmental organizations. Students should recognize that, while it is important, government is not the *only* focus for civic community. Civic and neighborhood groups (e.g., neighborhood watches, world affairs councils, chambers of commerce, Rotary and Zonta International), and groups organized around common needs and interests (e.g., welfare rights and environmental groups), are quasipublic institutions. Their goals are related to public life, and they should be challenged to identify and work toward the public good.

Students can also be challenged to use their own school and youth groups in this way, as centers of civic community. How can student organizations work, not just to represent the interests of students, but to benefit and improve the school as a community? How can youth groups like the Boy and Girl Scouts, Campfire, SADD, and others be engaged in identifying the public good as well as serving the community? Recent interest in national youth service can be a potent force for strengthening citizenship, but only if young people are empowered in the process.

Attitudes Toward the Efficacy of
Local Communities

One of the most fundamental causes of political alienation in the modern world can be summed up in a simple dichotomy: power resides in one place, participation in another. To be meaningful and efficacious, participation must be centered in small-scale, local settings. Unfortunately, the power to mobilize sufficient resources to address public needs effectively is all too often located in large-scale, remote institutions like national governments. The fact that our lives are routinely influenced by the decisions and actions of people in distant parts of the world and that such pressing problems as unemployment and homelessness in part result from our place in the global economic system only worsens this basic dilemma. In short, the trend toward increasing scale in modern life seems destined to increase political alienation.

As we have learned about the complexity of social, political, economic, and ecological systems, we have become painfully aware that local communities cannot solve many problems on their own. But, has our emphasis on the power of national governments and international cooperation been myopic as well? Have we lost sight of critical ways in which local communities can and must contribute to recognizing and addressing public needs? Some problems may best be addressed within local communities. Many of those problems that require national or international policies may also be solvable only if small-scale institutions effectively mobilize individual concern and cooperation. Much of the current thinking on management and corporate effectiveness supports this idea. As organizations grow larger, they must work harder at listening to workers at all levels and at involving even the smallest work group in decentralized management (Bennis & Nanus, 1985; Blanchard & Johnson, 1982; Heller, Van Til, & Zurcher, 1986; Ouchi, 1981; Pascal & Athos, 1981; Peters & Austin, 1986).

The only solution to the alienating effects of giantism may well be a vibrant localism, and here, too, the schools can play a vital role. Educators can encourage a more realistic image of the power of local communities, not only in matters of purely local concern but also in matters of national and international concern. Students should recognize that one local community cannot alter the trends that are leading to a warming of the global climate. But they should also recognize that it may be impossible to alter those trends if local communities are not involved in discussing the problem, finding acceptable solutions to it, and implementing those solutions.

Attitudes Toward Citizens as Leaders

For most political scientists, citizenship within the political arena implies "active" participation in politics. It may be more accurate, however, to say that citizenship has been seen as "reactive" participation. Citizenship, in this view, has to be treated as the equivalent of "followership," not leadership. The latter, the more proactive role in political life, is primarily associated with positions of authority. Leaders are people who sit atop the management hierarchy of organizations. Sometimes charismatic leaders emerge from the masses, but, by virtue of their ability to inspire and mobilize other people, even these people ultimately take their places atop organizational hierarchies. Citizens, almost by definition, are the people who follow these leaders. The equation of citizenship with followership has the happy consequence of making the role of citizen accessible to everyone. If citizenship requires little skill other than being able to make personal judgments and decisions in a voting booth, then virtually anyone can be a good citizen.

Unfortunately, equating citizenship with followership also has insidious side-effects. For one thing, it absolves the average citizen from the need to exercise leadership, whatever the crisis or need. When problems arise, we look to those in authority to respond, and we bemoan the lack of leadership if they cannot. No one looks to the average citizen to exercise creativity or leadership in the public realm. What has been widely regarded as a leadership crisis in America today stems largely from the unwillingness of average citizens to exercise leadership in the public arena.

By equating citizenship with followership, we also deflate the role of citizen itself. Citizens become part of a lesser class that observes and judges political life, but can do little more. We define citizens as inefficacious when we see them merely as observers. We also deprive citizenship of any allure. By contrast, in their private lives people can be proactive. They can participate in setting agendas. They can create the basis for their own futures. Business entrepreneurs, union officials, and Girl Scout leaders *lead*. In civic life, these same people—as citizens—merely follow.

The schools can play a vital role in reasserting the leadership dimensions of citizenship. Opportunities for developing skills and capabilities associated with leadership should be made available to a broad spectrum of students. Education about the practice of citizenship should place far greater stress on the more active modes of participation, like community organizing. Given the commonly accepted assumptions about the complexity of issues and the pull of private life, it may seem counterproductive to stress these more intensive modes of citizen participation. Indeed, it would be inappropriate to denigrate the less intensive modes such as voting. The *overall* role of citizen, however, must be elevated to something more than just observing and judging, if we want that role to be compelling to young people. Only if students perceive that they have opportunities to take the initiative in setting public agendas and mobilizing groups to address public needs, independent of any formal position of public authority, can we expect to capture the kind of entrepreneurship that most "leaders" now reserve for their private lives.

Attitudes Toward the Public Good

Greater participation in civic life may lead to a healthier citizenship. It may also make "alienated participation" more widespread. The fundamental difference between healthy citizenship and alienated participation lies in the search for the public good. Political participation only reflects a healthy citizenship if it balances the pursuit of private interests with a genuine concern for achieving what is best for the civic community as a whole.

One of the chief failings of the American political system over the past half century has been its inability to encourage average citizens to participate in the search for the public good. While Americans may feel loyalty toward their community, their state, and their nation, they feel little or no responsibility to help define the public good, especially with respect to issues that involve their own private interests. Within representative systems, citizens are sometimes encouraged to advocate their particular viewpoints and interests to elected officials. But it is the elected elite, not citizens, who aggregate those interests into some vision of the public good. Those who care too much for the public good may find themselves at a disadvantage vis-à-vis those who seek only their private interest. It is hardly surprising, therefore, that most citizens feel little personal responsibility for the public good and lack the skills necessary to participate in defining it.

A key goal of citizenship education should be to reassert the role of average citizens in seeking and defining the public good. Educators should reinforce and nurture students' interest in the public good and their commitment to searching for it. Young people should be rewarded for being concerned with the public good. They should have opportunities to encounter role models who have made the public interest an important part of their lives.

At the same time, educators need to nurture in their students a valid image of the public good and the process through which it is defined. We must not encourage images of the public good or the civic community that are unrealistic or that do not accept the validity of dissent. Conflicts over private interests are endemic in any human group, from the family to the entire world. Genuine conflicts over what constitutes the public good are just as endemic. The public good and the best way to achieve it are almost never clearly defined. The most realistic images of the public good only emerge from discussions in which many points of view are recognized as legitimate and listened to carefully. Even then, our image of the public good remains tentative—an imperfect vision based on limited human understanding. Unless we teach young people to expect and legitimize conflict within their communities, we encourage disillusionment. Unless we encourage them to participate in the search for the public good, we can never encourage a healthy citizenship.

REFERENCES

Alger, C. F. (1977). "Foreign" policies of U.S. publics. *International Studies Quarterly, 21*(2), 277–318.

Alger, C. F. (1978, Summer). Extending responsible public participation in international affairs. *Exchange, 14,* 17–22.

Almond, G. A. (1961). *The American people and foreign policy.* New York: Praeger.

Almond, G. A. (1980). The intellectual history of the civic culture concept. In G. A. Almond, J. S. Coleman, & L. W. Pye (Eds.), *Civic Culture Revisited* (pp. 1–36). Boston: Little, Brown.

Apter, D. E. (1964). Introduction: Ideology and discontent. In D. E. Apter (Ed.), *Ideology and discontent* (pp. 15–46). New York: Free Press.

Banfield, E. C. (1961). *Political influence.* New York: Free Press.

Barber, B. R. (1984). *Strong democracy: Participatory politics for a new age.* Berkeley and Los Angeles: University of California Press.

Bauer, R. A., Pool, I. D. S., & Dexter, L. A. (1972). *American business and public policy: The politics of foreign trade* (2nd ed.). Chicago: Aldine-Atherton.

Bennis, W., & Nanus, B. (1985). *Leaders: The strategies for taking charge.* New York: Harper & Row.

Berger, P., & Berger, B. (1983). *The war over the family.* London: Hutchinson.

Berger, P., & Neuhaus, R. (1977). *To empower people.* Washington, DC: American Enterprise Institute.

Berry, J. (1977). *Lobbying for the people.* Princeton, NJ: Princeton University Press.

Blanchard, K., & Johnson, S. (1982). *The one minute manager.* New York: Berkley Books.

Boyte, H. C. (1980). *The backyard revolution: Understanding the new citizen movement*. Philadelphia: Temple University Press.

Brady, R. A. (1978). The puzzle of political participation in America. In A. King (Ed.), *The new American political system* (pp. 287–324). Washington, DC: American Enterprise Institute.

Burnham, W. D. (1982). *The current crisis in American politics*. New York: Oxford University Press.

Chittick, W. O. (1982). Macromotives and microbehavior: A prescriptive analysis. In G. K. Bertsch (Ed.), *Global policy studies* (pp. 205–229). Beverly Hills, CA: Sage.

Citrin, J. (1981). Changing American electorate. In A. Meltsner (Ed.), *Politics and the Oval Office: Towards presidential governance* (pp. 37–39). San Francisco: Institute for Contemporary Studies.

Cobb, R. W., & Elder, C. D. (1972). *Participation in American politics: The dynamics of agenda-building*. Baltimore: Johns Hopkins University Press.

Crenson, M. A. (1983). *Neighborhood politics*. Cambridge, MA: Harvard University Press.

Dahl, R. A. (1961). *Who governs?* New Haven, CT: Yale University Press.

Dahl, R. A. (1963). *Modern political analysis*. Englewood Cliffs, NJ: Prentice-Hall.

Dye, T. R., & Zeigler, L. H. (1978). *The irony of democracy*. North Scituate, MA: Duxbury Press.

Heller, T., Van Til, J., & Zurcher, L. A. (Eds.). (1986). *Leaders and followers: Challenges for the future*. Greenwich, CT: JAI Press.

Henry, N. (1984). *Governing at the grassroots: State and local politics* (2nd ed.). Englewood Cliffs, NJ: Prentice-Hall.

Huntington, S. P. (1975). The United States. In M. J. Crozier, S. P. Huntington, & J. Watanuki (Eds.), *The crisis of democracy* (pp. 59–119). New York: New York University Press.

Lane, R. E. (1972). *Political man*. New York: Free Press.

Lees, J. D., & Turner, M. (Eds.). (1988). *Reagan's first four years: A new beginning?* Manchester, England: Manchester University Press.

Mansbridge, J. J. (1980). *Beyond adversary democracy*. New York: Basic Books.

McClosky, H., & Saller, J. (1984). *The American ethos*. Cambridge, MA: Harvard University Press.

Medcalf, L. J., & Dolbeare, K. M. (1985). *Neopolitics: American political ideas in the 1980s*. Philadelphia: Temple University Press.

Milbrath, L. W. (1968). The nature of political beliefs and the relationship of the individual to the government. *American Behavioral Scientist, 12*(2), 28–36.

Milbrath, L. W., & Goel, M. L. (1977). *Political participation: How and why do people get involved in politics?* Chicago: Rand McNally.

Newfield, J., & Greenfield, J. (1972). *A populist manifesto: The making of a new majority*. New York: Warner.

Nisbet, R. (1972). *The twilight of authority*. New York: Basic Books.

Nordlinger, E. A. (1981). *On the autonomy of the democratic state*. Cambridge, MA: Harvard University Press.

Novak, M. (1974). *Choosing our king.* New York: Macmillan.

Ortega y Gasset, J. (1957). *The revolt of the masses.* New York: Norton.

Ouchi, W. (1981). *Theory Z: How American business can meet the Japanese challenge.* Reading, MA: Addison-Wesley.

Pascal, R., & Athos, A. (1981). *The art of Japanese management.* New York: Simon & Schuster.

Pateman, C. (1970). *Participation and democratic theory.* New York: Cambridge University Press.

Pateman, C. (1980). The civic culture: A philosophic critique. In G. A. Almond, J. S. Coleman, & L. W. Pye (Eds.), *Civic culture revisited* (pp. 97–102). Boston, MA: Little, Brown.

Peters, C. (1983, May). A neoliberal's manifesto. *The Washington Monthly,* pp. 9–18.

Peters, T., & Austin, N. (1986). *A passion for excellence: The leadership difference.* New York: Warner Books.

Raskin, M. G. (1986). *The common good.* New York: Routledge & Kegan Paul.

Reich, C. A. (1970). *The greening of America.* New York: Random House.

Rifkin, J. (1977). *Own your own job: Economic democracy for working Americans.* New York: Bantam.

Rosenau, J. N. (1974). *Citizenship between elections.* New York: Free Press.

Saffell, D. C. (1984). *State politics.* Reading, MA: Addison-Wesley.

Shafer, B. E. (1983). *Quiet revolution: The struggle for the Democratic Party and the shaping of post-reform politics.* New York: Russell Sage.

Thompson, D. F. (1970). *The democratic citizen.* New York: Cambridge University Press.

Verba, S. (1969). Political participation and strategies of influence: A comparative study. In J. D. Barber (Ed.), *Readings in citizen politics* (pp. 3–26). Berkeley and Los Angeles: University of California Press.

Verba, S., & Nie, N. H. (1972). *Participation in America: Political and social equality.* New York: Harper & Row.

Verba, S., Nie, N. H., & Kim, J. (1971). *Modes of democratic participation: A cross national comparison.* Beverly Hills, CA: Sage.

3 The Historical Perspective

The Contribution of History to Citizenship Education

KERRY J. KENNEDY

The place of history in the school curriculum has been contested throughout the twentieth century. Ravitch's (1985) analysis has shown that up to 1915 there was strong endorsement of history as an essential component in the education of all students. That role increasingly came to be questioned by progressive educators who adopted a social efficiency view of the curriculum, rather than one based on the academic disciplines. The result was a social education curriculum that favored relevance and current events as the basis of a liberal education. Keller (1984) has argued that this progressive influence was still strong as late as the middle 1970s. She has characterized an agenda for the reform of the social studies drawn up in 1975 by the Social Science Education Consortium as "echoing the *Progressive Education*'s agenda of the 1930's and, perhaps, the 'Seven Cardinal Principles' of 1918" (p. 81).

During the 1980s, however, the tide seems to have turned once again. Among the many recent reforms advocated for American schools during the 1980s has been the inclusion of history as part of the common curriculum for all students (Adler, 1984; Boyer, 1983; Sizer, 1984). A number of prominent historians have recently championed the cause of history (Gagnon, 1988; Ravitch, 1985), and the Bradley Commission on the Study of History in Schools has been established. If Keller (1984) is correct, and the place of history in the curriculum is now secure, there remains the task of making some assessment of the specific contribution history is able to make to a general education.

HISTORY IN THE CURRICULUM: PROBLEMS AND PROSPECTS

Making an assessment of what history can offer is by no means easy. There are, for example, extreme views that highlight the propagandist function of history. As Merriam (1934) states, "Each group cultivates the enobling of its past as a sign of its present claim to power, and even in vanished dignity and prestige finds a valid claim to the renewal of what once was" (p. 89). While Merriam rejects such a function in relation to the teaching of history, he nevertheless proposes equally instrumental reasons:

> It is also possible that history might consider a larger concern for the future . . . , that it may conceive its mission more expressly as that of contributing to the progressive reorientation and reconstruction of life than heretofore; . . . with a franker and more open recognition of the utility of historic data as material for weaving new patterns of human behavior in a more consciously controlled social organization. [p. 92]

A similar, although perhaps better articulated, social utilitarian view of the teaching of history has recently been advocated by Gagnon (1988). He has argued that there is a strong link between history and civic education. For him, courses in civics and government simply provide information about the basic tools of government. History, on the other hand, develops a sense of judgment about the sweep of human events, including the crises that have risen. It is this judgment about the past that is able to guide and inform decision making in the present:

> The chances for democratic principles to survive such crises depend upon the number of citizens who remember how free societies have responded to crises in the past, how free societies have acted to defend themselves in, and emerge from, bad times. Why have some societies fallen and others stood fast? Citizens need to tell one another, before it is too late, what struggles have had to be accepted, what sacrifices borne and comforts given up, to preserve freedom and justice. [p. 44]

As social utilitarians, Gagnon (1988) and Merriam (1934) agree that history has lessons to teach, which should be a part of the education of all students.

Such a view is not shared by all historians. Ravitch (1985), for example, has argued strongly that history must be taught for its own sake, rather than as a means to an end:

> History will never be restored as a subject of value unless it is detached from the vulgar utilitarianism that originally swamped it. History should not be expected to teach patriotism, morals, values clarification, or decision making. . . . [History] endows its students with a broad knowledge of other times, other cultures, other places. It leaves its students with cultural resources on which they may draw for the rest of their lives. These are the values and virtues that are gained through the study of history. Beyond these, history needs no further justification. [p. 132]

The distinction between Ravitch's view and the more utilitarian views has been referred to as the distinction between socialization and education (Egan, 1983). The purpose of the latter function is "to come to understand the past in its own terms, in its uniqueness, for its own sake and the sake of the pleasure of understanding" (p. 202). However, as Egan goes on to say, the socialization function

> is not concerned simply with building a picture of what happened, but is concerned with involving us in the picture—it is *our* picture—and with orienting our feelings and the elements which make up the picture. In teaching American children about the Declaration of Independence, for example, one does not seek to present such knowledge for "its own sake." It is a potent part of the American socializing story. It is not enough that children learn about the events and the characters. Clearly they are to approve of the events and identify with certain sentiments and characters. [p. 202]

Yet the dividing line between education and socialization may not be as clear as Egan (1983) is suggesting. Intrinsic and instrumental justifications for the teaching of history may not be mutually exclusive. Ravitch (1985) argues, on the one hand, that the teaching of history should be asked to serve no purpose at all; yet, in writing about the role of history in the elementary school, she acknowledges the need for students to be culturally literate. She argues that one means of inducting students into a common culture is by introducing them to historical persons and events. Perhaps the lesson is that, while history deserves a place in the curriculum for its own sake, it is also capable of contributing to significant educational objectives.

This is certainly the view of a number of recent writers. Keller (1984), for example, has pointed to the cultural function history is able to serve:

History is, simply, the collective memory of mankind, and all people need to partake in the memory. History is the account of how the human species developed over time: its triumphs, its tragedies, its pattern of life in different cultures and eras. Knowledge of history is one of the things that distinguish civilized people from the barbarians: the civilized person is one who has learned, and continues to learn, from the experiences of past generations. Those who are without knowledge of history are cultural amnesiacs: they cannot know who they are, because they do not know whence they came. [p. 82]

In a similar vein, the American Federation of Teachers (1987) has argued that history provides the context in which current events and social science concepts can be best understood: "History alone affords the perspective that students need to compare themselves realistically with others—in the past and elsewhere on earth—and to think critically, to look behind assertions and appearances, to ask for the 'whole story', to judge meaning and values for themselves" (p. 17).

It seems, then, that there must be an acknowledgment of both the uniqueness of history as a component of the school curriculum and a recognition that it is able to contribute to more general educational aims. It may be, as Gilbert (1984) has argued, that the distinction between instrumental and intrinsic justifications for the teaching of history is probably little more than a difference in levels of abstraction. Nevertheless, it is an important distinction to keep in mind throughout this chapter, as the relationship between history and citizenship education is assessed. There is the possibility that an overly instrumental approach will focus too much on the socialization function of history teaching, while too much emphasis on the teaching of history for its own sake will miss out on the valuable lessons that young people can learn as a result of studying history. The following discussion will keep these potential problems in mind.

CITIZENSHIP EDUCATION AND HISTORY: CONCEPTS AND IDEOLOGY

If history is to contribute to the education of an intelligent citizenry, there must in the first place be a recognition that citizenship education is more than a list of competencies devoid of any specific content. Such a list was constructed by Remy (1980), and, while it would be possible to use historical content to help students develop certain of the competencies, the point to note is that it would be possible using Remy's scheme to teach an entire course in citizenship education without reference to any history at all.

Gross (1958), on the other hand, seems to advocate an important role for history in citizenship education when he writes, "We are a young nation, successful and powerful, and our history has been both a source of pride and reassurance. Because of our prodigious growth, we have believed that we can find many of our values in the national record and we can chart our future by the light of these former experiences" (p. 162). Such a view sees the specific content of history as a powerful source of values and possibly even inspiration for young people. In this context history clearly has a role to play in citizenship education. It is far removed from the view of Remy (1980), who seems to attach no value to any specific content.

A compelling argument for highlighting specific content is made by Oldenquist (1980), who proposes that "it is necessary to give children more than skill and method. They must be made to care, feel and identify in certain ways. This is what it means to internalize a principle or attitude and it is only this that can create an inner and direct interest in the good of one's community" (p. 33). The danger in such an approach is the direct links suggested between citizenship education and moral education. While Oldenquist (1980) argues that the two should not be seen as identical, there are those who advocate that moral education ought to be the single most important component of citizenship education (e.g., Bell, 1977). Such a view in relation to history is somewhat simplistic, since it is full of examples of people who have had to sacrifice private morality for the public good. Acting morally and acting as a good citizen may not be one and the same thing. As Oldenquist (1980, p. 33) points out, "Sometimes a good person is required to be a bad citizen." In this context, history has the potential to demonstrate how individuals and nations have grappled with moral issues, but it cannot be used as a substitute for moral education. History has multiple lessons to teach, and some of them may contribute to moral education, but most of them will raise as many issues as they resolve.

The issues discussed so far cannot be divorced from a consideration of the general aims of schooling. History must contribute in a significant way to a general education, an important part of which is citizenship education. Yet there are indications that schools would have difficulty at the present time in insuring that history could be available for all students. The reasons are not unrelated to the issues referred to already. The remainder of this section will be concerned with examining in more detail the general purposes of schooling and their relationship to citizenship education.

The Importance of Content in the Curriculum

It may seem strange to want to affirm the importance of content in the curriculum. After all, isn't that what curriculum is all about? Isn't the basic curriculum question concerned with identifying which knowledge is of most worth? For the past two decades, however, the answer to this question has tended to relativize curriculum content. On the one hand, it has been argued that, for subjects like mathematics, social studies, science, and language studies, it is not so much the content as the process that is important. This has meant that there has been an overwhelming emphasis on identifying processes that students can acquire and hopefully utilize in contexts other than the specific one in which they were learned. On the other hand, there has been a reluctance to accept that there are fundamental forms of knowledge. The result has been a fragmentation and proliferation of areas of knowledge, each staking an equal claim to its place in the curriculum.

The rationale for adopting these approaches seemed convincing at the time. The diversity of the school population seemed to require a diverse range of subject offerings. Not all students were academically oriented and college bound, so it did not seem appropriate to offer them a traditional academic education. Even for those who were capable, there was the argument that the "information explosion" made it impossible to be able to teach every known fact, since there was simply too much information. Thus students were introduced to broad conceptual frameworks, often in the context of inquiry-oriented learning. Content was seen as a means to an end for both the academic and nonacademic student, but not as having any intrinsic value.

Lawton (1975) get to the heart of the issue when he links curriculum to its broad cultural function: "Common schools are meaningless unless they transmit a common culture and provide an adequate means for individual development within the general framework of the culture. Without an insistence on a basic minimum understanding of the forms of knowledge which we regard as important, talk of equality of opportunity is no more than a sham" (p. 80). Indeed, the curriculum of schools must be concerned with powerful knowledge that has the potential to unlock the culture for young people. The concept of "worthwhile knowledge" is therefore central to education. If such knowledge is not at the heart of school programs, then schools can hardly be said to be performing their role, either for individuals or the nation as a whole. Young people must be able to appreciate their past and be capable of shaping the future, and this they can do if they are introduced to a powerful knowledge base that will lead them to question the status quo and become active in seeking solutions to society's problems, and help them to understand that they are part of a much larger world that relies on everyone to make a meaningful and purposeful contribution.

Citizenship Education in the Curriculum

If the inclusion of worthwhile knowledge in the curriculum of schools is seen to be central to education, then citizenship education has a significant contribution to make. Finkelstein (1985) talks about the need to transform civic education into "a sensitive and effective weapon against contemporary assaults on freedom and dignity" (p. 14). She refers to a number of writers who seek to promote such a notion. One is Giarrel (1983), who argues that civic education "involves preparation in the intellectual qualities which allow us to envision new possibilities for public life [and acquire] the social and moral qualities to resist domination and work with others in collective projects" (p. 57). Another writer is Morrill (1982), who states that "education for democratic citizenship involves human capacities relating to judgement, to choice and to action. To be literate as a citizen requires more than knowledge and information; it includes the exercise of personal responsibility and active participation" (p. 365).

These are not calls for rote learning of predigested facts about the U.S. Constitution and the distant past, nor are they concerned with simply involving students in ritual and ceremony. Rather, they are visions of how an intelligent citizenry should think and act. They focus on the creation of a public consciousness or what Finkelstein (1985) calls a "reconstructed public spirit" (p. 14). They point toward the possibility of common values that can guide action and relationships in a diverse society.

Such views are not confined to the United States. Tomlinson (1986) also argues in the British context that the public good is best supported

> by promoting free, independent minded individuals who also have the moral awareness of themselves and others which confers the sense of fraternity. It gives the fundamental value to the idea of citizenship and creates the common ground—a sense of our common humanity upon which, alone, civilised society (and a complex economy) are possible. [p. 27]

In a similar vein, Butts (1980), an American, captures the spirit behind citizenship education, arguing that citizens must acknowledge pluralism and diversity in society yet be prepared to act not for private interests but in the public good:

Civic education must honor cultural *Pluribus*, but it must also strengthen political *Unum*. Somehow civic education must promote and protect the rights of all persons to hold a diversity of beliefs, but it must also develop a commitment to actions that uphold the common bonds of a free government as the surest guarantee of the very holding of a pluralism of beliefs. [p. 117]

This is to be achieved in the school setting by relying

upon scholarly knowledge and research without becoming bloodlessly intellectualized or rigidly circumscribed by the arbitrary boundaries of the separate and specialized academic disciplines, and without degenerating into random discussions or entry games. We must protect the rights of privacy without retreating into the privatism of purely personal experience as the norm of public morality. [p. 117]

It follows from this that the challenge of citizenship education is not so much to identify a single body of knowledge that can inform future citizens. Rather, it is to provide students with the opportunity to range across areas of knowledge, examining fundamental ideas, processes, and values that have shaped and continue to shape people and the societies in which they live. At the same time, students must become aware that they themselves are capable of shaping the future—that they are not simply passive reactants to forces over which they have no control.

Yet action is not an end in itself; it must be directed toward the interest of all citizens, rather than carried out on behalf of self-interests. There are common bonds and ties that unite a nation of diverse individuals, and it is this commonality that ought to govern actions and lead toward a just and equitable distribution of the rewards that society has to offer. Unjust societies can expect to be challenged, because, where access to the benefits society has to offer is inequitable, there can be no common bond. Justice as an operational principle, therefore, is indispensable if individuals are to be asked to act on behalf of public rather than private interests.

The preparation of students for citizenship, then, is not a matter of "adding on" a separate course of study for that purpose. It is a question of insuring that the whole school community takes on the task. It will mean that teachers in all subject areas will be involved in a concerted effort to insure that young people are introduced to an essential core of knowledge that will enable them to view issues in the perspective of both past and present concerns. It will mean that the whole of school life will be directed at *encouraging participation* and *action* for the *common good*. It will mean that the school must become a model that will encourage a critical and reflective stance toward knowledge and promote the necessity for action when the common good is threatened.

Schools, of course, must do much more, but this is their particular function in relation to the preparation of citizens. It is a function that complements and supports the central role of the school in focusing students' attention on valued and worthwhile knowledge. For, in the end, access to knowledge is an empowering process that allows individuals to move beyond their own private concerns. It provides a broader context for both thought and action. Without an expanded knowledge base, students will always be limited by the present, by their immediate environment, and by their commitment to self rather than others.

BACKGROUND ISSUES RELATED TO THE ROLE OF HISTORY IN CITIZENSHIP EDUCATION

If history is to play its role in the education of an intelligent citizenry, there must be a recognition that it has a unique contribution to make. There are three broad issues that help to establish such a contribution:

1. A recognition that historical knowledge is a fundamental form of knowledge and therefore must be available to all citizens;
2. An understanding that history is able to create a sense of an inclusive community to which all citizens belong and to which all, both past and present, contribute;
3. A realization that historical situations are demonstrators of civic intelligence in action, showing us how others have taught and acted in seeking to solve societies' problems in the past.

This section examines each of these areas.

History As a Fundamental Form of Knowledge

It is cogently argued by Hirst (1974) that there are fundamental forms of knowledge that are the "basic contributions whereby the whole of experience has become intelligible to man, . . . the fundamental achievements of mind" (p. 40). While such a view has not gone unchallenged (Phillips, 1974), it nevertheless provides a useful way of conceptualizing epistemological issues related to the curriculum. Hirst (1974) has identified four characteristics of the so-called "fundamental forms of knowledge." In operational terms, these can be described as follows:

1. Each form involves central concepts that are distinctive.
2. Each form has a distinctive logical structure.
3. Each form has distinctive statements testable against experience.
4. Each form has developed methodologies for exploring and testing experience.

If human experience is indeed structured in a number of unique forms, then students ought to have access to all the forms, if their education is to be an opening up of the possibilities for the future. To deny access to a way of organizing human experience is to limit the student's knowledge base and therefore the possibility of action. The full range of valued knowledge ought to be made available to students, so as to maximize their potential in coming to understand themselves and the world in which they live. At the same time, they must be equipped with knowledge that will assist them in transforming the world; otherwise they will be left with the status quo.

Skilbeck (1979) argues in agreement with Hirst (1974), that historical knowledge represents a fundamental form or mode of knowledge that should find a place in the curriculum of any general education. Students are able to experience these events and ideas in a mediated way, through access to historical documents and artifacts or by examining the work of professional historians whose task it is to study the relationships among various people's experiences over time. The data of history can be made readily available to students, who can then describe, analyze, and evaluate it both in relation to themselves and to others. No other discipline is able to make these experiences available to students.

Egan (1983) also points to the unique contribution that history is able to make to the education of students. He rejects out of hand the "socializing" function of history, that is, its use to involve students uncritically in a nation's story. Rather, he argues, along with Collingwood (1946) and Dray (1964), that the main purpose of studying history is to recapture thoughts, events, and idea within the contexts that have created them and that made them meaningful. In this sense, history broadens the experience of young people by introducing them to the experiences of historical characters. As Egan (1983) puts it,

The focus of teaching would be on making the alienness and difference of those thoughts and reasons comprehensible to modern students. Now obviously one cannot completely get inside the thoughts of others and of course there will always be some ethnocentric and present-centric reductionism involved. But the hard discipline of history is centrally about overcoming the reduction of past experience to present experience and about the expansion of present experience and understanding into those alien worlds and lives which preceded ours. [p. 204]

At the same time, Egan (1983) argues that this aim cannot be achieved if history is considered simply as an element of the social studies curriculum. The educative function of history can best be preserved in the school curriculum when it is recognized that as a distinct discipline it has its own logical structure, its own methodology, and its own criteria for public accountability. These traits tend to become quite blurred in the context of a social studies education, in which, more often than not, the general aim is to understand the present and its role expectations. The study of the past becomes simply another way of understanding the present, and those aspects of the past that cannot contribute in this way are excluded from the curriculum. Such an approach ignores the unique contribution that history has to make to the education of students.

If history does represent a unique way of organizing human experience, then it follows that all students must have access to it. This argument rests in an assumption articulated by Hirst (1974), that "one of the central functions, if not the central function, of education, is the introduction of pupils to those forms of thought and knowledge which we think peculiarly valuable" (p. 69). It should not be expected that students can become competent citizens if areas of fundamental knowledge have not formed part of their education.

This does not mean that any "history" will do. Rather, it means that the history found in the school curriculum must recognize the qualities of the discipline that make it a fundamental area of knowledge—its logical and conceptual structure, the public testability of its statements, and its distinctive methodology. It is the discipline of history, and not simply stories about the past, that has a role to play in the education of citizens.

History and the Creation of an Inclusive Community

If the aim of teaching history for citizenship education is to recapture the events, thoughts, and ideas of historical agents, then it becomes a question of who will be included in the process. Traditionally, as Finkelstein (1985) points out, certain groups such as women, minorities, and ordinary people have been excluded: "The national community, the civic community [has been] an exclusive one, and for many an irrelevant one. For public life [has been] exclusively that of the voter, the worker, the manager and the governor, not the lover, the nurturer, or the spirit. Thus stripped of moral content, public processes become uninspiring as well as exclusive" (p. 19).

The breakdown of this exclusive nature of much history is referred to by Shenton and Jakoubek (1980). They point to the collapse of consensual historiography in the wake of the civil rights movement which brought the realization that there was in the United States not one nation but two, black and white. To this breakdown has been added the feminist critique that has shown how women can be made the focus of historical attention, once presuppositions about politics as the central function of the past are removed. In addition there has been a growing interest in the history of the American working class and the various ethnic groups that have contributed to the diversity of its values and cultures. These trends are summed up under the rubric of the "new social history" and its attempt to recreate an inclusive past. As Shenton and Jakoubek (1980) write, "In their interest in the general and the whole, social historians seek to democratize the meaning of history. In the broadest sense, the present historical effort is toward an understanding of the whole American people in all their diversity, complexity and humanity" (p. 469).

It is the emphasis on inclusiveness that is most relevant for citizenship education. All citizens—women and men; ethnics and anglos; upper, middle, and working class—must feel that the past is theirs. The creation of a sense of national community can only come about when all citizens are made to feel a part of that community. If history as acted out by middle-class white men and written about by middle-class white men is all that is transmitted to students, then it will convey only a portion of what is significant. This kind of history can be very limited and constraining, creating what Finkelstein (1985) calls "conceptual prisons" (p. 19). If students are not taken outside of these prisons to be shown a broader, more inclusive picture of the past, then there is the danger that those who have been excluded from the national or civic community will not feel at all constrained in acting against the public good. An inclusive history allows for the recapturing of the thoughts, feelings, and ideas of all citizens. It provides the foundation for a national community that has responded and will continue to respond to the needs of all its citizens. It is above all in the shaping of this sense of national community that history is able to contribute to the education of citizens.

Historical Situations As Demonstrations
of Civic Intelligence in Action

Murchland (1985) refers to four kinds of intelligence. Three of them are characterized by their essentially private nature: gathering facts, assigning meaning to them, and theorizing about them. A fourth kind of intelligence is quite different, and is called "we thinking together." It is described in the following way, "This is the essential mark of our intelligence, and its purpose is the creation of public consciousness. . . . Sound public philosophies and good public practices are among the highest creations we are capable of" (p. 34). This kind of thinking is also referred to as "civic intelligence."

History allows students to focus on the way in which other people in other times have come together to exercise their civic intelligence. It provides images of how the process of thinking together has created both inclusive and exclusive communities, just and unjust societies, and good and bad public practices. These can all be understood and evaluated in the context of the times that produced them and as part of the drama and excitement that makes historical study unique. Students will never meet the protaganists, but they can encounter their thoughts, ideas, and feelings through written accounts, artifacts, and historical interpretation, in a manner and form that other disciplines are unable to offer.

When historical situations are considered as demonstrations of civic intelligence in action, there emerges a powerful rationale for selection of specific content in the school curriculum. Egan (1983) complains that the narrowness of present social studies frameworks makes it almost impossible to include a study of Ancient Greece, except on the dubious grounds that a knowledge of the past enriches students' understanding of the present. Yet, if it is important to study examples of civic intelligence in action, then clearly the study of Ancient Greece has an important role to play in any curriculum. The emphasis is not on facts or their interpretation, or on theories that can be derived from them. Rather, the emphasis is on how people came together, the covenants they made, the outcomes they expected. How did they think publicly, and whom did they empower? This is the essence of civic intelligence, and history can provide students with the insights and ideas that shaped and molded "thinking together" in the past. It may or may not help students to understand the present, although, significantly, it can demonstrate that a preoccupation of humankind has been to promote a common set of values and ideas for the public good. Concepts about the latter have certainly changed, but the quest has continued, and this is the lesson only history can teach.

CRITICAL ISSUES ASSOCIATED WITH CITIZENSHIP EDUCATION AND HISTORY

There are two critical issues that remain to be examined in relation to citizenship education and the teaching of history. One has to do with making decisions about the type of history to be taught. Should it be U.S. history, world history, ancient history, or European history? Given that citizenship education is the goal, how does one choose among them? A second issue is concerned with recognizing that learning history has a number of constraints associated with it. Unless these constraints are recognized, teachers may have difficulty in selecting an appropriate approach for specific grade levels. Each of these issues will be discussed in turn.

Which History?

Butts (1980) refers to the need for linking efforts in civic education and international education: "Now I believe we are beginning to recognise that we are entering a third formative period when the idea of national citizenship must take account of the vast changes in the world situation that have suddenly burst upon our consciousness since the end of World War II" (p. 154). Alder and Lindhardt (1981) argue that a consideration of issues in world history can be linked to citizenship education. They take the concepts of "partisanship" and "propaganda" to show how case studies taken from international examples can sharpen students' critical thinking, enlarge their sense of community, and assist them in understanding that all societies have been subject to common pressures. In this sense, world history is not removed from the concerns of future citizens, but is an essential part of them.

Anderson and Rivlin (1980) refer to the demands of citizenship education in a global age. They argue that there is an increasing global interrelatedness that means individuals must exercise their citizenship in the context of a global age. The implications for school programs are outlined and include the need (1) to recognize the importance of both the Western and non–Western worlds and that regions are parts of a global whole, (2) to encourage toleration and appreciation of cultural difference, and (3) to encourage participation in the global arena. Citizenship exercised in relation to only a single nation–state ignores the realities of a shrinking global environment and the demands for global citizenship.

These views are instructive for considering which history should be included in a school curriculum designed to promote citizenship education. They prevent the simplistic answer that only U.S. history is capable of contributing to the education of citizens. Rather, they point to the need for considering a range of historical contexts and situations, if future citizens are to be well prepared. That is to say, if future citizens are not to be ethnocentric or too narrowly nationalistic, then they should be exposed to the history of other regions of the world, apart from the United States. This will include studies of Australia, Asia, and Africa, as well as such neighbors as Latin America and Canada, along with more traditional European studies.

This is not to say that U.S. history should not be the core of historical studies in American schools: It surely should be. Yet it cannot be the only history studied. The history of the United States was itself shaped by forces external to the country, just as students' lives today are faced by forces beyond U.S. control and influence. Contemporary examples include the oil crisis of the 1970s, the value of the Japanese yen, and the agricultural pricing policies of the European Economic Community. Such factors exert an enormous influence over the lives of citizens, and they must be able to understand them not only in narrow nationalistic terms, but in the broader context of the historical factors that brought them into existence. This involves a broadly based historical study that includes both U.S. and world history in such a way that global interrelatedness is both understood and appreciated.

Student Understanding of History

Curriculum specialists have devoted a great deal of effort to considering which content should be taught to which students at what age. In the social studies area the dominant approach has been one in which students start off by considering the world around them—themselves, their homes, and their community—and then move in later years to focusing on their state, the nation, and the world. This approach has been criticized (Egan, 1983), and in the past two decades considerable research has been done specifically in the area of history education to suggest that more attention should be paid to the psychological constraints that govern student understanding of history (Collis & Biggs, 1979; Coltham, 1971; Hallam, 1970; Jurd, 1972; Kennedy, 1983; Zaccaria, 1978). These constraints have been related to Piaget's stages of development. The crucial difference, as shown in Figure 3.1, is the age at which students are said to be able to engage in complex historical thinking. Such thinking, it seems, cannot be expected of students until about 15 years of age.

The implications of this for the teaching of history are considerable and have been outlined by Hallam (1970). He has suggested that, for the high school students up to the age of 14, material ought not to be too abstract. Emphasis should be placed on helping students improve their reasoning skills, keeping in mind that formal operational thinking is the mark of the professional historian. Teaching strategies should be developed to insure that students are not fixated at a particular stage of development. While acceleration from one stage to another may not be possible, thought should be given to ways in which students can be confronted with increasingly complex situations.

These views, however, have not gone unchallenged and do not represent the only lines of research on historical cognition. Laville and Rosenweig (1982) criticize the approach of Hallam (1970) and others by claiming that it represents a static view of the nature of history and that more dynamic and critical methods of introducing students to history would overcome many of the problems associated with students' intellectual development. Kennedy (1983), following a neo–Piagetian psychological view, attempts to demonstrate that it is limitations on information processing capacity that account for student limitations in understanding historical material. This tends to place the emphasis on

FIGURE 3.1. Piaget's Developmental Levels and Age Levels Related to Historical Understanding

Stage of Development	Characteristic	Piaget	Historical Understanding
		Hypothesized Age Level	
Preoperational	Unable to relate discrete items	0–5	0–12
Concrete	Focused on a single event or piece of data	5–8	12–14
Formal	Understands relationships and proposes hypotheses	8–12	14–16

instructional strategies rather than the selection of content. Lee (1978) and Hallden (1986), while not following any particular psychological model, nevertheless point to qualitative differences in students' ability to reason about historical phenomena. Egan (1978) goes even further and suggests that there are indeed stages of historical understanding that are qualitatively different, but these are not based on psychological development. Rather, they are deductively derived categories that are based on children's orientation to knowledge in general and historic events in particular. Recent empirical research by Levstik (1986) and Levstik and Pappas (1987) tends to support this view, and their work demonstrates how very young children can have a lively interest in and concern for history and historical events.

Thus there is no consensus on the exact nature of the problem, yet there is agreement that young students certainly think differently about history than older students and adults and that these different modes of thinking need to be taken into consideration when planning appropriate content. It is unclear at this stage whether sufficient attention has been paid to the different ways students can come to know history or whether some expanded theory of cognition and concept formation is needed, along the lines suggested by Eisner (1982). Yet one thing is clear: Great care must be taken in presenting history to students. Consideration needs to be given to the age of students, the cognitive demands of the content, and the outcomes that are expected.

In a somewhat speculative fashion, it may be that what history teachers need to do is play up the dynamic between local, national, and global content. Such an interplay would certainly provide for the discussion of citizenship issues in the history curriculum. This would mean not isolating content into discrete areas so that only young students deal with local content and older students with some remote continent. Students of all ages need to be reminded that they are part of a very broad canvas, and this can be achieved by promoting the local, national, and global dimension of citizenship. Very often the drama and mystery of events that lie beyond the experience of young students can be the very things that motivate and sustain interest in the historical process, although eventually this interest needs to be grounded in local concerns. In the same way, adolescents are intensely interested in self, and that might be an ideal starting point for an exploration of global issues.

All this would require curriculum planning of the highest quality, to insure that an adequate scope and sequence was determined and that specific activities were well articulated and cohesive. The main issue for teachers to keep in mind is that it is not the content itself that poses problems for students—it is the information processing demands that teachers themselves make concerning the content. These demands need to be simple for younger children and increasingly more complex for older children.

For this reason, some attention must be made to insure that appropriate teaching strategies are matched with specific content. Teaching strategies, once the sole concern of educators, have more recently attracted the interest of policy makers as well (Garman, 1987). This is in large part because public perceptions about lack of standards in schools have focused to some extent on methods of teaching. Student-centered, open-plan classrooms, where teachers are facilitators rather than instructors and where decisions about what is taught are made by students rather than teachers, are sometimes seen to be important influences that have accounted for a decline in standards both academically and morally. Great care needs to be taken in making such cause-and-effect attributions about different teaching strategies. A century of educational research has been unable to establish clear relationships between variables such as method of instruction and student performance. The main variable influencing student performance seems to be academic learning time—the amount of time a student allocates to a work task. The more time a student spends working on a task, the better she will do. While this is an important finding, its implications for instructional models are not absolutely clear.

Thus, in the context of history and citizenship education, care must be taken when it comes to prescribing particular teaching strategies. It would be inappropriate, for example, to assume that methods of direct instruction emphasizing didactic teaching best suit the nature of history and the promotion of citizenship. Indeed, Torney-Purta (1985) has argued that just the opposite is the case if the aim is to improve civic understanding and encourage the development of civic values. Drawing on a wide range of research, she has shown that classroom processes that make use of discussion and questioning have a direct relationship to an increase in students' civic knowledge and attitudes. She recommends a balance between content and process so that significant issues can be subjected to critical reflection and inquiry. Students who are encouraged to recognize different points of view, analyze the differences, and consider the implications of alternative outcomes are more likely to develop positive civic attitudes while at the same time acquiring significant knowledge about citizenship. If a balanced approach yields such results, it ought to be encouraged in classrooms across the nation.

In the end, positive classroom climates must contribute to the promotion of citizenship education. Certainly content is important, but the environment must also be supportive. If students cannot see citizenship being modeled in their immediate surroundings, and if the values being expounded upon are not also the values being lived out, then the impact of significant content may be minimal. This does not mean resorting to classrooms where "anything goes" and freedom is interpreted to mean "do your own thing." Rather, concern for the public good should be the guiding principle for the democratic classroom, just as it should guide the democratic society.

CONCLUSION AND RECOMMENDATIONS

History has a significant role to play in promoting citizenship education. As a fundamental form of knowledge it introduces students to a way of thinking and a mode of experience that is unique. It has the potential to create an inclusive national community to which all belong and to which all can contribute. It shows how groups have acted in the past to solve problems and create communities. Teachers must become sensitive to the demands history places on students' cognitive ability and select content that, while challenging, can also be integrated into existing knowledge and understanding. If citizenship education is to be successful, teachers must recognize that a positive classroom climate will contribute more than anything toward the achievement of desired objectives. These are significant demands to place on teachers, yet there is little doubt that a concerted effort in all these areas will be for the good not only of individual students but for the nation as a whole.

Given the significance of history in the education of an intelligent citizenry, the following recommendations are made:

1. History should be a part of the common curriculum for all students. It should find a place in both the elementary and secondary school curriculum.

2. A national committee should be set up to define essential history content to be included in college and school curricula. Guidelines should be provided to all school districts and colleges, to help them make decisions about the selection of specific history content.

3. The National Assessment of Educational Progress should include a battery of history items reflecting nationally significant history content and skills.

4. College history courses should provide specialist training for history teachers, who must be educated in both depth and breadth. These courses should continue past initial training to provide ongoing professional development for all teachers of history.

5. History professors should take a special interest in the preparation of history teachers, so that courses focus on the most recent historical scholarship and interpretation. Special efforts should be made to insure that history teachers cover broad chronological periods as well as more specialized studies.

6. A cooperative program between the federal and state governments should establish centers of excellence for the teaching of history. These should involve teachers, scholars, and educators in a national effort to improve the teaching of history in schools and colleges.

REFERENCES

Adler, M. (1984). *The Paidea proposal*. New York: Macmillan.

Alder, D., & Lindhardt, S. (1981). World history: Building conceptual understanding. *Social Education, 45*(8), 548–549.

American Federation of Teachers. (1987). *Education for democracy*. Washington, DC: Author.

Anderson, L., & Rivlin, G. (1980). Citizenship education in a global age. *Educational Leadership, 38*(1), 64–65.

Bell, T. (1977). Values and morality. In U.S. Department of Health, Education and Welfare, *Education and Citizenship—A Conference Report*. Washington, DC: Author.

Boyer, E. (1983). *High school*. New York: Harper & Row.

Butts, R. F. (1980). *The revival of civic learning: A rationale for citizenship education in American schools*. Bloomington, IN: Phi Delta Kappan Educational Foundation.

Collingwood, R. (1946). *The idea of history*. Oxford, England: Claredon Press.

Collis, K., & Biggs, J. (1979). *The structure of learning outcomes in history*. Unpublished paper, University of Newcastle, Newcastle, Australia.

Coltham, J. (1971). *The development of thinking and the learning of history*. London: The Historical Association.

Dray, W. (1964). *Philosophy of history*. Englewood Cliffs, NJ: Prentice-Hall.

Egan, K. (1978). Teaching the varieties of history. *Teaching History, 21*, 20–22.

Egan, K. (1983). Social studies and the erosion of education. *Curriculum Inquiry, 13*(2), 195–214.

Eisner, E. (1982). *Curriculum and cognition*. New York: Longman.

Finkelstein, B. (1985). Thinking publicly about civic learning: An agenda for education reform in the 80's. In A. Jones (Ed.), *Civic learning for teachers: Capstone for educational reform* (pp. 13–24). Ann Arbor, MI: Prakken.

Gagnon, P. (1988, November). Why study history? *The Atlantic Monthly, 262*(5), 43–66.

Garman, N. (1987, April). *An interpretive analysis of the Madeline Hunter clinical supervision movement in Pennsylvania*. Paper presented at the annual meeting of the American Educational Research Association, Washington, DC.

Giarrel, J. (1983). The public, the state and the civic education of teachers. *Journal of Teacher Education, 34*(6), 57.

Gilbert, R. (1984). *The impotent image: Reflections of ideology in the school curriculum.* London: Falmer Press.

Gross, R. (1958). United States history. In R. Gross & L. Zeleny (Eds.), *Educating citizens for democracy: Curriculum and instruction in secondary social studies* (pp. 162–214). New York: Oxford University Press.

Hallam, R. (1970). Piaget and thinking in history. In M. Ballard (Ed.), *New movements in the study and teaching of history* (pp. 162–178). London: Temple Smith.

Hallden, O. (1986). Learning history. *Oxford Review of Education, 12*(1), 53–66.

Hirst, P. (1974). *Knowledge and the curriculum.* London: Routledge and Kegan Paul.

Jurd, M. (1972). Adolescent thinking in history-type material. *The Australian Journal of Education, 17*(1), 2–17.

Keller, C. (1984). Improving high school history teaching. In C. E. Finn Jr., D. Ravitch, & R. T. Fanchar (Eds.), *Against mediocrity: The humanities in America's high schools* (pp. 87–98). London: Holmes and Meier.

Kennedy, K. (1983). Assessing the relationship between information processing capacity and historical understanding. *Theory and Research in Social Education, 11*(27), 1–22.

Laville, C., & Rosenweig, L. (1982). Teaching and learning history. In L. Rosenweig (Ed.), *Developmental perspectives on the social studies* (pp. 67–81). Washington, DC: National Council for the Social Studies.

Lawton, D. (1975). *Class, culture and curriculum.* London: Routledge and Kegan Paul.

Lee, P. (1978). Explanation and understanding in history. In A. K. Dickinson & P. J. Lee (Eds.), *History teaching and historical understanding* (pp. 72–93). London: Heinemann.

Levstik, L. (1986). The relationship between historical response and narrative in a sixth-grade classroom. *Theory and Research in Social Education, 14*(1), 1–20.

Levstik, L., & Pappas, C. (1987). Exploring the development of historical understanding. *Journal of Research and Development in Education, 21*(1), 1–15.

Merriam, C. (1934). *Civic education in the United States.* New York: Charles Scribners.

Morrill, R. (1982). Educating for democratic values. *Liberal Education, 68*(4), 365–376.

Murchland, B. (1985). Civic education: Passing the problem. In A. Jones (Ed.), *Civic learning for teachers: Capstone for educational reform* (pp. 33–36). Ann Arbor, MI: Prakken.

Oldenquist, A. (1980). On the nature of citizenship. *Educational Leadership, 38*(1), 30–35.

Phillips, D. (1974). Perspectives on structure of knowledge and the curriculum. In P. W. Musgrave (Ed.), *Contemporary studies in the curriculum.* Sydney: Angus and Robertson.

Ravitch, D. (1985). *The schools we deserve: Reflections on the educational crises of our time.* New York: Basic Books.

Remy, R. (1980). *Handbook of basic citizenship competencies: Guidelines for comparing materials, assessing instruction and setting goals.* Alexandria, VA: Association for Supervision and Curriculum Development.

Shenton, M., & Jakoubek, R. (1980). Rethinking the teaching of American history. *Social Education, 44*(6), 461–466.

Sizer, T. (1984). *Horace's compromise.* Boston: Houghton Mifflin.

Skilbeck, M. (1979). The nature of history and its place in the curriculum. *Journal of the History Teachers' Association of Australia, 6,* 2–9.

Tomlinson, J. (1986). Public education, public good. *Oxford Review of Education, 12*(3), 211–222.

Torney-Purta, J. (1985). Evidence for balancing content with process and balancing answers with questions: The contribution of psychology to the civic education of teachers. In A. Jones (Ed.), *Civic learning for teachers: Capstone for educational reform* (pp. 91–99). Ann Arbor, MI: Prakken.

Zaccaria, M. (1978). The development of historical thinking: Implications for the teaching of history. *History Teacher, 11*(3), 335–344.

4 The Economic Perspective

Economic Literacy and Citizenship Education

RONALD A. BANASZAK

Today, citizens in our democracy cannot function effectively without an understanding of the economy. Kenneth Boulding (1969), a former president of the American Economic Association, has declared,

> An accurate and workable image of the social system in general, and the economic system in particular is . . . increasingly essential to human survival. If the prevailing images of the social system are unrealistic and inaccurate, decisions which are based on them are likely to lead to disaster. . . . Economic education, therefore, along with education in other aspects of the social system may well be one of the most important keys for man's survival. . . . In a complex world, unfortunately, ignorance is not likely to be bliss, and a society in which important decisions are based on fantasy and folk tales may well be doomed to extinction. [pp. 10–11]

Though understanding our economic system is as important to good citizenship as understanding our political system, too frequently citizenship education has been limited to only political education. Such a narrow view is inappropriate, for it is difficult to think of a political issue that does not have a significant economic dimension. Ignoring economics distorts students' understanding of social realities, reducing their ability to cope with them and depriving students of the knowledge needed to understand the economic consequences of social action and policy. Economically literate citizens are essential to a healthy, well-functioning democracy.

In our democracy, the government and the economy are managed by everyone who participates. How we vote on election day and how we vote with our dollars have important consequences. How informed and how thoughtful we are directly affects the quality of our choices and the effectiveness of our political and economic systems. As Hansen (1982) explains, "Ours, after all, is a democracy—the presence of too many economic illiterates could well lead to faulty public policy, if it hasn't already. Widespread economic understanding seems to be a must in a free society where the rule of one-person-one-vote prevails" (p. 23).

Economic understanding is not sufficient for citizenship, of course. Citizens of the United States simultaneously exist in a democratic polity, a largely capitalist economy, and a pluralistic culture. Citizens need to understand and support each system. Each affects the others, and each requires the informed involvement of citizens. Economic understanding has particular relevance today, for it is both a body of knowledge and a way of thinking about complex choices citizens have to make on both societal and personal levels. Economic literacy is not casually acquired by merely surviving in our economy. It requires formal instruction that should be part of the education of all citizens.

The purpose of this chapter is to define economic literacy, make a strong case for teaching about our economy in elementary and secondary schools, and discuss some important issues related to creating an economically literate citizenry.

DEFINING ECONOMICS AND ECONOMIC LITERACY

Alfred Marshall (1948), a British economist, stated clearly how pervasive economics is in our lives: "Economics is a study of mankind in the ordinary business of life" (p. 41). Indeed, we encounter economics as we work, save, buy, and participate actively as citizens in a democracy. In this section, economics and economic literacy will be defined and some related issues discussed.

Economics As a Discipline

Economics is the discipline concerned with the allocation of limited resources among unlimited wants. The economy, composed of economic institutions, is the organized way we transform resources into desired goods and services. Economics is the study of how this process works.

Economics is both a body of knowledge and a way of thinking about certain phenomena. It provides "a kit of tools with which to analyze the complexities of the real world" (National Task Force on Economic Education, 1961, p. 17). These tools are concepts, generalizations, theories, and models that describe the ways in which limited resources are allocated. Economics also is a methodology for investigating and understanding better how the economy works. John Maynard Keynes (1930) expresses this view well when he defines economics as "a method rather than a doctrine, an apparatus of the mind, a technique of thinking, which helps its possessor to draw correct conclusions" (p. 6). Keynes's "technique of thinking" is the scientific method that economists use in their search for generalizations that have broad application and predictive power. This scientific method teaches that the acquisition of knowledge must be independent of the economist's personal values. Like other scientists, economists must be objective or positive, that is unprejudiced, following truth wherever it leads, focusing on "what is," not "what should be." As Milton Friedman (1953) declares, "Positive economics is, or can be, an 'objective' science, in precisely the same sense as any of the physical sciences" (pp. 4–5). Economics does not involve providing practical advice about which economic policies should be adopted, but rather how to predict the consequences of those policies. Making, judging, and influencing economic policy, as citizens must, requires economic literacy.

Economic Literacy

Through our everyday experiences, we learn about the economy. Some of what we learn is correct, but much is incorrect and incomplete. Hansen (1982) suggests that the goal of economic education is to move the ordinary citizen from a "folk" knowledge of the economy to the more comprehensive knowledge of professional economists. Thus, becoming economically literate can be viewed as the process of gaining a more complete and accurate knowledge of the economy.

Economic literacy needed by citizens involves more, however. It is not synonymous with the discipline of economics, but draws on that discipline. It is different in several ways. The discipline of economics seeks to discover new knowledge. Economic literacy involves citizens' knowing and applying fundamental economic ideas to make rational decisions about the use of limited resources. Economically literate individuals have a general understanding of the institutions that comprise our economic system and an accurate understanding of basic economic knowledge. Such individuals are equipped to conduct an objective, reasoned analysis of economic issues. Further, according to a study by O'Brien and Ingels (1987) such individuals feel more fully in control of their economic futures after studying economics.

Economic literacy also differs from the discipline of economics in its normative, or values, dimension. Through economic reasoning, individuals try to manage the use of their limited resources in ways that will lead to the most complete fulfillment of their goals. In general, a resource should be diverted from less important to more important uses. Doing so requires an understanding of what one personally values. While the discipline of economics can be descriptive and value free, the application of economic knowledge cannot be separated from the values of those using it.

Thus, being economically literate must include a knowledge of what we value, both individually and as a society. The generally shared economic goals that affect economic policy and personal decision making in the United States are discussed in more detail in the next section.

DOMINANT CONCEPTS AND IDEOLOGIES
OF CITIZENSHIP ECONOMICS

Economic literacy has both personal and social applications. We use it daily in our personal economic roles as producers, consumers, and savers, every time we make decisions about the allocation of our personal resources. In our citizenship role, we also call upon our economic understanding to make decisions about public policy.

It would be presumptuous to attempt to present a comprehensive treatment of economic concepts and ideologies needed for citizenship in this short chapter, but it is possible to highlight major ideas and deal briefly with the dominant ideological orientation among economists in the United States. Doing so does not deny the insightful critiques that some economists have voiced of mainstream economics (Bergmann, 1987; Culbertson, 1987; Galbraith, 1987; Heilbroner, 1987; Kuttner, 1985; Strober, 1987; Thurow, 1987).

Citizen Involvement

Citizens in our democracy participate in three distinct but interrelated systems: a representative government, a mixed-market economy, and a network of social and cultural institutions. Novak (1982) argues that "political democracy is compatible in practice only with a market economy. In turn, both systems nourish and are best nourished by pluralistic liberal culture" (p. 14). He claims that democracy and capitalism proceed from the same historical impulses to control the power of the state and liberate the energy of individuals.

These political and economic systems are separate, yet they influence each other and in turn are influenced by the ideas and values produced through the social system. For example, stable prices, full employment, and economic growth are three valued goals for the operation of our economy, goals that the government has charged itself to help achieve. Through fiscal and monetary policy, the federal government influences the operation of the economy to help achieve such socially determined goals.

A mixed-market economy, in a democracy, is largely managed by the population as a whole; that is, everyone who participates helps manage the system. Both individuals and groups make decisions, but, as Lasswell and Kaplan (1969) describe the process, "The group is constructed as a pattern of individual acts. An act is always that of a single person and when we speak of 'group acts' a pattern formed by individual acts is to be understood" (p. 3). While obviously some individuals, due to their position or status, have more influence on our economic, political, and social systems than others, those systems are constructed in ways to maximize the power and influence of independently motivated and acting individuals. While Lee Iacocca can provide leadership to Chrysler Corporation and work to reinvigorate that company, his success will depend on thousands of consumers evaluating Chrysler's automobiles and independently deciding whether or not to buy one, thus ultimately determining the success of Mr. Iacocca's efforts.

Our political and economic systems are based on the belief that the collective wisdom of many individuals is superior to that of a few. Clearly, our founders, in writing the U.S. Constitution, attempted to limit the power of the government and to maximize the potential for human freedom. Adam Smith, in describing the emergent capitalist system in 1776, similarly trusted in the wisdom of the individual. Novak (1982) reasons that "individual rationality, close to the emergent texture of daily events, in the end adds up to a far more rational form of economic order than a rationality imposed upon the collective from some distance above daily events" (p. 79). The belief in the collective wisdom of individual decision makers is one of the central realities of the American experiment.

But that collective wisdom needs to include an understanding of how the economy operates. Schug (1985) believes that, "indeed, the welfare and improvement of our economic system—and ultimately of the republic itself—require such an informed citizenry" (p. 6). This is because citizens interact with the economy in at least three ways. First, through the political process, citizens set the nation's broad economic goals and the rules under which the economy must function. Second, they also make daily decisions about the distribution of resources, goods, and services among citizens. Third, citizens regularly make more specific economic decisions by voting on such items as bond issues and taxes.

Further, without a knowledge of how the economy operates, citizens can be more easily misled by politicians, the media, and business leaders. Economic literacy gives citizens the ability to ask the right questions of their leaders and candidates for office and to evaluate the information they receive from news sources and advertising. Wood (1985) cautions, "It is hard to imagine the harm that has been done by insufficient public understanding of the principle of opportunity cost, or to imagine how much good might be done by public understanding of the costs of protectionism" (p. 32).

The Need for Universal Economic Literacy

Economic literacy is essential for all citizens partially because economics is pervasive, so many of today's issues are economic in nature or have an economic dimension. For Stigler (1983), the matter is simple: "The public has chosen to speak and vote on economic problems, so the only open question is how intelligently it speaks and votes" (p. 64). But more important, economic reasoning is a very powerful thinking tool, applicable in a wide variety of situations. As Stigler further argues, economic principles are "integral to all rational behavior, and they work in ways so subtle that their comprehension cannot be left to intuition or general training in other disciplines" (p. 62).

Finally, economic experts cannot be easily employed to advise citizens on economic policy issues, because such issues involve the nature of fundamental social goals rather than technical economic knowledge. Arguments over subsidized housing, welfare, and urban renewal are not answered by technical knowledge of economics, though that knowledge can be helpful in understanding the situation and the consequences of various policy actions. The conflicts involved in these issues are conflicts over social goals, and economics cannot solve these debates. Citizens cannot rely solely on the advice of economists to set public policy, because any such advice is based on those economists' own views of which social goals are important. Therefore, citizens need to be knowledgeable enough about economics to reflect intelligently on public policy issues and make informed decisions.

Economic Values and Citizenship

At the heart of citizenship in our democratic society is the need for citizens to make decisions. As we have seen, those decisions are made to achieve valued ends. As Myrdal (1944) and many others (e.g., Newmann & Oliver, 1970; Oliver & Shaver, 1966) have argued, human dignity is the fundamental value of American society, from which all other values flow. Citizens need to accept allegiance to that and those other basic values of our society that transcend historical eras or cultural boundaries. For Novak (1982), the "cultural system is the chief dynamic force behind the rise both of a democratic political system and a liberal economic system" (p. 185).

Individuals and society hold a variety of goals for our economic system. The most important of these are economic freedom, economic efficiency, equity, security, full employment, stability, justice, and a minimum standard of living for everyone (Saunders, Bach, Calderwood, & Hansen, 1984). These goals provide not only guidance in making individual decisions, but criteria for evaluating progress toward reaching these goals over time. Unfortunately, these goals are often in conflict, and difficult choices or trade-offs have to be made among them. For example, farm price supports, though promoting security for farmers, also reduce efficiency; consumer protection legislation, while providing more security for consumers, may reduce freedom in the marketplace; minimum-wage laws, designed to promote income equity, may increase teenage unemployment; and wage/price controls, designed to restrain inflation, also reduce freedom and efficiency. Citizens need to understand these goals and how to choose among them when they conflict. The discipline of economics can inform those choices, but it cannot make them. Each citizen must reflect on the issues and personally reach a decision.

Other values are necessary for our economy and our democracy. Our belief in the value of individual decision makers is based upon an equally firm belief in the virtue of our citizens. That virtue is largely influenced by our cultural heritage, which helps hold in check individualism and self-interest. Democracy requires trust in the quality of the informed judgment of citizens when involving them in policy decisions. Equally important is our belief that the world can be made better through human effort—that the future can be better than the past. Without such a belief, it becomes impossible to maintain confidence in our participatory systems. If the world were either totally irrational or totally predictable, so that we could have no influence on it, there would be no reason for us to participate as individuals. There would be no point in trying to improve the world if those efforts had no chance of succeeding.

Economic Concepts for Decision Making

Goals are implemented through our collective decisions. Because its core concept is choice, economics is an ideal subject for developing decision-making skills. In the conduct of everyday life, citizen choices have both a personal as well as a societal effect. Personal choices about which goods to purchase help determine what and how much the economy will produce. How well workers choose to do their jobs impacts the quality and efficiency of their work and affects the competitiveness of the United States in world markets.

Economic decision making is a logical, reasoning process using economic concepts and generalizations. The common model of economic decision making consists of these six steps:

1. Clearly identify the details of the decision situation.
2. Determine what personal and social goals are to be attained.
3. Identify alternative decisions.
4. Consider each alternative and its consequences.
5. Decide on the best alternative for reaching the desired goals.
6. Review and evaluate the decision.

This decision-making model is not unique to economics. Knowledge of economic relationships informs citizens applying this model to policy issues, especially during steps three and four. The economic relationships most useful as citizens identify and evaluate alternatives and their consequences are the laws of supply and demand, scarcity, opportunity cost, production possibilities, cost/benefit analysis, long-term effect, marginal analysis, and sunk costs.

Schur (1985) argues that the *laws of supply and demand* are perhaps the most important. The law of demand states that, as price increases, the quantity of a good or service that is demanded decreases. The law of supply states that, as price rises, producers are willing to increase the quantity supplied. As price falls, the quantity producers are willing to supply also falls. The economy tends to move toward an equilibrium price at which the quantity producers are willing to produce is identical to the quantity consumers are willing to buy. Some government policies, such as a minimum wage, are designed to modify the free action of the laws of supply and demand, but no action of government is able to eliminate fully the operation of these laws. Even in command economies, where government policy has officially supplanted the laws of supply and demand, they are seen in black markets, free markets, and the like.

Productive resources are *scarce* compared to the uses we have for them. Thus we need to make choices about alternate uses of productive resources. Ultimately choices are made between the most desirable and the next most desirable alternative use. These choices can be measured in terms of lost opportunity, or the *opportunity cost*. But decisions about the use of productive resources seldom are mutually exclusive. We do not choose between automobiles and skyscrapers, but between relative amounts of automobiles and skyscrapers, or various *production possibilities*.

Every decision has *costs and benefits*. By examining the costs associated with each decision in relation to the expected benefits, we attempt to make choices that maximize benefits for the least cost. When examining the consequences of a decision, it is important to consider the *long-term effect* as well as the immediate one. A choice that has a less desired short-term effect still may be the better choice if it has a more desirable long-term effect.

Marginal analysis is used in economic decisions to determine the value of producing or consuming an additional unit of the same good or service. It is an effective way of informing us about choices designed to maximize output and satisfaction. The law of diminishing marginal utility teaches that additional quantities of goods yield successively smaller increments of satisfaction. Marginal productivity measures the additional output achieved by adding an additional unit of resources as input.

Each economic decision should be made on its own merit and not be influenced by previous decisions. Past use of resources in a particular way is known as a *sunk cost*. Since this use has already occurred, there is no way to change it. Often individuals believe that, since resources have been spent in a particular way in the past, it would be wasteful not to continue spending resources in the same way. However, if continued expenditure of resources in that way is not an efficient means to achieve the desired end, that pattern of resource use should be discontinued.

Economic Concepts for Citizenship

Besides those economic concepts helpful for decision making, a few others are needed by all citizens so they will possess an overview of the major features of the operation of our economy and be able to participate effectively in it.

To begin with, our economic system uses *incentives* to influence human behavior, by offering financial rewards that permit some individuals the ability to make larger claims for products and services. Understanding and employing incentives is a powerful way to influence the economy, for individuals attempt to make choices that maximize output and satisfactions, thus promoting self-interest. Consumers seek to maximize their satisfaction, workers their wages, producers their profits, and investors their return. Incentives are only effective when they are equally available to all citizens, but achieved by only some because of their actions. A society with a *free-enterprise*-based economy can expect unequal results because individuals have varying talents, opportunities, and desires. An incentive-based system requires us to take risks, embrace uncertainties, and arrive at variable results. However, our desire to promote our own *self-interest* cannot be unbridled. It must be rational and socially responsible. This means that self-interest is constrained by our cultural heritage and that our interests usually are best served by making decisions that result in long-term benefits, even if doing so means foregoing short-term advantages.

The principal feature of our economy is the *market*. The market is not a place where buyers and producers meet, but rather the process through which the decisions of individuals and businesses determine the allocation of resources. The forces of *supply* and *demand* interact, seeking an equilibrium and registering decisions through price. *Exchange* occurs within the market and involves trading resources, products, or services. When exchange is voluntary, both sides believe they have gained. Exchange is fundamental, permitting *specialization* and resulting in more efficient use of resources.

All products and services are created using *productive resources*. These resources can be *human*, *natural*, or *capital*. Natural resources are the gifts of Nature such as land, water, and petroleum. Human resources include all the physical and mental capacities of people. Capital resources are produced from natural resources through human effort and include such items as machinery and factories. It is the quantity of capital resources, more than any thing else, that determines the level of *economic development* of a country. Developed countries have more capital resources, while developing countries have fewer.

In our *mixed-market economy*, economic decisions are made by individuals and institutions in a process that involves the least necessary amount of government intervention to achieve economic goals. Of course, the government must provide the *infrastructure* (laws, currency, etc.) within which our economy functions, but beyond those basics the extent of government involvement in the economy is an evolving and ever-changing one. Today the government attempts to manage the economy to produce price stability, growth, full employment, and other val-ued ends through *fiscal* and *monetary policies*. The government is also a major consumer and producer of goods and services. Finally, through the government we attempt to mediate the circumstances of individuals who do not benefit from our economic system. Citizens have asked the government to provide support to those in need. So the government participates in programs that transfer income from individuals who are more successful in the economy to individuals who receive inadequate income from the marketplace. Also, the government sets and enforces the rules of the economy, to prevent individuals or groups from gaining an unfair advantage.

RECENT EVENTS IN ECONOMIC EDUCATION

The repeated calls during this century for more instruction about economics as an essential ingredient in the education of citizens give testimony to the continued absence of economic education in the na-tion's schools. Little progress was made until the influential Committee for Economic Development (CED) decided in the late 1940s to focus on the issue of economic education. Economists, educators, and represen-tatives from business, labor, government, and private research organiza-tions met at a CED-funded workshop in 1948 to consider the issue of widespread public ignorance of economics and to propose solutions (Baker, 1950). Frankel (n.d.) reported that this group "focused on the schools not only as the best place for economic education, but as the *only* place for most Americans" (p. 1). During the workshop, the nature of economic education was heatedly debated. Those in favor of teaching economics as an academic discipline won out over those who wanted to focus economics education on economic institutions and on consumer or personal economic topics. This direction has been dominant ever since, influencing both the content and presentation of economics.

Economic Education Organizations

The Interim Committee on Economic Education, established at the CED conference, became the Joint Council on Economic Education (JCEE) in 1949. Economic education now had a national advocate whose stated major goal was "to foster, promote, conduct, encourage and fi-nance scientific research, training and publication in the broad field of economic education in order to bring about a wider knowledge and understanding of the principles and operation of our American economy" (Frankel, n.d., p. 1). Inadequate economics education for teachers, old-fashioned instructional techniques, and a paucity of adequate materials were the initial issues addressed by the JCEE.

The JCEE prides itself on a strong local presence throughout the nation. Most of its programs are delivered on the local level through affiliated state councils and individual centers. Currently, the JCEE has a council in every state and the District of Columbia, and more than 250 local centers on college and university campuses. Through this local presence, the JCEE is able to promote the teaching of economics, deliver teacher training, and assist school districts with implementation of economics education.

The JCEE is not alone in its efforts to promote economic literacy. A recent directory identified 198 major organizations involved in providing business and economic education information for precollegiate students (Banaszak, 1985). While most are regional, Junior Achievement and the Foundation for Teaching Economics have national constituencies and deserve special mention.

Founded in 1919, Junior Achievement (JA) has developed a network of over 230 "field operations" that deliver educational experiences directly to students. It began by offering an after-school program that allowed students to create and run their own businesses with help from business volunteers. This continues to this day. Beginning in the 1970s, JA experimented with in-school economics programs, first for junior high school students, then for fifth and sixth graders, and most recently for twelfth graders. These programs have expanded rapidly and had an impact on a million students in 1987 (Junior Achievement, 1987, 1988).

Another group, the Foundation for Teaching Economics (FTE), focuses its efforts on materials development for young adolescents and on curriculum change to promote more economics instruction in Grades 7 through 10. The most significant effort of the FTE has been to explore ways of explaining economics that are especially appropriate for young adolescents, and the results have been well received by educators around the nation. The FTE's approach uses real-world, people-oriented case studies. It is popular with both students and teachers and seems to facilitate students' internalizing and using the economic content (Banaszak, 1987).

Variety of Materials

All three organizations—the JCEE, JA, and FTE—depend largely on donations from business. Chamberlin (1979) estimated that economic education has received more money from business sources than all the other social sciences combined. Unfortunately, in the past much of this funding has been spent on providing biased instructional materials to schools at no cost. One estimate is that U.S. firms spent $50 million in 1956 alone on free materials for school use, with a considerable proportion directed toward economic education (Baker, 1960). Fortunately, many corporations are more sensitive today to the need for unbiased materials and are willing to fund materials development projects of reputable economic education organizations.

In addition, commercial publishers, sensing an increasing market, have also produced economic education materials. Movies, filmstrips, computer software, supplementary texts, and textbooks abound. More important, these materials have begun to focus on adapting the discipline of economics to the developmental perspective of the target age group.

The most significant of the publications guiding economics education is the *Master Curriculum Guide in Economics: A Framework for Teaching the Basic Concepts* (Saunders et al., 1984), produced by the Master Curriculum Guide Project of the JCEE. That publication grew out of earlier works sponsored by the Committee on Economic Development and the American Economic Association. The two organizations sponsored the National Task Force on Economic Education that in 1961 issued a report calling for the teaching of basic economic concepts and controversial issues in the schools and stressing the use of a reasoned approach to thinking about economic issues. The second part of the Master Curriculum Guide Project was the creation of exemplary lessons, by grade level, illustrating how teachers could instruct their students about economics (Banaszak & Clawson, 1981; Clow, Ristan, Hartoonian, Senn, & Thomas, 1985; Davison, 1977; Kourilsky, 1978; Morton, Buckle, Miller, Nelson, & Prehn, 1985; Niss, Brenneke, & Clow, 1979; O'Neill, 1980a, 1980b; Weidenaar, 1982; Wentworth & Leonard, 1988). Grade placement of economic content has been further refined in the recently published *Economics: What and When* (Gilliard, Caldwell, Dalgaard, Highsmith, Reinke, & Watts, 1988).

Extent of Economics Instruction

There has been a considerable increase in enrollment in economics programs in recent years. Traditionally, economics has been taught almost exclusively to a few college-bound high school seniors. A 1951 survey found less than 5 percent of all high school students took an economics course (McKee & Moulton, 1951). In the 1960s and 1970s, that pattern began to change as economics was taught with more regularity in the elementary and secondary schools. In a 1981 survey conducted by Yankelovich, Skelly, and White, Inc., teachers reported that increased percentages of students were taking economics compared to three and five years earlier. Economics teachers in that survey also reported that students were studying economics in earlier grades than in the past. Two-thirds of the junior high school economics teachers reported that the subject was taught in the sixth or seventh grades in their schools, and over half of the senior high school teachers reported that economics was introduced in the ninth or tenth grades in their schools. The survey concluded that 87 percent of the nation's junior and senior high school students were enrolled in schools that teach economics.

Almost half of the economics teachers surveyed indicated that economics was a required subject, mandated by state law (Yankelovich, Skelly, & White, Inc., 1981). In a 1982 survey of state requirements, Banaszak and Brennan found that 24 states required schools to offer instruction in economics. In 7 of these states, economics was a required course for high school graduation. The same survey repeated four years later (Brennan, 1986) found the number of states requiring economics had risen to 27. More significantly, 15 states required a one-semester course in economics for high school graduation. This dramatic increase in mandating economics education at the high school level means that 46 percent of all high school graduates have passed a one-semester economics course. Mandated high school courses have contributed to increased enrollments in economics courses at lower grade levels, since many districts have implemented economics education programs in the elementary and middle schools to help prepare students for the new high school requirement.

Content of Economic Education

The selection of economics content is based primarily on a structure-of-the-discipline approach. This analytical social science approach is reflected in the JCEE's *Master Curriculum Guide in Economics: A Framework for Teaching the Basic Concepts* (Saunders et al., 1984) and in most economic education materials. It emphasizes specific economic content that is considered to be core to the discipline of economics, as well as the methods of inquiry used by economists. In the 1970s and 1980s, however, educators renewed their interest in consumer and career education programs. This reexamination of practical or personal economics was partially due to frustration with the structure-of-the-discipline approach, which caused students to think of economics as too esoteric. The fact that students were learning economics simply to pass course tests was evident from surveys showing how little students really knew about economics (Johnson, 1975). Further, few students voluntarily elected to take economics courses. Hansen asked in 1977 how economic educators could "find the right mix of personal and citizenship economics to promote greater student motivation and better match . . . the willingness of educators to provide economic education" (p. 66).

Another dilemma for the structure-of-the-discipline approach is the tendency of textbooks to present economic knowledge as an assured reality instead of an unfolding field of inquiry that continually produces new theories to explain economic phenomena. Economics, like the rest of human understanding, is a collection of evolving theories, replete with debate and dissension on even some of the most basic economic ideas. Further complicating the teaching of economics is the widespread perception that economists do not agree. In the Camelot days of the Kennedy Administration and the founding of the Council of Economic Advisors, it seemed that economists had the keys to promoting continuous growth without inflation or recession. The events of the 1970s shook economists, and public confidence in the field of economics has not recovered. The breakdown in the consensus of economists on macroeconomic issues has reminded teachers anew of the feeling that economics is difficult to teach because economists do not agree. It is easy to forget that economists have far more agreement than disagreement on basic principles and procedures of analysis.

CRITICAL ISSUES OF CITIZENSHIP ECONOMICS

While more students are now studying economics, there are still three critical issues about the content and teaching of economics that need to be addressed by economic educators concerned with citizenship. The first is the ambivalent attitude most Americans have toward our economy. The second is the lack of popularity of economics in the school curriculum, due to its manner of instruction. Third is the widespread erroneous understanding of the economy by citizens.

Ambivalent Public Attitude Toward the Economy

The most critical issue of economic education for citizenship is the reluctance of educators to help students develop a generally positive attitude toward our economic system. Although Americans take pride in their political system, readily describing it as exemplary, they have an ambivalent attitude toward their mixed-market economic system, and this makes it difficult for them to recommend it to youth. Yet every society needs to transmit its systems and values to its youth, and educational institutions play an important role in this process. Young Americans must come to accept the legitimacy of a mixed-market system, if it is to continue and be strengthened. Of course, no system is perfect. There are justified criticisms of both our political and economic systems, but each has a flexibility that encourages evolutionary improvements, and these come as a result of active citizen participation. Without a positive attitude about the systems and their capacity to change for the better, it is difficult for citizens to believe seriously that their participation will make a difference. Educators are at least partially responsible for developing those positive attitudes.

Student acceptance of our economy must be an informed acceptance, so students need to know about other economic systems and be able to compare their advantages and disadvantages to ours. Reaching that state of informed acceptance requires a developmentally appropriate process. Leming (1987) argues that, with very young students, nonrational methods of instruction need to be used to promote a positive view of our economy. As students mature, such methods should be relied on less. As he explains, "What is taught children must be developmentally appropriate. In the political and economic domains, as with morality, children must be taught to first feel positive toward cultural values. . . . As children mature, and as their reasoning ability develops, the basis for allegiance to these norms will change" (p. 64).

Students, as they mature, need to reflect critically on our economic system and realize that it can be criticized on a number of dimensions. It is not appropriate to teach youngsters that our economy is faultless and perfect, as they eventually will discover how they have been deceived, and this will only contribute to cynicism. As D'Amico, Daly, Wallace, and Wilson (n.d.) warn, "Often as children realize their preparation is inadequate or irrelevant, they turn against the institutions that have been misleading them" (p. 12).

In part, the ambivalence of Americans toward the economy can be explained by their lack of understanding of its basic operating principles. It is difficult to understand a complex market-driven economic system, wherein the search for individual self-interest is supposed to produce the greatest good for all of us, so long as self-interest is channeled into meeting consumer demands through competition of sellers in a largely open, free marketplace. In such a system, we can claim a high level of efficiency in the allocation of scarce resources to meet human wants, rapid progress toward producing more of what we want, and broader dispersion of economic power among many individuals and institutions. Yet it seems implausible that individuals and businesses seeking their own self-interests could somehow serve the highest good. It is much easier to imagine that, with each person pursuing self-interests, some will become very wealthy and seize more and more of what is produced for themselves, leaving less for the powerless members of society. With such reasoning, profit becomes a "rip-off" of the working poor by the rich. Only knowledge of the workings of our economy through economic education can counteract such misconceptions.

Our ambivalence toward the economy is also a consequence of the emotionality of economic issues that affect our standard of living. It is clear that some individuals in our incentive-based economy succeed while others do not. Poverty remains a persistent and disturbing problem, as does entrenched wealth. Still, in our system, we feature incentives to encourage individuals to make the most of their talents and abilities. Equality of opportunity necessarily leads to inequality of results. Cooper (1985) argues that, "when people are free, everyone will surpass the majority of his or her fellows in some respects" (p. 58). Through welfare and other assistance programs, we attempt to ameliorate some of the harshness of the market-driven system and provide a minimum standard of living for everyone. As a society we have decided to leave the incentives built into our mixed-market economy undisturbed, for they result in a higher standard of living for the vast majority of our citizens. Other societies, with other values for their economies, make different choices.

There is also ambivalence expressed toward business. While businesses provide the jobs, goods, and services that we need, as Bach (1982) explains they also have "vast power which can be used either for good or ill, the public feels, and that power is focused too exclusively on trying to make profits" (p. 13). Bach suggests that the source of fear of business is the concentration of power in immense multinational institutions. Individuals feel powerless against such entities. In addition, business malpractices are regularly reported in the press, and the resulting public perception is that all businesses are corrupt. Only a fuller understanding of how our economy truly functions will help citizens reach a more balanced view of business.

For these reasons, educators often feel compelled to withhold approval of our economic system. Yet, if that system is to continue and improve, students must learn that the economy is worthy of their support, come to an understanding of it, and develop a commitment to the basic values we try to achieve through it.

High-quality Economics Instruction

Another critical issue in preparing economically literate citizens is related to the lack of recognition by educators and the general public of the importance of economics instruction in the schools. This is partially due to the general perception that economics is a difficult and dull subject providing few direct personal benefits. Such a perception stands in stark contrast to Americans' general interest in economics, as evidenced by the enormous quantity of discussion about economic issues; the popularity of the *Wall Street Journal, Money,* and similar specialized publications; and the quantity of economic news in general magazines and newspapers. Why, then, is economics in the schools such an unpopular topic? A look at economics instruction, teaching materials, curriculum, and teacher training will help explain why economics has a reputation as a dull subject.

"Complexity and unreality—these are the two great barriers to vitalizing economic education," declared Harold Clark, an economic education reformer, in 1940. His comment, referring to both the selection of economic content and the manner of its instruction, is almost as true today as then. In many classrooms, economics instruction is little more than memorization and regurgitation of facts and terminology, with minimal attention given to student understanding. Such teaching results in a tyranny of jargon in which labeling of phenomena is believed to be equivalent to comprehension. In a study of school district curriculum guides, Armento (1986) discovered that economics is often presented "as a series of definitions rather than a dynamic, interrelated, constructed inquiry into the economic world" (p. 107). Economic content needs to be presented in ways that establish an understanding of our dynamic economic system. Students need to apply economic logic to a wide variety of situations they might encounter as consumers, workers, savers, and citizens. No amount of knowledge of isolated economic concepts will ever result in economic understanding or help citizens become capable of economic reasoning.

Too often, economics has been viewed only in terms of the content in a college course. While appropriate for training professional economists, such a view is not appropriate for the vast majority of citizens. Economics needs to be more closely related to the uses citizens will make of their economic knowledge. For example, citizens are consumers of government services. Economics classes, however, seldom consider the knowledge, skills, and problems associated with the consumption of government services. This situation is further complicated by most teachers' lack of training in economics. They often have such a superficial understanding of economics that they are not able to comprehend its usefulness or relevance and its ability to contribute to students' understanding their surrounding world.

The manner in which economics is taught also contributes to its reputation as a dismal science. Although the last 50 years have seen the development of a variety of innovative teaching strategies that involve students in their own learning—including simulations, role plays and debates—many economics students are still taught almost exclusively through lectures and textbook readings (Fancett & Hawke, 1982). Unfortunately, these are much less conducive to developing citizenship competencies than are the newer, student-centered techniques. A further complication is that the discipline of economics has become highly mathematical, so mathematical tools such as supply-and-demand graphs are often used to explain economic content to elementary and secondary students. This is done despite the fact that the mathematical skills of those students typically are not sufficient to allow them to understand such graphs. Instead of helping students to understand, such tools may only obfuscate. This sort of teaching does little to help students see the relationships among the study of economics, their lives, and current issues such as foreign trade and domestic protectionism, the plight of the family farm, and industry deregulation/regulation.

One final note is necessary regarding instruction. Economics is often claimed to be taught effectively by an infusion method, whereby it is included in other course content such as American history and geography. While this provides a potentially powerful way to include instruction about economics, there is evidence that it has not been implemented in a manner that effectively increases student understanding of our economy (Brickell & Scott, 1976; Walstad & Watts, 1985b). Walstad and Watts' (1985a) research strongly suggests that infusion of economic content throughout the curriculum, without a separate twelfth-grade economics course, is not nearly as effective in producing economic knowledge as the separate course. This is partially because many teachers have little training in economics, but it is also due to the poor quality of economic content in other social studies textbooks, as documented in repeated surveys of those texts by economists (American Economic Association, 1963; Davison, Sgontz, & Shepardson, 1975; Main, 1977; Miller & Rose, 1983; O'Neill, 1973). It may be counterproductive to expect teachers—if they have little training in economics and are using textbooks that contain errors in the economic explanation—to teach economics.

Public Misunderstanding About the Economy

Economic educators must also overcome misunderstandings about our economy. Daily participation in the economy breeds familiarity and an illusion of understanding. But, as noted earlier, it is very difficult to develop an accurate understanding of the economy by merely participating in it. The portrayal of business and economic events on television and in the movies contributes to such misunderstanding. There are errors that need to be corrected and lapses of knowledge that need to be filled in.

An additional source of misunderstanding is the press. Great quantities of information about our economy are relayed by journalists. Unfortunately, journalists, like teachers, are seldom trained in economics. They are not expected to educate the public, but simply to report current events. Too frequently they focus on a startling fact and use an attention-grabbing headline to draw readers into a story. They tend to focus on personalities, not issues, and look at things in the short run, rather than the long run. Further, reporters are commonly trained to use an adversarial model when reporting the news. This model requires winners and losers in each situation, while it is usually mutual gain that more accurately describes the situation in our economy. The adversarial model makes it difficult for news reporters to discuss such issues as efficiency, one of the most important concepts in economics. Instead, they are much more likely to discuss issues associated with the distribution of goods and services, because there always seems to be winners and losers in this area.

Economic education is needed to overcome this pervasive misinformation about our economy, for, only when citizens understand our economy can they make decisions intelligently.

RECOMMENDATIONS

In this section, the following seven recommendations for improving the education of future citizens about the economy are discussed:

1. Economics should be taught in ways that facilitate its use by citizens.
2. Economic instruction should stress the teaching of economic reasoning.
3. Economics education needs to develop commitment to goals and the general features of our economy.
4. Treatment of economic content in the social studies curricula needs to be increased, with an appropriate weighting of infused and specific treatment.
5. Continuing attention should be paid to creating, evaluating, and improving economics education materials.

6. Training in economics should be required of economics teachers.

7. Research that is needed to inform instruction, curriculum, and materials development should be undertaken immediately.

Accessibility and Utility for All Citizens

For too long, educators have assumed that college-level teaching of economics provides an appropriate model for precollege economics instruction. For example, most economic units begin with scarcity, a concept that may be very difficult for younger students to grasp with true understanding, because it is a relational concept and because it seems contrary to the abundance of products they see in stores. Dewey (1933) warned that, when using disciplinary-based studies, there is a danger that teachers and students will isolate their intellectual activities from "ordinary affairs of life [and] tend to set up a chasm between logical thought . . . and the specifics and concrete demands of every day events" (p. 62).

The logical structure of economics may not be an effective paradigm for instruction at all grade levels. It is not appropriate to expect youngsters to learn economics as adults do. Youngsters simply are not small adults. They construct meaning out of the world in different and unique ways, depending on their level of cognitive development and experiences with the world. We need to provide students with an overview of the economy that creates a general frame of reference for understanding economic relationships from their perspective. Students then will be better able to add to this general framework as they gain additional knowledge.

In order for economics to have genuine meaning to students, it must be relevant to their observed world. Economic content should be explained to students using real-world examples that are part of their experiences. With young students, economics can be explained using examples from their families and local community. With older students, current local, national, and world events can be related to economics. Using real-world examples helps build a bridge between the normally abstract content of economics and the uses students are to make of their economic knowledge. Such instruction requires the inclusion of both positive economics (economic content) and normative economics (economic policy to achieve valued ends). Citizens must make choices based on their knowledge of economic consequences and the goals they hope to achieve through their choices. They need to practice such decision making in the classroom, using real or hypothetical examples they might encounter as voters, workers, consumers, or savers.

In addition, economics readily lends itself to a variety of student involvement activities, such as role plays and simulations. Using such activities has at least five important pedagogical benefits. First, these strategies, because they are real-world and issue oriented, are conducive to developing and practicing citizenship skills. Second, personal experiences are much more conducive to learning than vicarious experiences. Third, an active learning role is more effective in gaining understanding than is a passive learning role. Fourth, participatory activities permit students actually to make decisions and bear the consequences of those decisions. Fifth, they also permit the mastery of new skills that may be required to complete the activities. By including unique, peculiar, or inconsistent examples in the activities, students' existing understanding can be challenged and their ability to transfer knowledge from known situations to new ones improved.

Teaching Economic Reasoning

One of the major goals of economics education is to promote more rational decision making in the allocation of resources; yet, far too often, instruction in economics is limited to learning the definitions of terms. Without the creation of situations in which students have to think about problems and issues in the classroom, little growth in economic reasoning can be expected. Through the use of activities, challenging situations, and public policy debates, students can practice economic reasoning. Direct instruction includes both instruction about how to think and, more important, practice in making economic decisions. Instruction in economic reasoning is so important that it should be given higher priority than instruction in economic content.

Developing Citizen Support for Our Economy

As noted at the beginning of this chapter, the *discipline of economics* can be—indeed, should be—neutral regarding any particular economic system. Economics as a discipline attempts to understand economic relationships for the purpose of establishing which ones have predictive value. To achieve that end, economics cannot be subverted to achieve any particular valued end. Just as physics cannot take a stand on approving or disapproving of the speed at which gravity attracts an object toward the Earth, economists cannot be allowed to posit desired ends and then analyze the economy to achieve those ends.

Economic literacy, on the other hand, cannot be neutral. Preparing citizens to participate effectively in our economy requires their commitment to the basic goals of our economy and to its general features. This should not be interpreted as meaning that students must slavishly accept all dimensions of our economy, nor should it be interpreted to mean that our economy is perfect and not subject to improvement. Rather, this recommendation would require us to treat our economic system in much the same way that we treat our political system. We do not hesitate to tell students that our political system is exemplary, though not perfect. We encourage allegiance to our political system to insure social vitality, cohesion, and stability. The same argument can be made for developing a generally positive disposition toward our economic system.

Increasing Economic Content in the Social Studies Curricula

Economic literacy will only increase when there is adequate treatment of economic content in the social studies curriculum. Currently the curriculum seldom calls for instruction beyond the definitional level and is highly repetitive from year to year. Armento's 1983 study of curriculum guides found that "concepts are dealt with at the introductory, definitional level whether the guide is intended for the ninth or twelfth grade" (p. 27). A sequence for the development of economic concepts by grade level should be created by each school district, and the content needs to go beyond the definitional level. Definitions and generalizations should be introduced in earlier grades and developed with increasing sophistication throughout the remainder of the curriculum.

The difficulties of infusing economic content throughout the social studies curriculum described earlier can be minimized if specific attention is given to the economic content. It is not sufficient to say that, because the Great Depression has been discussed in an American history class, economic ideas related to depressions have been adequately explained.

In addition, substantive treatment of economics should take place in the middle school or early high school years, either as a separate one-semester course or a major unit within an existing course. Among the powerful reasons for this placement are the cognitive development of students, their involvement in the economy, the formative period of their values and attitudes, and their continued presence in school prior to the extensive dropout problem (Davis, 1987). The traditional twelfth-grade one-semester course in economics should certainly continue to be offered. The combination of infusing economic content throughout the curriculum and a major treatment in the middle or junior high school will allow the twelfth-grade economic course to become more substantive, dealing with public policy issues and sophisticated economic reasoning.

Creating, Evaluating, and Improving Instructional Materials

The quality of economics instructional materials is critical to achieving economic literacy. In a review of research about economics education, Highsmith (1987) concluded that, "even when used by educators unfamiliar with economics, good materials help bring economic understanding to students" (p. 219). While the quality of economics instructional materials has increased considerably over the last 20 years, progress is still needed in both content and pedagogy. Since much of economics is taught in conjunction with other social studies courses, the economic content of social studies textbooks needs to be continually monitored so that errors, both of omission and commission, can be corrected. Further, the developers of materials should be sensitive to incorporating the principles of good instruction, as discussed in the first recommendation. Economic textbooks also need to examine carefully what is included and what is excluded, compared to the uses we expect students to make of the knowledge they are gaining. It is inappropriate to teach youngsters the discipline of economics and then expect them to know how to make public policy decisions without having had any practice.

Requiring Teacher Training

Since each state establishes its own requirements for teacher certification, there is considerable variation from state to state. Often it is possible for teachers to teach economics without any advanced training in the subject. In California, for example, teachers of the new twelfth-grade economics course, required for graduation, may never have had a college course in economics. Teacher training programs that consist only of after-school workshops of a few hours' duration are insufficient to provide the understanding necessary for teachers to do an adequate job with economic content. Instead, semester-length courses should be required, preferably while teachers are still in training. For those already in the classrooms, specialized economic education courses, such as those delivered by the Joint Council on Economic Education, should be required.

Undertaking Needed Research

Economic education suffers from a lack of understanding of how students construct economic knowledge from their experiences and how they use that knowledge. Comprehensive research should be undertaken to explore what economic decisions citizens make, what values citizens hold related to the economy, how economic socialization of students occurs at various ages, and how economic content should be sequenced to facilitate learning. Such research would provide needed information for more informed decisions about content and instructional methods. This information would guide teachers, curriculum developers, and creators of instructional materials. Unfortunately, without this research base, much of what will be done in economic education in the future will be based upon little more than the untested hypotheses of those making the decisions.

REFERENCES

American Economic Association. (1963). Economics in the schools: A report by a special textbook committee on economic education. *American Economic Review, 52*, Part 2 Suppl.

Armento, B. J. (1983). A study of the basic economic concepts presented in DEEP curriculum guides, grades 7–12. *Journal of Economic Education, 14*, 22–27.

Armento, B. J. (1986). Promoting economic literacy. In S. P. Wronski & D. H. Bragaw (Eds.), *Social studies and social sciences: A fifty-year perspective* (pp. 97–110). Washington, D.C.: National Council for the Social Studies.

Bach, G. L. (1982). Economic education and America's love–hate affair with business. In W. H. Peterson (Ed.), *Economic education: Investing in the future* (pp. 11–21). Knoxville, TN: University of Tennessee Press.

Baker, G. D. (1950). The Joint Council on Economic Education. *The Journal of Educational Sociology, 23*, 389–396.

Baker, G. D. (1960). Economic education. In C. W. Harris & M. R. Liba (Eds.), *Encyclopedia of Educational Research* (3rd ed.). New York: Macmillan.

Banaszak, R. A. (Ed.). (1985). *Directory of organizations providing business and economic education information.* San Francisco: Foundation for Teaching Economics.

Banaszak, R. A. (1987, April). *Teaching economics to young adolescents: Program of the foundation for teaching economics.* Paper presented at the annual meeting of the Association of Private Enterprise Education, Atlanta.

Banaszak, R. A., & Brennan, D. C. (1982). *A study of state mandates and competencies for economics education.* Stockton, CA: Center for the Development of Economics Education.

Banaszak, R. A., & Clawson, E. (1981). *Strategies for teaching economics: Junior high school level (grades 7–9)*. New York: Joint Council on Economic Education.

Bergmann, B. R. (1987). "Measurement" or finding things out in economics. *Journal of Economic Education, 18,* 191–202.

Boulding, K. (1969). Economic education: The stepchild too is father of the man. *Journal of Economic Education, 1,* 10–11.

Brennan, D. C. (1986). *A survey of state mandates for economics instruction, 1985–86.* New York: Joint Council on Economic Education.

Brickell, H. M., & Scott, M. C. (1976). *Effectiveness of economic education in senior high schools.* New York: Policy Studies in Education.

Chamberlin, D. (1979). Should business support economic education in our schools? *Minnesota Business Journal, 3,* 10–12.

Clark, H. F. (1940). Vitalizing economic education. *Social Education, 4,* 397–403.

Clow, J. E., Ristan, R., Hartoonian, H. M., Senn, P., & Thomas, R. (1985). *Teaching strategies: Consumer economics (Secondary).* New York: Joint Council on Economic Education.

Cooper, J. W. (1985). The moral basis of equal opportunity. *Educational Leadership, 43,* 57–59.

Culbertson, J. M. (1987). A realistic international economics. *Journal of Economic Education, 18,* 161–176.

D'Amico, J., Daly, S. L., Wallace, J. D., & Wilson, J. (n. d.). *Words into action: A classroom guide to children's citizenship education.* Philadelphia: Research for Better Schools.

Davis, J. E. (1987). *Teaching economics to young adolescents.* San Francisco: Foundation for Teaching Economics.

Davison, D. G. (1977). *Strategies for teaching economics: Primary level (grades 1–3).* New York: Joint Council on Economic Education.

Davison, D. G., Sgontz, L. G., & Shepardson, R. (1975). *Economics in social studies textbooks.* Iowa City: University of Iowa.

Dewey, J. (1933). *How we think.* Boston: D. C. Heath.

Fancett, V., & Hawke, S. (1982). Instructional practices in social studies. In Project Span Staff (Eds.), *The current state of social studies: A report of project SPAN* (pp. 207–264). Boulder, CO: Social Science Education Consortium.

Frankel, M. L. (n. d.). *The history of the Joint Council on Economic Education.* New York: Joint Council on Economic Education.

Friedman, M. (1953). The methodology of positive economics. In M. Friedman (Ed.), *Essays in positive economics* (pp. 1–14). Chicago: University of Chicago Press.

Galbraith, J. K. (1987). On teaching a fractured economics. *Journal of Economic Education, 18*(2), 213–226.

Gilliard, J. V., Caldwell, J., Dalgaard, B. R., Highsmith, R. J., Reinke, R., & Watts, M. (1988). *Economics: what and when.* New York: Joint Council on Economic Education.

Hansen, W. L. (1977). The state of economic literacy. In D. Wentworth, W. L.

Hansen, & S. Hawke (Eds.), *Perspectives on economic education* (pp. 61–79). New York: Joint Council on Economic Education, National Council for the Social Studies, and Social Science Education Consortium.

Hansen, W. L. (1982). Are Americans economically literate? In W. H. Peterson (Ed.), *Economic education: Investing in the future* (pp. 22–37). Knoxville: University of Tennessee Press.

Heilbroner, R. L. (1987). Fundamental economic concepts: Another perspective. *Journal of Economic Education, 18*(2), 111–120.

Highsmith, R. (1987). The research core of economic education. *Theory Into Practice, 26*(3), 216–222.

Johnson, S. S. (1975). *Update on education: A digest of the National Assessment of Educational Progress.* Denver: Education Commission of the States.

Junior Achievement. (1987). *Annual report.* Stamford, CT: Author.

Junior Achievement. (1988). *Fact sheet.* Stamford, CT: Author.

Keynes, J. M. (1930). *The scope and method of political economy.* New York: Macmillan.

Kourilsky, M. (1978). *Strategies for teaching economics: Intermediate level (grades 4–6).* New York: Joint Council on Economic Education.

Kuttner, R. (1985). The poverty of economics. *The Atlantic Monthly, 255*(2), 74–84.

Lasswell, H. D., & Kaplan, M. (1969). *Power and society.* New Haven, CT: Yale University Press.

Leming, J. S. (1987). On the normative foundation of economic education. *Theory and Research in Social Education, 15,* 63–76.

Main, R. S. (1977). Economics in social studies texts. In *National Conference on Economic Education and the Future of Capitalism: Proceedings.* Washington, DC: National Association of Manufacturers.

Marshall, A. (1948). *Principles of economics* (8th ed.). New York: Macmillan.

McKee, W., & Moulton, H. (1951). *Survey of economic education.* Washington, DC: The Brookings Institution.

Miller, S. L., & Rose, S. A. (1983). The Great Depression: A textbook case of problems with American history textbooks. *Theory and Research in Social Education, 11*(1), 25–29.

Morton, J. S., Buckle, S. G., Miller, S. L., Nelson, D., & Prehn, E. C. (1985). *Teaching strategies: High school economics courses.* New York: Joint Council on Economic Education.

Myrdal, G. (1944). *An American dilemma.* New York: Harper & Row.

National Task Force on Economic Education. (1961). *Economic education in the school.* New York: Committee for Economic Development.

Newmann, F. M., & Oliver, D. W. (1970). *Clarifying public controversy.* Boston: Little, Brown.

Niss, J. F., Brenneke, J. S., & Clow, J. E. (1979). *Strategies for teaching economics: Basic business and consumer education (secondary).* New York: Joint Council on Economic Education.

Novak, M. (1982). *The spirit of democratic capitalism.* New York: Simon & Schuster.

O'Brien, M. U., & Ingels, S. J. (1987). The economics values inventory. *Journal of Economic Education, 18,* 7–17.

Oliver, D. W., & Shaver, J. P. (1966). *Teaching public issues in the high school.* Boston: Houghton Mifflin.

O'Neill, J. B. (1973). *Economics in social studies textbooks: An evaluation of the economics and the teaching strategies in 11th and 12th grade U.S. and world history textbooks.* New York: Joint Council on Economic Education.

O'Neill, J. B. (1980a). *Strategies for teaching economics: United States history (secondary).* New York: Joint Council on Economic Education.

O'Neill, J. B. (1980b). *Strategies for teaching economics: World studies (secondary).* New York: Joint Council on Economic Education.

Saunders, P., Bach, G. L., Calderwood, J. D., & Hansen, W. L. (1984). *Master curriculum guide in economics: A framework for teaching the basic concepts* (2nd ed.). New York: Joint Council on Economic Education.

Schug, M. C. (1985). Introduction. In M. C. Schug (Ed.), *Economics in the school curriculum, K–12* (pp. 6–8). Washington, DC: Joint Council on Economic Education and the National Education Association.

Schur, L. (1985). What economics is worth teaching? In M. C. Schug (Ed.), *Economics in the school curriculum, K–12* (pp. 21–32). Washington, DC: Joint Council on Economic Education and the National Education Association.

Smith, A. (1930). *An inquiry into the nature and causes of the wealth of nations.* E. Cannan, Ed. London: Methuen & Co., Ltd. (Original work published 1776)

Stigler, G. J. (1983). The case, if any, for economic literacy. *Journal of Economic Education, 14,* 60–66.

Strober, M. H. (1987). The scope of microeconomics: Implications for economic education. *Journal of Economic Education, 18,* 135–149.

Thurow, L. C. (1987). Evaluating economic performance and policies. *Journal of Economic Education, 18,* 237–245.

Walstad, W., & Watts, M. (1985a). The current status of economics in the K–12 curriculum. In M. C. Schug (Ed.), *Economics in the school curriculum, K–12* (pp. 8–20). Washington, DC: Joint Council on Economic Education and the National Education Association.

Walstad, W., & Watts, M. (1985b). Teaching economics in the schools: A review of survey findings. *Journal of Economic Education, 16,* 135–146.

Weidenaar, D. J. (1982). *Strategies for teaching economics: Using economics in social studies methods courses.* New York: Joint Council on Economic Education.

Wentworth, D. R., & Leonard, K. E. (1988). *Teaching strategies: International trade.* New York: Joint Council on Economic Education.

Wood, W. C. (1985). The educational potential of news coverage of economics. *Journal of Economic Education, 16*(1), 27–35.

Yankelovich, Skelly, & White, Inc. (1981). *National survey of economic education, 1981.* New York: Playback Associates.

5 The Geographical Perspective
Geography's Role in Citizenship Education

NICHOLAS HELBURN

From early on, geographers involved in education have been explicitly concerned that their students (and their students' students) be effective citizens. With great consistency, geographers have expressed the responsibility for preparing students to solve public policy problems, both near and far. Three themes persist:

1. The interaction of local society with its environment,
2. The interdependence of one's own society with others around the world,
3. The recognition and acceptance of cultural differences.

WHY GEOGRAPHY IS IMPORTANT

Geography is important because students must *know* and understand it well enough to make intelligent decisions about society and the global environment. Further, they must *feel* enough concern to participate in finding and carrying out solutions to worldwide problems. As Joe Russel Whitaker (1948) writes,

> We have a keen appreciation of the duties and privileges of citizenship in our own country, but we must accept the challenge presented by the evolving world community. Terrestrial unity exists whether we choose to recognize it or not. Life is on a global basis today. To take part in this global community places an enormous strain on our educational system, but one which it dares not to reject. It we are to join with the people of other lands in furthering common interests, such as the preservation of the freedom of the seas and the creation of the freedom of the air; if we are to work with others on the problem of living

together with the least friction and the maximum of mutual aid, we must prepare ourselves to take a more intelligent, vigorous place in the world community—we must become citizens of the world. [p. 10]

Forty years later, Backler's (1988) admonition is strikingly similar:

Today's young people—the adults of tomorrow—will soon be responsible for making informed and rational decisions about issues affecting the interactions of the world's inhabitants and the relationships of all humans to the earth. They must understand how their actions influence the lives of people living in other regions of the world and how the actions of those people affect them. They must know where and why events are occurring if they are to apply their intelligence and moral sensitivity to improving the quality of human life on this planet. They must, in short, receive a sound education in global geography. [p. 4]

Natoli and Gritzner (1988), in a similar vein, state,

Geographical literacy demands that all students gain a common knowledge of their immediate and world environments. One important characteristic of geography is its concern for the earth as an ecological system. This equips us with a global perspective for analyzing world problems. Such knowledge about and appreciation of the world can lead students to satisfying lives and improve their participation as citizens in this democratic society and as partners in the world community.

    We can no longer sanction the practice of isolating ourselves from the global community. As each year passes, our relationships in the complex mosaic of nations become an increasingly inextricable part of our passage through life. Knowledge of geography will improve the meaning, safety, and enjoyment of this journey. [p. 9]

While none of these statements attempt to define citizenship, it is clear that each author understands that knowledge and intellectual skills must be accompanied by a sense of responsibility and a sense of obligation to help solve social and environmental problems.

GEOGRAPHY IN THE SOCIAL STUDIES

Libbee and Stoltman (1988) analyze the debate about the definition of citizenship in the social studies. Reviewing the work of other authors (Barr, Barth, & Shermis, 1977; Engle, 1960; Kurfman, 1977) and the guidelines of the National Council for the Social Studies (1971), they found three traditions:

1. Social studies taught as citizenship transmission,
2. Social studies taught as social science,
3. Social studies taught as reflective inquiry.

Libbee and Stoltman (1988) conclude that diversity is valuable, that all three traditions are appropriate, that citizenship transmission is "most common and perhaps most appropriate in the elementary schools and that the social science and reflective inquiry traditions [are] more important in middle and secondary schools" (p. 32).

Perhaps a more profound insight can be obtained by relating geographers' concern for citizenship to the rubric proposed by Haas (1979) and summarized in Figure 5.1. Haas sees citizenship transmission as "conservative cultural continuity" (CCC). This is the mainstream rationale which others are trying to reform. The process of reflective inquiry (PTR), analysis of public issues (API), modes of inquiry (MOI), and education for citizen action (ECA), are all reform rationales originating primarily within the social studies community in schools of education. Intellectual aspects of history and/or the social sciences (IHSS) embrace most of the reform attempts by academic disciplines in colleges of arts and sciences including geography.

FIGURE 5.1. **Mainstream and Reform Rationales in Social Studies Education**

Mainstream Rationale	Reform Rationales	IHSS
CCC: Conservative cultural continuity	PTR: Process of thinking reflectively	Intellectual aspects of history and/or the social sciences
	API: Analysis of public issues	
	MOI: Modes of inquiry (also related to IHSS)	
	ECA: Education for citizen action	

GEOGRAPHY AND CITIZENSHIP:
VIEWS FROM THE LAST FORTY YEARS

Among geographers there is some tension about attitudes and values within the IHSS rationale for reform. Some have been uneasy with the attitudinal objectives of citizenship, while others have been clear and explicit about the value positions they hold and hope will be adopted by their students.

The Question of Values

Whitaker (1948), in his "Talks on Values and Problems," is urging a modification of the mainstream CCC rationale:

> Geography provides for building up an understanding and apprecia-
> tion of the problems and the achievements of other people. This, I take
> it, is one of the essentials on which to build a world order. In the
> hands of an effective teacher, geographic study can promote interna-
> tional understanding and good will: distant places and the problems
> of the people there become real; their problems are understood in
> terms of the circumstances under which they have developed; their
> achievements are appreciated; and their right to a place in the pageant
> of progress of the whole earth is made clear. [p. 20]

He goes on to say that

> the future of mankind must surely depend . . . on the achievement of a
> greater degree of co-operation. And wholehearted co-operation must
> be based on a sympathetic understanding of others. We must have
> some appreciation of their problems, their fine traits, and their ideals
> if we would rid ourselves of prejudice and hatred, eternal barriers to
> full co-operation. [p. 22]

Finally, Whitaker states the value position most clearly with respect to the education of teachers:

> The most effective geography teacher will have a genuine sympathy
> and liking for men of all lands. The narrow, the bigoted, the intensely
> nationalistic, the belligerent individual may convert geography into a
> school of hate, of odious comparison. If geography is to function in
> the most effective way in furthering an understanding and apprecia-
> tion of other peoples, whether in our own nation or in foreign lands, it
> is necessary that the teacher himself be thoroughly imbued with re-

gard for his fellow men. . . . He will possess the kind of inquiring, sympathetic mind that views men all over the world as brothers in the common problems of living the best kind of life possible on this earth. [p. 160*f*]

The New Geography

Sixteen years later, Gilbert F. White (1962), the originator and protector of "the new geography," was quite humble in his "Critical Issues Concerning Geography in the Public Service":

> The contributions which geographic thought can make to the advancement of society are relatively few, simple, and powerful. They are so few and simple that a significant proportion of them can be taught to high school and beginning undergraduate students. They are so powerful that failure to recognize them jeopardizes the ability of citizens to deal intelligently with a rapidly changing and increasingly complex world. These include an understanding of the extraordinary diversity of combinations of surface features around the world, and an understanding of patterns of the major distributions such as those of population, livelihood, climate, and land forms. Closely related is an understanding of the processes which give unity to the explanation and regularities of those peculiar patterns. Among these processes are energy and water balance, the diffusion of culture, and the location of economic activity. While properly mindful of great deficiencies in knowledge of both distributions and processes, geographers have an obligation to teach and interpret the tools they have forged. [p. 279]

White (1965) later expanded on the role of geography in education. By comparison with the earlier charting of the planet, he claimed,

> The new exploration of the earth . . . has profound implications for education. . . . [I]t is an effort to understand the order and regularity of features of the earth.
>
> Attention to unfamiliar places need not inhibit discovery of the familiar. The corner store or local park or the journey to school may provide the base from which a new, disciplined way of looking at the world can grow.
>
> Geography is a major teaching challenge in American society today. From it come approaches to several persistent problems troubling man. Knowledge about the dimensions and character of the earth responds in a concrete way to the concept of one world which gradually has emerged with improvements in modern communica-

tions and with the elaboration of international responsibilities. The world of the United Nations is no political theory: it is a mosaic of real people on real land.

Man continues to be deeply disturbed by doubt about the capacity of the earth to support rapidly expanding population at reasonable living levels. He soberly asks how resources can be marshaled to meet new needs, and how he can deal helpfully with the tremendous tensions provoked by deep disparities from place to place in level of living and in resource endowment.

To these problems, exploration of the kind I have suggested brings a combination of understanding and mode of thought from both social sciences and the natural sciences and offers one of the bridges which joins them in the service of man. To supplement the historical approach and the analysis of social process there is much to be said for a mode of thought which views events in their spatial setting and probes their relations to each other in earthly places. . . . This is a kind of discovery of the earth that can leave the student deeply excited by problems upon whose solution the outcome of the human adventure depends. [pp. 9 & 10]

Geography Versus Ethnocentrism

Broek (1966), in *Compass of Geography*, written specifically for social studies teachers, deals with citizenship in the very first pages:

There are, of course, many gradations between pure curiosity at the one extreme and the direct usefulness of geography at the other. Somewhere in between lies the value of geography as part of the intellectual equipment of every citizen of every country. In particular, how can the citizens of the United States, a great world power and a democracy, exercise their rights and perform their duties if they are geographically illiterate?

At home, too, we need better geographic understanding to solve our domestic problems. Depopulation of agricultural areas, rapid growth of the suburbs, change in character of the central business districts, Negro migration, exhaustion of mineral resources, pollution of air and streams, and other matters of concern must be understood better by the general public so that it will actively support efforts toward solutions. Above all—and this is true of international as well as national affairs—problems must be seen in their regional context. Justice, freedom, democracy, and equal rights are high ideals. Their wise application demands an awareness of different conditions in different places. "Global unity" does not mean world-wide uniformity. We must not simply assume that our own interpretation of ideals is the right one which we can confidently project on all other peoples as the standard model for imitation. Awareness of conditions and ways of life in other countries helps us to frame more realistic attitudes. [pp. 2–3]

Like Whitaker (1948), Broek (1966) is fighting the ethnocentrism and narrow patriotism that he must have ascribed to the conventional indoctrination—citizenship transmission, or CCC. Fourteen years later, when the volume was revised (Broek, Hunker, Muessig, & Cirrincione, 1980), the authors repeated the statement almost verbatim, but with updated examples. They concluded the book with a quotation from Norman Cousins (1976):

How to educate for a decompartmentalized world? How to gain acceptance for the idea that life is the highest value? How to prepare for citizenship in the human community? The place to begin, it seemed to me, was with the fact that the universe itself does not hold life cheaply. Life is a rare occurrence.

This demonstrates once again that the geographer defines citizenship in global terms, setting ideals in terms of all humanity. Values of tolerance, cooperation, and humane concern for others are not spelled out in behavioral terms. They are, however, clearly implicit.

Controversy Over Attitudinal/Affective Objectives

As Director of the High School Geography Project, I was aware of the aesthetic and emotional impact that *Geography in an Urban Age* would have on students' motivation. I understood, as did the rest of the staff, that the materials must necessarily influence the attitudes and values of the students. However, since much of the political support for the project had to come from the "scientific" community, I did not relish opening a possible controversy over attitudes and values. In the 1960s and 1970s many geographers still considered their work value-free. They were more comfortable identifying only objectives in the cognitive domain, with emphasis on what Remy (1980) called "citizenship competencies."

Kasperson, writing about his participation in HSGP (1967), addressed both cognitive and attitudinal objectives while at the same time expressing the hesitancy of the social scientist with respect to identifying the values implicit in curriculum materials. After describing informational and conceptual objectives, he continued:

Attitudinal objectives represent a substantially smaller degree of effort in the Political Unit. It is difficult both to define and to confront this type of objective. Should, for example, political geography aspire to make students more world-minded? Less authoritarian? Should the material purposefully champion a peaceful settlement of international conflicts? The curriculum innovator should realize that a set of values and beliefs will be implicit in the unit. If, for example, political geography demonstrates the often amoral operation of international politics, what effect, if any, does this have upon student ethics? The Political Unit has only one explicit attitudinal objective—that students should enjoy studying geography—although there is some sensitivity to these other considerations. (p. 287)

Three years after the first edition of *Geography in an Urban Age* (1969/1976) was in print, writing for an international readership, I came out of the "objective" closet and expressed myself clearly about goals in the attitudinal/affective domain (Helburn, 1972):

Decisions about geography curriculum are severely influenced by national and local needs and goals. I'm not familiar with the recent educational history of Yugoslavia, but it would be safe to predict a long-standing struggle over how much of the geography curriculum in Croatia should be devoted to learning about Croatia and how much to the other parts of Yugoslavia. The desire to perpetuate the individuality of Scotland vis-à-vis England will be reflected in the selective emphasis of geography in Scottish schools.

   Curriculum decisions must always select:

> what information do we emphasize,
> what do we withhold,
> what kind of information do we give about
> what places and people,
> what proofs do we respect,
> what authorities do we quote,
> which controversies do we open for free inquiry,
> which do we assume to be settled our way.

All these are all powerful influences upon the thinking of those who study with us.

   An extreme example exists in the former colonies of major powers. Imagine the problems of the young Puerto Rican studying for admission to Harvard, the Nigerian preparing for First Class Honors at the University of London. Can it be so different from the Quechua-speaking Indian at the University of Quito, the Tibetan in Peking or the Uzbek in Moscow?

   Given the power of nationalism in the world, even today, who speaks for the world? As the most privileged members of the geographic profession, we carry a special responsibility:

> To reflect as realistic a view as possible of the region in the nation, and of the nation in the world,
>
> To raise rather than to obscure the choice of value positions about controversial issues,
>
> To stand firm against the natural tendency of governments to use schools as an instrument of national power by substituting indoctrination for education.
>
> To assert this responsibility is to take a value position oneself. It is a judgment which derives from the widest view of the role of education in the modern world.
>
> Students find their norms of society and their role in society in part from their school experience: their text and assignments, the social processes of the classroom and the organization (the distribution and use of power) of the school. Most of us will make the choice to foster intellectualism versus its opposites, to foster science over myth or magic. Choices between fostering socialism versus capitalism or individualism versus communalism are less likely to be agreed upon. [pp. 48–49]

In the same article, I then extended the values discussion beyond the subject matter of geography, to the distribution of power within the school and the teaching strategies in the classroom:

> Curriculum materials, if they approach completeness, take into account the processes within the classroom. They influence the degree to which teachers foster competition as against cooperation. Some of the simulation games designed for classroom use cannot be won by individual student action, only by cooperation. Role playing activities can be designed to illustrate the value and the techniques of negotiation and compromise.
>
> Group problem-solving activities can demonstrate the greater reliability of decisions reached with inputs from all members of the group. When teachers widen their teaching strategies beyond didactic texts, lectures, recitations, and exams to include these more participative activities, [then] skills of leadership and cooperation, of creativity and initiative become important outcomes of the school experience.
>
> Geographers may ask what has this to do with me? — leadership is not a goal of geography. But such social skills are goals of education. The geographer who ventures into curriculum development must realize that he will be influencing the social structures of the classroom. If he does not offer teachers the material for effective group work, he will be encouraging a school experience in which the principal social skill learned by children is to sit quietly in rows facing the teacher until called upon. Such practice in unqualified obedience to authority

over 12 to 16 years of formal education has implications that cannot be ignored by geographers, or anyone else. [pp. 49–50]

Now, nearly two decades later, I believe that most thoughtful geography educators would agree that attitudes and values *are* taught in the social studies classroom and it is best to be self-conscious and explicit about the attitudinal/affective domain. They would concur with Newman (1985) and with Parker and Jarolomek (1984) that the social studies, geography included, have a responsibility to develop citizens who not only know what they need to know about citizenship, but also feel a loyalty to democratic values and a sense of obligation to participate in the political process.

PROFESSIONAL CONSENSUS
ON IMPORTANT GEOGRAPHIC KNOWLEDGE AND SKILLS

What, then, are the contributions school geography can and should make to the intellectual development of the future citizen? It is understood there are strong private reasons for geographical skills and knowledge, understandings that contribute to the enrichment of life as well as skills and knowledge that are useful in making a living. There is much overlap. For example, cartophiles love maps and believe that all people should have the opportunity, within a liberal education, to fall in love with maps. Cartography is a valued profession in its own right. But here we deal only with map skills as tools for transmitting and understanding information and ideas about public policy issues and as territorial symbols of the polity.

Guidelines for Geographic Education, prepared by the Joint Committee on Geographic Education (1984) of the National Council for Geographic Education and the Association of American Geographers, is the best source for extracting the cognitive contributions of school geography to citizenship. Its codification of the cognitive objectives of geographic education has been widely accepted with minimal dissent. Much of the discussion is organized around five themes:

1. *Location*: Position on the earth's surface, not only the absolute location, but also relative location in respect to other pertinent phenomena;
2. *Place*: The characteristics of places, both physical and human, and the ways those characteristics have been changed over time;
3. *Relationships within places*: Humans and environments;

4. *Movement*: Interactions across the surface of the earth, and relationships between and among places;
5. *Regions*: How they form and change, nodal and uniform.

These guidelines extend to all aspects of geographic education. Here I select from each theme a few objectives that are especially pertinent to the student's competence as a citizen.

Location

The JCGE (1984) guidelines emphasize the following points with regard to location:

- "Be able to explain how location influences activities and processes in different places" (p. 24). The location of the United Nations in New York City might be a case in point.
- "Be able to describe how physical and cultural attributes of one location interact with attributes of other locations" (p. 24). The cultural attributes of Jerusalem and Palestine are significant in their interaction with other locations, both near and far.
- "Be aware that the significance and importance of locations change as cultures change their interactions with each other and with the physical environment" (p. 24). The Duchy of Muscovy had a very different significance and importance in medieval time from what it has now.
- "Be able to identify and locate a large number of important places and features in many parts of the world" (p. 24).

The JCGE hedged here, unable to specify the number of places or even the criteria for delimiting the places and features whose locations should be in the student's memory. No one denies that knowing locations is important, but to secure agreement among committee members as to what is really worth memorizing may be more than could have been expected. Every author who writes a place-name unit for the curriculum must make those decisions; and each of us, as we use such units, must make the decisions again.

There is some perspective to be found in the probably apocryphal story of the recent graduation of a Ph.D. candidate in geography, whose grandmother challenged the young man after the ceremony to "spell-down" the capes and bays of Africa. He was able to list 2 to her 35. Clearly the profession has no official position for us in this regard.

An even more important skill is finding locations on maps and in atlases. My personal recommendation is that much place-name memorization should occur in the lower elementary grades, when conceptual objectives are relatively difficult to achieve and the memorization comes easily. Here, games, puzzles, "bees," and map exercises can help to make the memorization fun. In upper elementary and higher grades, place-name memorization must always be related to the significance of places, and must always be carried out in the context of the subject matter. For an extraordinary example of such teaching and learning, see Smith's "Making Maps from Memory" (1989).

If the knowledge of locations is not used, it fades; therefore, throughout the social studies, at all grade levels, place-name knowledge must be used. Those students who are approaching the end of their formal education and do not know the names, locations, and some of the features of most of the nations of the world and most of the states of the United States clearly need remedial work. Even in remedial work in the tenth through twelfth grades, place names are better taught in the context of the significance of those locations.

It should be clear, however, that all responsibility for place-name illiteracy cannot be laid at the feet of the social studies. The sciences and humanities can also reinforce place-name knowledge acquired earlier. At home, an atlas in the living room, a globe in the dining room, and repeated reference to relative location in the family's discussion of world affairs maintains place-name literacy. The brief exposure of a map behind the television newscaster does not do the job.

Place

The JCGE (1984) guidelines emphasize the following points with regard to place:

- "Be able to relate how human activities and culture create a variety of different and similar places" (p. 25). Tolerance of differences may be related to understanding of how they occur.
- "Describe ways in which people define, build and name places and develop a sense of place" (p. 25). Applied to political territory, this is a crucially important understanding.
- "Explain how intensive human activities can dramatically alter the physical characteristics of places and that places can be damaged, destroyed, or improved through human actions or natural processes" (p. 25). Environmental protection and ecological understanding are built upon this principle.

Relationships within Places

Two of the JCGE (1984) outcomes listed here are closely related to the objectives just given for place:

- "Give examples of how human alterations of physical environments have had positive and negative consequences" (p. 25).
- "Understand why humans attempt to control the quality of the natural environment and to mitigate the effects of hazardous natural events such as drought, floods, earthquakes, and hurricanes" (p. 25).

Movement

This JCGE (1984) category includes interconnectedness and therefore encompasses many of the bases for understanding world interdependence:

- "Be aware that movements reflect global patterns of interaction" (p. 26).
- "Know that few places are self-sufficient" (p. 26).
- "Describe how changes in . . . technology influence the rates at which people, goods, and ideas move from place to place" (p. 26).

Regions

The brief list of JCGE (1984) outcomes under regions includes the following:

- "Know that region is a conceptual tool to help make general statements about complex reality" (p. 26).
- "Describe how the concept of regions relates local places in a system of interactions and connections" (p. 26).
- "Give examples of nodal and uniform regions" (p. 26).

Skills

In addition to objectives in the foregoing five areas, the JCGE (1984) guidelines include skills that students should acquire, such as asking the "where" and "why there" questions; acquiring, presenting, and analyzing information; and developing and testing generalizations. Map skills and the use of other graphics also get a heavy emphasis.

SOME CONTROVERSIAL OBJECTIVES
FOR THE GEOGRAPHY CURRICULUM

Reaching beyond the easily arrived-at consensus, there are several objectives that I believe need to be added to the geography curriculum — or at least need to be given greater emphasis.

Maps and Citizenship—Again!

Map and globe skills are so uniformly included in the educational objectives of geography that it seems mundane to bring them up again. But too many of us feel we have done enough if our students understand longitude and latitude, can find specific places, and can interpret the meaning of common symbols. This is not enough. Map distortions have a powerful effect on the way we see the world. In citizen decisions, as in other decisions, it is the image that counts. We draw our images necessarily from maps. Unless our citizenry is alert to "cartohypnosis"—to the distortion of map projections and to the choice of symbolism for propaganda purposes—we can expect some very wrong decisions (Boggs, 1947; Pepper & Jenkins, 1985).

Seeing the World As a Single System:
The Global View

More than any other discipline, geography reiterates the global view. If there are those among us who object to "globalism," they must prefer that students live in ignorance. They must be counted among the enemies of education. I find the global view indispensable on both the physical and human sides of the discipline. The effects of increments of radioactivity or of carbon dioxide on the whole world are part of what the citizen needs to know, for we make policy decisions within our boundaries that affect all the world. Through our moral and diplomatic leadership we may be able to influence the decisions of other countries. Our lack of moral leadership can be equally influential.

If, at the end of their formal education, students understood the world's nation–state system, it might be redundant to include it in the objectives of geography. There is plenty of evidence, however, that students' experience and learning, in and out of school, in social studies and in other subjects, has left them naïve and ignorant about international political structures and interactions. While there are those who would question whether the word *system* should be applied at all to these structures and interactions, surely it is essential that most citizens know

1. The division of the world into sovereign states,
2. The elements that contribute to the cohesiveness of the state,
3. Something of the ways these units get along with each other, and
4. The fragile institutions that oversee this interaction.

The interdependence of states gets what amounts to a lot of lip service as an educational goal, in spite of having been there for most of this century. Few would question that students should be aware of our economic and cultural interchanges with the rest of the world. But American education has been less candid about the realities of political, diplomatic, and military power in international relations. Further, students need to know about the processes of underdevelopment, including the tendency for the center to prosper while the periphery is impoverished. Citizenship in the twentieth and twenty-first centuries requires the ability to assess and interpret the strength of nations, the foundations of national power, and the existence of great powers and less powerful nation–states.

The existence of dissatisfied minorities within the states falls within this general heading. *The New State of the World Atlas* (Kidron & Segal, 1984) refers to these minorities as "nations against the state." How well do we deal with Tadjiks in the Soviet Union, Kurds and Palestinians in the Middle East, Québeçois in Canada, Native Americans and Chicanos in the United States? These "nations" without territories that they can really call their own are part of the knowledge citizens need, and they illustrate powerful themes in both contemporary and historical political geography. We organize into polities in the hope that we can change our society toward an ideal, but different group (classes, genders, and ethnic groups) have different ideals.

Territory and Sovereignty

Geography has something special to say about the concepts of territory and sovereignty, upon which the present system is based. Looked at geographically, the land surface of the world is divided into political regions we call nations, countries, or states; and each of which in turn is divided into provinces, states, or republics; and each of these into districts, counties, parishes, communes, or municipalities. This illustrates the concept of a nested hierarchy of regions. The division of power among the several levels of government is a common theme in civics, but social studies in American education has given too little attention to the nature of the territory governed and the way in which the characteristics of the territory influence the resulting society.

Our constant problem is how to make *unum* out of *pluribus*, for we are committed to a uniform system of laws that must be applied to a widely varying territory and to a citizenry almost as varied. The nested hierarchy of political regions is one of the major mechanisms we use to adjust the legal uniformity to the territorial variety. The Swiss canton high in the alps has quite different problems from those of the cantons adjacent to Zurich or Basle. Each must have authority to solve its unique problems, but how much authority?

Each of us can find our favorite examples of policy issues deriving from the variability of territory. A current example involves a fraction of the semidesert plateau of Northern New Mexico. Most of the intermontane plateau from the Rockies to the Cascades and Sierras is managed by the federal government, and some of this has been allocated to Native Americans in the form of reservations, both through federal legislation and treaties with the Native American nations. Where uranium ore and coal have been discovered on Black Mesa in New Mexico, suddenly these Native Americans are being forced to move, forced to give up their homes and farms. In the unequal power relations among units of government, the values of economic growth and development are pitted against the values of personal rights in real property and the sanctity of the home. The controversy focuses on the resource endowment of the territory, but also involves the boundaries of the region and the distribution of populations with specific cultures and economies and with limited employment alternatives. Scudder (1982), in *No Place to Go*, gives a vivid and insightful study of the controversy.

The first activity of the High School Geography Project unit on political geography illustrates this point (1969/1976). It consists of a role-playing activity called "Section," in which students "portray citizens and legislators in the hypothetical state of Midland. The problem on which they work is the allocation of the state's $25-million budget among a number of worthwhile projects. The state is divided into five regions, or sections, each rather (stereo)typical parts of the nation, each with particular concerns and needs" (p. 1). Three educational objectives express the hope that "students will be better able to":

> 1. Explain and give examples of how physical, cultural, and economic differences within a political territory give rise to associated differences in political goals and ideals.
> 2. Explain or give examples of how interest groups can coalesce across territorial lines yet remain confined to seeking their objectives through political processes of the territory in which they reside.
> 3. Describe the legislative process wherein the always limited resources of a political territory are allocated to its various and virtually unlimited needs. [p. 3]

Gottman (1973) has given his scholarly attention to the issue of territory in his Page and Barbour Lectures at the University of Virginia. He makes the paradox between security and opportunity central to his essay. While we organize political space to protect ourselves within the limits of our own territory, in so doing we isolate ourselves from others and their territories. So, while we assure ourselves of the opportunities within our territories, we deny ourselves the wider opportunities of the rest of the world.

In this light, interdependence means we are making use of the resources and opportunities in other people's territories and want to continue to do so. Our foreign policy must be tuned to maintaining those opportunities. To our one-sided view of the world, there are a couple of general policy derivatives from such statements that seem to need to be "learned" (read, "inculcated") in school social studies. First, we must be ready to support a diplomatic and military establishment sufficient to maintain our economic freedom within other people's territories; and second, we must allow a certain amount of economic penetration of our territory by foreign interests.

We begin to see sovereignty as divisible into political, economic, and cultural realms and perhaps other realms as well. But even political sovereignty that we hold most sacred is not absolute, as exemplified, say, in the ability of Israel to influence budget decisions in the U.S. Congress or the various U.S. efforts to modify the government of Nicaragua.

I like to think of political boundaries not as the sharp black lines on the map between pink Czechoslovakia and green Austria, but more like the membrane around an organic cell: semipermeable, more permeable in one direction to some things and more permeable in the opposite direction to other things. The inability of the United States or Canada to close their southern borders to immigration and to protect their lands and waters from acid-bearing clouds illustrates this permeability nicely.

Local Social Ecology

The other major field of geography that needs special emphasis for citizenship education might be called *social ecology*. I avoid the term *human ecology*, for it already has several meanings and it tends to emphasize individual human beings in their relationship to their surroundings. But human groups live in settlements—farmsteads, villages, camps, towns, and cities—and as societies they learn to use the environments of those settlements more or less harmoniously. Indeed, they learn to design the settlements for efficient and satisfying conduct of their lives and the achievement of group goals. The quality of our lives is powerfully affected by the harmonious adjustment of our towns and cities to their physical and biological environments (Helburn, 1982).

Hill and McCormick (1989) make this point at the beginning of their volume, *Geography: A Resource Book for Secondary Schools*:

> A democratic society cannot continue to function effectively with uneducated citizens in this increasingly technological, complex, and interdependent world. If people do not carefully appraise key issues to make informed decisions, problems accumulate. When citizens no longer have the knowledge to make informed decisions, they lose the power to control their environments. In losing control, they become controlled, victims manipulated in a world plagued by problems. [p. 2]

Intelligent decisions are needed about the design of settlements. For instance, they should be placed so as to avoid floods and minimize the impact of heat waves. A careful eye should be given to allocating and controlling the use of the life-supporting resources of the environment, such as soil that must last as long as society and air that must be kept breathable. To make such decisions intelligently, citizens must understand something of the functioning of the natural environment and the human impacts on the more sensitive and delicate parts of those natural systems.

The understanding of social ecology and the interactive adjustments of human societies with their environments is needed across the whole range of scales, from local to global. Here are just a few pertinent facts:

- The orientation of one's house on its lot influences the amount of solar energy received.
- Shrinking or swelling soils and subsoils must be identified before a neighborhood is developed, to avoid continuing trauma to homeowners long after the developer has moved on.
- The health and safety of the inhabitants of the whole city depend on good planning for flood avoidance and earthquake preparedness.
- Regionwide catastrophes can be minimized by preparation for rare but serious drought or heat wave.
- Excessive air pollution in one region kills forests and fish in another.
- Germany and the Netherlands suffer the consequences of a toxic spill into the Rhine in Switzerland.

- The Chernobyl nuclear accident caused terror throughout northwestern Europe as well as in much of the Soviet Union.
- Increases in carbon dioxide, nitrogen oxides, and other gases threaten to upset the existing climate equilibrium through global warming. The social consequences of this increasing "greenhouse effect" remain largely unexplored.

In some schools the understanding of natural systems is achieved in earth sciences and biology classes. In others it is included in geography. The study of impact of human actions on natural systems, and the ways that public policy can minimize the negative impacts, belongs in geography and the social studies. Good citizenship requires these "conservation" understandings at local, regional, national, and global scales, and at a profound rather than just a casual level.

MOTIVATION FOR EFFECTIVE CITIZENSHIP: LOYALTY TO PLACE

If the foregoing discussion addresses the more important cognitive skills and knowledge that geography contributes to citizenship education, what, then, is geography's contribution in the attitudinal/affective domain? The following excerpt from *The Prophet* (Gibran, 1923) contains a powerful and appropriate metaphor. The speaker—the prophet—is addressing his listeners on various subjects of spiritual significance. He has just been asked by a priestess to speak to them of reason and passion. He says,

> Your soul is oftentimes a battlefield, upon which your reason and your judgment wage war against your passion and your appetite.
> Would that I could be the peacemaker in your soul, that I might turn the discord and the rivalry of your elements into oneness and melody.
> But how shall I, unless you yourselves be also the peacemakers, nay, the lovers of all your elements?
> Your reason and your passion are the rudder and the sails of your seafaring soul.
> If either your sails or your rudder be broken, you can but toss and drift, or else be held at a standstill in mid-seas.
> For reason, ruling alone, is a force confining; and passion, unattended, is a flame that burns to its own destruction. [pp. 50–51]

The poet's *reason* translates to the academic's cognitive domain. The poet's *passion* translates to the academic's affective domain. Just *knowing* what good citizenship involves will not move most of us to action, and just *feeling* that we ought to "do something" may result in random actions, usually to no avail.

When Gifford Pinchot started the conservation movement with Theodore Roosevelt in the first decade of the twentieth century it was not their knowledge of forestry and hydrology that set the two apart from others. Many people knew as much or almost as much. It was their *passion* that moved them to action. Americans became concerned about apartheid in South Africa not so much by *knowing* that blacks were suffering, but more by sharing the *feelings* of blacks as shown through television images of riots and demonstrations. Once the feelings were there, citizens were moved to get Congress to invoke sanctions. As Che Guevera is credited with saying: "At the risk of sounding ridiculous, let me say that all revolutionaries are moved by profound feelings of love."

Attachment to home, loyalty to region, love of country, concern for Mother Earth, are some of the *emotions* that emerge from geography that is well taught. Matched with *knowledge*, they will help create citizens who not only *know* what to do but are ready to go out and *do* it.

Bearing in mind this essential relationship between reason and passion, the pertinent questions for geography instruction are

1. What part can geography play in increasing the motivation of the future citizen to participate in the political process?

2. Can school geography increase the loyalty to hometown and home neighborhood and thereby increase the readiness to set aside personal chores in favor of participation in the preservation and improvement of the local environment?

3. Can school geography contribute feelings of patriotism, and, if so, should it?

4. Can school geography extend the sense of civic obligation beyond national frontiers, so that students identity and empathize with the inhabitants of the whole Earth and want to share in the protection of the world's ecosystems?

There is no question about the existence and power of such attitudes. Patriotic platitudes are all too real. Gottman (1973) quotes from George Scelle: "The concern for the preservation of habitat is a passionate reflex in all human communities" (p. 14).

When I first raised this concern with a colleague, his response was that the loyalty was to the group, not to the place. "Do or die for dear old Rutgers" reflects a loyalty to a social institution. But, when the Boston Braves moved to Milwaukee, while a few fans continued their loyalty, I suspect that it was mostly a new group of fans, place-rooted Milwaukeans, who supported the team. It must have been a deep place loyalty that made the fight so intense to keep the Oakland A's in Oakland, and by that time both Kansas City and Philadelphia had been forgotten.

Perhaps the truth is some of both—that loyalty is to a place-rooted group. Tribes and clans are such. Even the family has a much more powerful pull when it remains in place. When we exiled the Choctaws and the Cherokees to Oklahoma Territory, powerful feelings of belonging were shredded.

It is probably academic to ask to what extent this is a survival of what Ardrey (1966) called the "territorial imperative," a deeply rooted, perhaps instinctive need to defend the family and the exclusive right to the mating prerogative. Likewise, the parallel to the emotions associated with property ownership is not perfect.

Mobility and Loyalty to Place

Certainly Americans and Australians have less place-attachment than the citizens of many other nations, in part because all of our ancestors (except our aborigines) moved here from somewhere else, within recorded history. Our African culture was weakened in the holds of those terrible slave ships. Our ethnic roots as Swedes were severely pruned when we settled in Minnesota. Our Irish Celtic culture was weakened in the process of coming to Boston. Sentimental attachment requires a past. With only a century or two of local history, our place attachment is understandably weaker than, say, the Turkish villager whose family has always lived in that place. Literally it may only have been a few centuries, but it might as well have been always. The current mobility of most of our American population further weakens our place loyalties.

There is a negative potential in this attachment to place, resulting in xenophobia and a kind of provincialism in which one's preference for home causes one to be disinterested in the rest of the world. This can result in what Gritzner (1981) describes so vividly:

> To individuals lacking a global "mental map," the world must be little more than a confusing hodgepodge: places without location, quality, or context; faceless people and cultures void of detail, character, or meaning; vague physical features and environments; . . . temporal events that occur in a spatial vacuum; and a host of critical global problems for which they have no criteria on which to base analyses, judgments, or attempts at resolution. Such individuals are prisoners of their own ignorance and provincialism.

Topophilia

Yi-fu Tuan (1974, 1977) is one of the geographers who has thought and written on the subject of emotional attachment to place. Tuan asserts that it all starts in infancy. Closeness to mother is a good. Remoteness from mother is fearful. But with age, stature, and experience, knowledge of the territory reduces the fear. One *knows* an area experientially—standing, sitting, lying there in different lights and temperatures; having stumbled from bed to bath or telephone or crib; having arranged and rearranged the furniture; having weeded and sprayed and mowed. In the same way one knows, albeit less well, the Pennsylvania Station or O'Hare Airport, the San Diego Zoo and Candlestick Park, Old Faithful and the Washington Monument. Knowing reduces the fear and tends to incorporate the area into the space one feels comfortable in.

The View from Above: Knowing a Place from Outside

Tuan (1974, 1977) goes on to point out that one knows a place in a rather different way by getting outside it and looking at it from a distance. Part of the appeal of the restaurant on Seattle's Space Needle or the one on the mountain high above Bergen, Norway, or any of their equivalents around the world, is the ability to see the whole community from the outside, to begin to know the community in this second way.

Perhaps this is the place where school geography makes a major and unique contribution to the prospective citizen's emotional commitment to participate in the political process. It can add to the experiential learning through field trips, but most important, it adds the overview. Chicago students would prefer to have dinner at the top of the Sears Tower and see the real city spread out along the lakeshore. But studying the map of the city may do more to help them to know the city from the outside, thus developing their external perspective and an associated emotional commitment.

The Map As Symbol of the Polity

The map also becomes a powerful symbol of the country, maybe as powerful as the flag. This is reinforced by the geographical allusions made in patriotic songs, such as "amber waves of grain" and "from sea to shining sea." Many have commented on the symbolic power of that first photograph of the Earth taken from the moon by the U.S. astronauts— the image of our blue and white spaceship Earth against the black backdrop of infinite space. On the global scale, this is the same external perspective that allows us to "know" our home in a different way. We can hope that the picture of the globe can help us all transcend the antagonisms and xenophobia we associate with parochialism, provincialism, and nationalism, moving instead toward an identification with all humanity.

In summary, the insider's knowledge of a place reduces its strangeness and increases the person's affection for the area. But the view from outside is also an important way of knowing an area, easily learned in geography. The map of the territory of the polity becomes a symbol of the political institution, defining the extent of the group to which one belongs. These generalizations apply across the several scales, from home and neighborhood through region and nation, to the world as a whole.

This affection combines with the knowledge of both natural and social systems working in the landscape to build a citizenry respectful of the community, the nation, the world; a citizenry both willing and able to protect and improve it. In this sense, modern geography is still in tune with Kropotkin (1885), writing in the nineteenth century:

> The task of geography in early childhood [is] to interest the child in the great phenomena of nature, to awaken the desire of knowing and explaining them. Geography must render, moreover, another far more important service. It must teach us . . . that we are all brethren, whatever our nationality. . . . [G]eography must be—in so far as the school may do anything to counterbalance hostile influences—a means of dissipating . . . prejudice and of creating other feelings more worthy of humanity. It must show that each nationality brings its own precious building stone for the general development of the commonwealth. [p. 942]

REFERENCES

Ardrey, R. (1966). *Territorial imperative: A personal inquiry into the animal origins of property and nations.* New York: Atheneum.

Backler, A. L. (1988). *A teachers' guide to global geography.* Bloomington, IN: Agency for Instructional Television.

Barr, R. D., Barth, J. L., & Shermis, S. S. (1977). *Defining the social studies* (Bulletin No. 51). Washington, DC: National Council for the Social Studies.

Boggs, S. W. (1947). Cartohyphosis. *Scientific Monthly, 64,* 469–476.

Broek, J. O. M. (1966). *Compass of geography.* Columbus, OH: Merrill.

Broek, J. O. M., Hunker, H. L., Muessig, R. H., & Cirrincione, J. M. (1980). *The study and teaching of geography.* Columbus, OH: Charles E. Merrill.

Cousins, N. (1976). Meaning, purpose, and belonging in life. In J. Baldwin, W. Von Braun, N. Cousins, A. Cox, M. S. Horner, & A. M. Schlesinger, Jr., *The nature of a humane society* (pp. 181 & 182). Philadelphia, PA: Fortress Press.

Engle, S. H. (1960). Decision making: The heart of the social studies. *Social Education, 24,* 301–306.

Gibran, K. (1923). *The prophet.* New York: Knopf.

Gottman, J. (1973). *The significance of territory.* Charlottesville: University of Virginia Press.

Gritzner, C. (1981). Geographic education: Where have we failed? *Journal of Geography, 80,* 264.

Haas, J. D. (1979). Social studies: Where have we been? Where are we going? *The Social Studies, 76*(4), 147–154.

Helburn, N. (1972). Implications of curriculum decisions. In A. M. Gunn (Ed.), *High School Geography Project: Legacy for the Seventies* (pp. 43–50). Montreal: Centre Educatif et Culturel.

Helburn, N. (1982). Geography and the quality of life. *Annals of the Association of American Geographers, 72,* 445–456.

High School Geography Project of the Association of American Geographers (Eds.). (1976). *Political geography: Geography in an urban age (Unit 4).* (rev. ed.). New York: Macmillan. (Original work published 1969)

Hill, A. D., & McCormick, R. (1989). *Geography: A resource book for secondary schools.* Santa Barbara, CA: ABC-Clio.

Joint Committee on Geographic Education. (1984). *Guidelines for geographic education.* Washington, DC: Association of American Geographers and National Council for Geographic Education.

Kasperson, R. E. (1967). On the process of curriculum reform. *Journal of Geography, 66,* 286–293.

Kidron, M., & Segal, R. (1984). *The new state of the world atlas.* New York: Simon & Schuster.

Kropotkin, P. (1885). What geography ought to be. *The Nineteenth Century, 18,* 940–956.

Kurfman, D. (Ed.). (1977). *Developing decision making skills.* Washington, DC: National Council for the Social Studies.

Libbee, M., & Stoltman, J. (1988). Geography within the social studies. In S. J. Natoli (Ed.), *Strengthening geography in the social studies* (pp. 22–41). Washington, DC: National Council for the Social Studies.

Maye, B. (1984). Developing valuing and decision making skills in the geography classroom. In J. Fein, R. Gerber, & P. Wilson (Eds.), *The geography teacher's guide to the classroom* (pp. 29–43). Melbourne, Australia: Macmillan.

Meinig, D. W. (1986). *The shaping of America: A geographical perspective on 500 years of history* (Vol. 1). New Haven, CT: Yale University Press.

National Council for the Social Studies. (1971). *Social studies curriculum guidelines.* Washington, DC: Author.

Natoli, S. J., & Gritzner, C. F. (1988). Modern geography. In S. J. Natoli (Ed.),

Strengthening geography in the social studies. Washington, DC: National Council for the Social Studies.

Newmann, F. M. (1985). *Educational reform and social studies: Implications of six reports.* ED 252 489. Boulder, CO: SSEC and ERIC.

Parker, W., & Jarolomek, J. (1984). *Citizenship and the critical role of the social studies* (NCSS Bulletin No. 72). Washington, DC: National Council for the Social Studies.

Pepper, D., & Jenkins, A. (1985). *The geography of peace and war.* Oxford, England: Blackwells.

Remy, R. C. (1980). *Handbook of citizenship competencies.* Washington, DC: Association for Supervision & Curriculum Development.

Scudder, T. (1982). *No place to go: Effects of compulsory relocation on Navahos.* Philadelphia: Institute for Study of Human Issues.

Slater, F. (1982). *Learning through geography.* London: Heinemann.

Smith, D. J. (1989). Making maps from memory. *World Monitor, 2*(5), 16–18.

Tuan, Yi-Fu. (1974). *Topophilia.* Englewood Cliffs, NJ: Prentice-Hall.

Tuan, Yi-Fu. (1977). *Space and place.* Minneapolis: University of Minnesota Press.

Whitaker, J. R. (1948). *Geography in school and college: Talks on values and problems.* Nashville, TN: George Peabody College.

White, G. F. (1962). Critical issues concerning geography in the public service. *Annals of the Association of American Geographers, 52,* 279–280.

White, G. F. (1965). Rediscovering the Earth. *American Education, 1*(2), 8–11.

6 The Cultural Perspective

Citizenship Education in Culture and Society

PHILIP WEXLER
RAYMOND R. GROSSHANS
QIAO HONG ZHANG
BYOUNG-UK KIM

In a lecture delivered almost 40 years ago, T. H. Marshall (1964) observed the irony that "citizenship has itself become, in certain respects, the architect of social inequality" (p. 70). He meant that a citizenship of individual rights—civil and political—legitimated a society of unequal social classes. At the same time, Marshall saw in the concept of citizenship a promise of equal social membership in a society comprised of individuals of equal social worth. This dual face of citizenship—both ideological and utopian—persists in current conceptions of citizenship and citizenship education, as well as in their broader cultural meanings.

As the concept of citizenship can function to obscure inequality, so, too, can it lead to a denial of the very basis of citizenship: social life. Citizenship or its derivative, citizenship education, stands for the ideal of social integration. However, when citizenship is extracted from social and cultural contexts, then citizenship education comes to play an ideological role. In this role, citizenship education poses as a representation of ideal social life, while at the same time it obscures the actual social and cultural bases upon which citizenship and citizenship education are built. In this role, citizenship education appears to address important social and cultural questions. When, however, the goals and processes of citizenship education are examined more closely, they are shown to rest on images of the individual and of society which are atomistic and fragmented, acultural and ahistorical.

In our view, citizenship, citizenship education, and research about citizenship education are all embedded in contexts of cultural meaning and social history. These contexts encompass all aspects of social life and a historical horizon of shared meaning. In what follows, we view citizenship education through these contexts. Our focus is American society, where, we suggest, concepts of citizenship and citizenship education have unintentionally buttressed ideological interpretations of social life. We attempt to re-embed citizenship and citizenship education into the broad cultural–historical context of society.

A CULTURAL APPROACH TO CITIZENSHIP AND CITIZENSHIP EDUCATION

From the outset, a fully social and cultural understanding of citizenship has been absent in the United States. By a cultural understanding, we mean an understanding of the contexts in which particular social structures and patterns of events occur. Such social action occurs in a symbolic context through which we represent the world to ourselves and ourselves to each other. Thus, culture is not simply style, taste, and preference; culture is the essential fabric of social life. By a social understanding, we mean an understanding of citizenship as membership in a social group and citizenship education as the normative experiences of individuals within groups. Citizenship is wholly social and takes form only within the context of interaction between and among people in their daily lives.

Because a fully social and cultural understanding of citizenship has been absent in the United States, citizenship education plays an increasingly ideological role in modern American culture. This role is best understood when citizenship is viewed broadly, as a historically variable cultural construct. Citizenship has varied historically in two important ways. First, its nature has changed with the scale of social organization. In primitive societies, familial structures based on age, sex, and lineage provided the foundations for social structures. According to Levi-Strauss (1961), the essential materials of social life and culture, which he indicates in the terms *contract* and *consent*, were present in primitive societies. As the scale of social organization changed, new forms of social life developed. Such loose associations of individuals and families who regulated their daily lives through face-to-face negotiations became more complex economic and political alliances based on increasingly abstract concepts of social regulation. Thus, we see citizenship as a variable cultural metaphor for human relationships as originally constituted within the family.

Second, the nature of citizenship depends on conceptions of individuality. Citizenship binds individuals to groups; however, it is not articulated in all social formations. Citizenship develops as a distinct abstract concept of membership when the individual is differentiated out of social organizations (families, tribes, clans) that share a collective consciousness. As Mauss (1938) points out, personhood, in the modern sense of individuality—despite its location at the core of modern consciousness—developed slowly and with great difficulty. The most important change in the form and context of sociality that bears on citizenship and citizenship education was the development of conceptions of oneself as a conscious, autonomous actor whose social membership is essentially voluntaristic. This change was paralleled by the development of a moral ethos unmediated by its relation to the social.

Durkheim (1938/1977) argues that the domination of the Western moral system by the "cult of the individual person" (p. 235) occurred in a specific sociohistoric moment: the Age of Reason, or the Enlightenment. It was in this period, the Enlightenment, that Westerners purposely posed questions concerning individual freedom and conscience and raised the possibility of personal communication with the transcendent. Also during this period, the modern nation–state emerged from the tangled alliances of feudal and monarchial states in Europe. Especially important to citizenship and citizenship education were the natural-rights theories of the philosophic movement in eighteenth-century France, which proclaimed the ideal of reason, justice, and liberty inspired by the dignity of the individual. For example, in *Du Contrat Social*, Rousseau argued for the creation of a useful citizenry as opposed to a refined and powerful minority and proposed an "abstract and universal basis of political rights for mankind" (quoted in Allen, 1922, p. 153).

In our view, this specification of natural laws for government legitimated by the popular majority signalled more than a new political theory. It was manifest individualism and rationalism, a new world view, which consequently stamped the shape not only of Europe but also of the New World.

CULTURAL HISTORY OF CITIZENSHIP IN THE UNITED STATES

The intellectual roots of the American founding generation were embedded in the Enlightenment ideals of individualism and rationalism. Some historians (Kettner, 1978; Reinhold, 1984; Rorabaugh, 1986) have shown how these ideals shaped the social and political foundations of the American republic. We include examples here to show how these ideals influenced the founders of the American republic. More important, these examples indicate that the rise of individualism and rationalism during the Enlightenment transformed the intellectual landscape and permanently altered ideas about the relation between individuals and society.

Reinhold (1984) shows how classical political and social models profoundly affected the values and ideals of the American founding generation. Educated during the high point of American classicism, the American founders envisioned an agrarian republic as the primary safeguard for liberty and stability. Their vision was based on the concepts of democracy and republicanism, which had been articulated and preserved for the West in the Greco–Roman classics. However, the specific nature of classical societies was unknown to the American founders. As Durkheim (1938/1977) notes, it was possible for early eighteenth-century intellectuals to apply the classics to their society only by "emptying them of their original content and spirit" (p. 325) and by retaining only the exterior form. Early eighteenth-century interpreters of the classical world, working from an incomplete record and without the technical aids available to modern historians, were unaware of the complex and rich nature of classical culture. Thus, the Enlightenment understanding of the classical world reflected the ideals of the seventeenth and eighteenth centuries as much as it reflected the realities of classical social organization. In contrast, twentieth-century scholars argue that the classical formulation of democracy was built on a culture of social integration. Culture, moral values, and politics were modeled after the traditional social patterns of communal life (Lords, 1982; Mauss, 1938).

Kettner (1978) explains how, during the seventeenth and eighteenth centuries, changes in traditional English law influenced the formal and informal bases of colonial American citizenship. It was during the Enlightenment that the English, through legal proceedings and in armed conflict, rejected the traditions of birthright citizenship based on natural principles of order and hierarchy. Instead, they favored citizenship based on Locke's natural-right theories, which stressed the freedom of the individual and recognized the "origins of allegiance in consent" (Kettner, 1978, p. 60). The notion that consent undergirded loyalty was critical in the thinking of the American founders who, in the Declaration of Independence, withdrew from George III their consent to be governed.

Enlightenment ideals had other effects on the American founding generation. One feature of Enlightenment individualism and rationalism that deeply influenced the political and social posture of the founders was a new perspective on the relationship between individuals and the transcendent. Termed *deism*, this intellectual approach to spirituality was widespread among the major social and political theorists of the Enlightenment and became the dominant form of spirituality among intellectual and upper-class Americans. Deists saw the evidence of God in Nature but rejected the existence of a God who intervened in human affairs. The major figures of the founding generation (Jefferson, Madison, Paine, Franklin, Adams, Washington) wrote deistic rationalism into basic American documents. Roelofs (1957) points out that many of the founders were deeply committed to the deistic world view, "even if the mass of the population had no comprehension of it" (p. 178). Just as the Declaration of Independence reveals the influence of Lockean doctrine on Thomas Jefferson ("life, liberty, and the pursuit of happiness"), it, too, reveals the influence of deism ("the laws of nature and nature's God"; "Divine Providence").

The world view of the American founders, then, was profoundly influenced by Enlightenment individualism and rationalism. This appeared in the founders' spiritual outlook, their individual intellectual achievement, and their collective intellectual achievement as represented in the basic American documents. The consequence of this world view is that the founders created an intellectual model for a new society, assuming that a certain moral frame of reference—individualist and rational—existed. However, their idealism had little connection to the everyday lives of the majority of the new nation's citizens. Indeed, in the early national period, Americans defined their citizenship through action, not through contemplation. Their actions betray them as wholly different people from those envisioned by the founders as their intellectual heirs.

A major consequence of the disjunction between the ideals of the founders and the social realities of the American people was the development, in the early years of the republic, of a two-tiered construct of citizenship. The ideology of republicanism, reflecting the founders' ideals, is located in the superstructure of this formulation. The culturally meaningful actions that have shaped American society occur at a deep structural level. This disjunction—between word and deed, thought and action—underlies the absence of a fully social and cultural understanding of citizenship and citizenship education.

Republicanism was already an ideology in the early national period. Although both Jefferson and Washington argued for the establishment of schools and colleges to promote the dispassionate intellectualism of their generation and class, these great men had less success founding schools than they had founding a nation. But their ideal persevered. As one citizen noted in the early republican era:

> By calling into active operation the mental resources of a nation, our political institutions will be rendered more perfect, ideas of justice will be diffused, the advantages of the undisturbed enjoyment of tranquility and industry will be perceived by everyone, and our mutual dependence on each other will be rendered conspicuous. The great result will be harmony. Discord and strife have always proceeded or risen upon ignorance and passion. When the first has ceased to exist, and the last shall be virtuously directed, we shall be deprived of every source of misunderstanding. [Samuel Harrison Smith, 1798/1965, p. 219]

The achievement of harmony was not so simple. In the first 20 years of the new republic, citizens had diverse interests; the possibility of harmony in their daily lives was denied by economic upheavals and massive intranational migrations. The relationship between state and federal government was as yet unspecified, and regional perspectives on political and economic issues proliferated. Collective social action centered on specific regional issues, like Shay's rebellion in Massachusetts and the rebellion in western Pennsylvania against the authority of the federal government to collect taxes on whiskey. In fact, republican ideology itself served to undercut traditional authority relations and did not promote harmony (Rorabaugh, 1986).

Also blocking the achievement of harmony was Evangelical Christianity, which swept back and forth across the young republic in its first half-century. This Second Great Awakening (distinct from the revivals of the middle eighteenth century) was enormously popular. More then the republican ideology of citizenship, this religious movement reflected the immediate needs and interests of the citizenry. People were encouraged to experience God directly, and frequently socialized in revivals and camp meetings. Contrary to both the republican and Christian ideals, such experiences heightened intolerance. By the second decade of the nineteenth century, Thomas Cooper, who was one of the last great Enlightenment thinkers in North America, published a commentary in which he insisted that American society become more accustomed to divergent views on religious matters (Miller, 1965).

The new nation's economy provides some clues as to the emerging nature of American citizenship. According to Rosenberg (1976), American industry before 1850 was characterized by its "intensive exploitation of natural resources which consisted in considerable abundance relative to capital and labor" (p. 35). Accordingly, "Americans were the

first people whose resources made it worthwhile to explore systematically the realm of highly resource-intensive inventions" (p. 45). In the
case of machine-tools and woodworking machinery, "there was a rich
harvest of inventions available to an economy which could afford to
trade off large quantities of natural resources for other factors of production" (p. 45). The seeming excess of natural resources and a constant
shortage of labor power with which to exploit these resources shaped
American culture. New forms of social interaction eroded and displaced traditional social patterns; by the 1820s the term *juvenile delin-
quency* was coined (Rorabaugh, 1986). Economic changes fueled rapid
social changes: industrialization, urbanization, and immigration. In response, new forms of collective social action emerged, most notably the
social reform movement. Early reform movements underscore the per-
sistence of such actions that stood in contradistinction to the ideals of
republican citizenship: Americans continued to define their citizenship
through action, yet had no overarching sense of an integrated social
order.

In the two decades preceding the Civil War, in addition to the
antagonisms between southern slave society and northern industrial
society, social life was deeply affected by economic boom-and-bust cy-
cles, rapid territorial expansion, and regional friction. From 1846 to
1856, as Bowles and Gintis (1976) point out, immigration was propor-
tionately greater than in any other period, including the pre–World War
I era. In terms of citizenship, Americans continued to wrangle over
what it meant to participate in a nation as opposed to a collection of
sovereign states. As the case of black Americans illustrates, the nation
had not yet agreed on what it meant to be human, let alone the finer
points of citizenship.

Kettner (1978) points out that the compromises of the U.S. Constitution that were tolerated for the sake of national union, as well as general
tensions over regional interests, were contributing causes to the Civil
War. Basic questions about the nature of American citizenship were
unresolved until, as conqueror, the North was able to impose the primacy of the Union on all the states. In the decade immediately after the
war, a number of legal questions about the nature of citizenship were
settled in suits concerning naturalization.

By the end of the 1870s, the social forces that contributed to the rise
of progressivism were massed. Among the most important were mass
immigration; the growth of nationalism, which followed the solidifica-
tion of the legal conception of citizenship and the settling of the state-
versus-federal debate; urbanization; and labor market upheavals. Also
by the 1870s the patterns of industrial life were set, marked by the

concentration of capital in fewer hands and the steadily increasing rationalization of labor processes. Patterns of schooling, too, were established, often in reaction to the social effects of industrialization, urbanization, and immigration. During the half-century from 1875 to 1925, scientific technology and corporate capitalism—the "twin forces which together gave shape to modern America" (Noble, 1977, p. xvii)—combined and developed into the modern corporation. By the outbreak of World War I, the nation was caught up in the goals of the corporation: social efficiency, mass consumption, and economic growth.

Despite this history of culturally meaningful structural change in American society, the basic ideals of republicanism persisted in an increasingly ideological form. Thus, the bases for citizenship and citizenship education came to rest on greater levels of abstraction and disassociation.

CITIZENSHIP EDUCATION: PRACTICAL CONCEPTIONS

In the history of American citizenship education, as in the cultural history of citizenship itself, there is a difference—a disjunction—between what people believe and what they do. The curriculum of citizenship education has remained relatively constant (Shaver & Knight, 1986), while practical conceptions of citizenship and pedagogies of citizenship education have changed.

We see in the literature four general approaches to citizenship education. Each of these approaches reflects a different practical conception of citizenship: individual character, formal nationalism, psychodynamic and cognitive development, and social participation. These practical conceptions, in turn, reflect the history of culturally meaningful change in American society.

Until about 1920, the first practical conception—individual character—prevailed. Individual virtues such as self-respect, ambition, courage, and character were emphasized. By the end of the 1920s, a second conception—formal nationalism—emerged. This conception emphasized the formation of a national spirit, one that would lead the United States to a position of international superiority and leadership. A third conception, inspired by Freudian and Piagetian theories prevalent during the 1950s and 1960s, focused on individual emotional attachment and cognitive development, in an effort to understand children's attitudes and knowledge of political institutions and roles. The fourth and most recent conception of citizenship education—social participation—emerged in the 1970s. Its proponents advocate practical experience and skill building, designed to promote political participation. Each of these conceptions of citizenship education can be placed in specific historical, social, and cultural contexts.

Individual Character

Barth and Shermis (1970) describe the individual-character focus of citizenship education, from the early republican era to the advent of the social studies movement, as "citizenship transmission" (p. 744). Throughout this period, the relationship between the individual and society was defined in terms of individual character. This practical conception is evident in the textbooks of that era, which, according to Butts (1977), were dominated by the values of Puritan New England: "hard work, honesty and integrity, the rewards of individual effort, and obedience to legitimate authority" (pp. 48–51). In addition to these themes, patriotism, liberty, equality, and democracy were presented uncritically to celebrate the ideals of American republicanism (Barth & Shermis, 1980).

The emphasis on individual character in approaches to citizenship education was constant throughout the nineteenth century and influenced the formalization of citizenship education in the social studies in the early twentieth century. In this period, according to Lybarger (1987), at least seven members of the first Committee on Social Studies were active in charity organizations or social settlement work. The role of citizenship education in the social studies curriculum originated in these reformers' perceptions of the need to Americanize and assimilate immigrants.

These charity workers, including the future chairperson of the Committee of Social Studies, Thomas Jesse Jones, and his colleague, James Hamilton, viewed poverty as the consequence of personal inadequacy. Charity organizations and settlement workers set two aims: first, to improve living conditions for their clients; and second, and more important, to influence what they called "the social evolution of the individual" (Lybarger, 1987, p. 184). In other words, these early charity workers wished to reshape individuals to Anglo–Saxon ideals and to impart to them a vision of higher ideals and nobility. Lybarger argues that committee members' early experiences encouraged them to enjoin teachers to approach the needs of urban children in much the same way that settlement and charity organization workers had dealt with their immigrant parents. Lybarger concludes, "The objective of school and settlement in addressing immediate needs was to make good citizens of the children of immigrants crowding into urban schools" (1987, p. 186).

The social judgment of charity organization and social settlement workers influenced early civics teachers' decisions about which ideals and traits they should incorporate into citizenship education. This practical conception of citizenship education as being designed to cultivate individual character was an aspect of a wider cultural mood and social process, a response to industrialization, immigration, and urbanization.

Formal Nationalism

At the time of the First World War, the second practical conception of citizenship education—formal nationalism—emerged in a specific social context. Formal nationalism was originally associated with the defense campaigns of conservative patriotic organizations. In a study that focused on the content and pedagogy of civic training, Merriam (1931) reviewed different techniques that were used to promote the growth of political loyalty and patriotism. He pointed out that the school had become an instrument of Americanization and that schools used tradition and symbolism as the principal elements in the organization of civic education. Too, Merriam found that school curricula focused on historical accounts of the founding and development of the nation and the biographies of national heroes like Washington, Jefferson, and Lincoln. Further, pedagogy centered on uncritical indoctrination rather than critical analysis and constructive synthesis. He argued that symbols such as the flag, patriotic songs, national heroes, monuments, and memorials, when woven together in the ceremonialism of modern political society, lost the essence of their meaning and became formalism alone. For example, in the 1920s legal measures were taken to insure that history instruction glorified national heroes (Merriam, 1931). During the late 1920s, primary schools were required by law to teach the principles of the U.S. Constitution and the government. Flag salutes, military training, and loyalty oaths were also required in public and private schools (Department of Health, Education and Welfare, 1976).

Psychodynamics and Cognitive Development

In the late 1950s and 1960s, the psychodynamic and cognitive-development conceptions of citizenship education arose in a more abstract context. These practical conceptions had their roots in the therapeutic and academic cultures shaped, respectively, by Freudian and Piagetian theories. With the "culture of professionalism" (Bledstein, 1976, p. 80) firmly established by this time, practical conceptions of citizenship education were increasingly drawn from the high-culture resources of academic institutionalized knowledge. Hyman (1959), for example, used psychodynamic theory to show the relationship between early forms of political participation and children's choice of ego ideal. He regarded the type of ego ideal chosen as a model of the child's conduct.

From a cognitive-development perspective, Dawson, Prewitt, and Dawson (1977) analyzed the politically oriented learning of children and adolescents. Focusing on how children dealt with abstract political relationships and roles, he found that the general patterns of preadult political learning were age related. Younger children had highly personal and emotional perceptions, while older children comprehended more abstract ideas and relationships. Also, the strong feelings of adolescents about political institutions, symbols, and authorities were supplemented with the knowledge of more specific roles and functions as they matured. Hess and Torney (1967) also took a cognitive-development view in their research on the development of political attitudes in children. They concluded that effective teaching would match concepts basic to the democratic system with the developmental sequence of children's political socialization. This conception is also linked to a broader social context.

The relation between a cognitive-development conception of citizenship education and wider curriculum changes in math and science during the post–Sputnik era, and how those changes were, in turn, linked to the societal context of militarization, is only now being explained (Noble, 1990).

Social Participation

After the turbulent 1960s, a seemingly more realistic and sophisticated practical conception emerged: citizenship education as social participation. Newmann and Oliver (1970) claimed that citizenship education should not transmit specific views of reality to students; rather, it should supply students with an analytical scheme and a repertoire of diverse viewpoints which they might use to clarify conflicting commitments in ways that make sense to them and that they can defend in public. Newmann and Oliver's approach to citizenship education permits students to engage in dialogues as a way to clarify their commitments and to develop their ability to use certain intellectual strategies for challenging and justifying public policies.

According to Newmann and Oliver (1970), public controversies are manifestations of conflict between the different values of "the American Creed" (p. 12). They define this creed as the set of values—phrased in general, abstract language—to which most Americans proclaim commitment. These include the fundamental values of the American political system as expressed in the U.S. Constitution, the Bill of Rights, and the Declaration of Independence. Other, less codified values include mercy, honesty, and efficiency. Newmann and Oliver believe that this creed contains values sufficiently diverse to embrace the ideals of many cultures and to respond to changing times. However, individual citizens are left to choose one value over another: Value conflict thus becomes a basis for public controversy.

Newmann and Oliver (1970) recognize that a curriculum based on public controversy could become as irrelevant as a more traditional one, if it does not relate the role of students as citizens to the exercise of power in the community. However, while Newmann and Oliver endeavor to move away from traditional citizenship curricula, their emphasis remains on a rational discourse of abstract values that includes both the ideology and cultural preferences of those curricula. The meaning of citizenship education, even in Newmann and Oliver's proposal for social participation, is still distant from the realistic culture of everyday life and ordinary social practice.

In this historical overview of citizenship education, we have seen variations in practical conceptions of citizenship education, and a connection between these conceptions and their cultural context. However, as we have shown throughout, the abstract values of citizenship remain those implicit in the original republican ideal. Such values remain rooted in individualism and rationalism, despite changes in both the cultural context of citizenship and the practical conceptions of citizenship education. Thus, citizenship education is ideological and static, like frozen ice on the surface of a running river.

CITIZENSHIP EDUCATION: CURRICULUM AND PEDAGOGY

The ideological nature of citizenship education, revealed in the disjunction between the constancy of its ideal and the variability of its culturally embedded conception and practice, also appears as we look at specific examples of citizenship education curriculum and pedagogy. At first glance, it is difficult to see the precise development of citizenship education curriculum, because it generally has not been treated independently in the curriculum, but rather as part of social studies, civics, or government courses. Nevertheless, in such courses we can discern examples of citizenship education, as well as changes in its content and pedagogy.

In citizenship education as an aspect of social studies education, there is relative constancy in the curriculum, despite a changing pedagogy. Research indicates a fairly stable set of content themes, including social responsibility, community participation, national history, geography, community need, and government (Carroll, Broadnax, Contreras, Mann, Ornstein, & Stiehm, 1987; Dunn & Harris, 1919; Michener, 1939; Torney, Oppenheim, & Farnen, 1975). This constancy corresponds to the static nature of the ideological bases of American citizenship, while changes in pedagogy correspond to changes in the culture of American society. This can be seen in the major changes or periods in citizenship education since the founding of the social studies movement, which include at least the following three phases: the "social studies movement," after the 1916 report of the National Education Association's Committee on Social Studies; the "new social studies movement" of the late 1950s and 1960s; and "contemporary trends" in effect since the 1970s (Alilunas, 1949; Barth & Shermis, 1980; Butts, 1977; Fraser, 1969).

The report of the Committee on Social Studies of the National Education Association (NEA) in 1916 was the starting point of modern social studies education. Barth and Shermis (1970) term this the period of the "teaching social studies as a social science" (p. 746), during which mastery of social science concepts and processes was emphasized. Also in 1916, the American Political Science Association (APSA) argued for the establishment of separate courses in civil government (Butts, 1977). However, the NEA's (1916) report prevailed; it incorporated citizenship education into the central aims of social studies. Civics and government would be taught in Grades 9 and 12, as part of the social studies curriculum. In the final report of the NEA's Commission on the Reorganization of Secondary Education (Cardinal Principles of Secondary Education, 1918), the social studies included a combination of subjects: history, civics, government, sociology, and economics (Alilunas, 1949; Butts, 1977). Thus, citizenship education, and the social preferences embedded in it, were incorporated into the subject matter of the social sciences.

In the period of war and economic crisis between the 1920s and 1950s, particularly in the Cold War and post–Sputnik eras, education in general and citizenship education specifically were reorganized on the basis of a combined emphasis on life adjustment and science (Kliebard, 1986). This reorganization reflected a general emphasis on scientism in American culture. Especially after the economic crises of the 1920s and 1930s, and the rise of interest in managerial efficiency and life-adjustment education (Kliebard, 1986), earlier methods of mental and moral training were replaced by methods that emphasized the logical acquisition of social information and knowledge. The learning of scientific skill and knowledge in social studies was emphasized over moral training and, indeed, over citizenship education itself. By the 1940s, learning to apply science to society was already included as an objective of citizenship education (Morgan, 1941).

Mathematics, science, and foreign languages became central in school curricula and were funded by the National Defense Education Act of 1958 and the National Science Foundation. These efforts mark the beginnings of the new social studies movement, which emphasized cognitive analysis, inquiry learning, and the discovery method (Butts, 1977; Weinland, 1975). The goals of pedagogy changed from the mastery of social science concepts to the acquisition of scientific methods, often termed "discovery" or "reflective inquiry" (Barth & Shermis, 1970, p. 748). Inquiry-oriented pedagogy remained influential in social studies curricula until the 1960s. A notable characteristic of citizenship education during this period was its relative indifference to the actual curriculum content of citizenship education. Instead, attention was directed to the instruction of scientific methods.

New approaches to citizenship education proliferated in the 1970s. These included a "law-related approach to citizenship education" (Butts, 1977, p. 66); approaches based on the academic disciplines of history and social sciences; and approaches that promoted the study of social problems, critical-thinking skills, and values clarification (Newmann, 1977). In sharp contrast to these changes in pedagogy, however, the most prominent element of the citizenship education curriculum was government (Oliner, 1983). For example, the Harvard Project, one of the new social studies projects, placed the role of government at the center in the teaching of civics and government (Shaver & Knight, 1986). In such projects, the curriculum remains frozen in place.

The change in social studies pedagogy, from an emphasis on affective moral training in the earlier periods to an emphasis on methodological training, reflects an important addition to the concept of patriotism promoted in citizenship education. Scientific prowess and technological achievement are incorporated into traditional symbols of patriotism. Further, in pedagogical practice, citizenship education itself is now considered as an aspect of the scientific enterprise, and curriculum construction itself becomes a technology (Cornbleth, 1985).

Along with these changes in the pedagogy of citizenship education and in education more generally, method becomes an end in itself. Rather than ask *what* to teach, the question today becomes *how* to teach;

the curriculum is taken for granted. The current emphasis on method, on pedagogical instrumentality, blocks the realization of at least two requisites of citizenship education. First, examination of citizenship education curriculum is displaced in favor of methodological interest. Second, examination of the relationship of citizenship education curriculum to its cultural and social context is precluded. Absorption with method, on the one hand, and the assumptions of an ahistorical privileged curriculum, on the other (Bloom, 1987), prevent an articulation of the concepts and practices of citizenship and citizenship education as informed by knowledge of culture and society.

CITIZENSHIP EDUCATION
IN CULTURE AND SOCIETY

Citizenship in America, as an ideology of the Enlightenment, has become a cultural "ideal" severed from everyday social life and practice. For citizenship education to work, as Janowitz (1983) argues, there must be a sense of civic consciousness and a deeply experienced commitment to the wider social community. In the present, as in the past, citizenship education instead supports an ethos of individualism. Such an ethos is enacted through schooling. Thus the error of republicanism, whereby belief was extracted from practical social relations and commitments, is repeated in the microcosm of the school. As we have shown, it is unlikely that "political socialization" can succeed in a cultural climate of individualism. Recently, however, this climate of individualism has come into question.

Such questioning occurs in various forms. The current cultural "restoration" in fundamentalist forms of religion is the most obvious. The reaction against individualism has not, however, been limited to this popularist phenomenon. A high-culture critique of individualism has emerged among disenchanted academics. In structuralism, post-structuralism, and hermeneutics, as well as in institutionally conventional academic knowledge, individualism is repudiated. Such critics as Lasch (1984) and Bellah, Madsen, Sullivan, Swidler, and Tipton (1985) seek the cultural bases of social commitment. The relationship between culture and an educated citizenry is expressed in their hope for a "public philosophy." Simultaneously, a critique of individualism is presented. Mass-culture criticism of individualism is expressed in such Hollywood films as *Wall Street, Broadcast News,* and *Baby Boom.* These films specifically critique greed, finance capital, and media hype. Here, the culture of individual consumer demand is rejected in favor of a culture of productive collective action. Mass culture reasserts the values of the social bonds of family, against the unrestrained egoism of corporate ambition.

The questioning of individualism opens the possibility of an alternative culture and society in which citizenship and the practice of social life are integrated. What is the current social basis for such an alternative? The present society contains the possibilities of a cultural reaction against individualism and for new forms of community and solidarity that may become the basis for a common citizenry. If the quest for a new community culture beyond individualism is to succeed, it will be integrated with contemporary social practice. Today, that practice is corporatist and professional. If a new "communalism" of belief—a public culture of citizenship—is to succeed and a new citizen to be defined, it will be built upon the possibilities offered by current social conditions. We know well the criticism and the dangers of corporatism and professionalism in society (Wexler, 1987). Yet, corporatism challenges the compartmentalization of current institutions; it opens the possibility of new forms of solidarity among previously segregated social fractions. Professionalism is potentially a new locus for communality and solidarity.

The practical question is whether or not these utopian aspects of corporatism and professionalism can be used to realize the cultural aspirations of any new communalism, of any new public philosophy. Such a possibility, however, necessitates abandoning an older view of citizenship education, and indeed of education generally, which locates educational practice in the person-to-person social relations of the school. The possibility of appropriating the structural and cultural possibilities of professionalism requires that we rethink citizenship education. Citizenship education will become socially transformative when it is fully integrated with the larger culture. This requires an understanding of and a commitment to education as a process of collective cultural formation of individuals (Wexler, 1987). This understanding takes account, as did Marshall (1964), not only of the culture and practices of the school and even the workplace, but also of citizenship as achievement of full social membership in a common endeavor.

Citizenship and citizenship education, in theory and practice, stand for the hope of nations for meaningful social integration. As we look at the history of citizenship education, curriculum, and pedagogy, and at the concept of citizenship itself, we see in the origin as well as in the different historical periods of citizenship and citizenship education that they remain rooted in the Enlightenment ideologies of individualism and rationalism. Our examination reveals that this ideological surface obscures a historical undercurrent of meaningful social and cultural change. As a practical result, citizenship and citizenship education deny the very bases of social life that contain the seeds of a fully social citizenry. The irony is that "citizenship," in its individual and rational formulation, prevents us from seeing its necessary cultural and social bases—the essence of a true citizenry and real citizenship.

What the study of citizenship education requires is not greater emphasis on measurement techniques for the variables of political socialization. Nor does citizenship education require schools to experiment with political participation. We suggest that citizenship educators abandon the "field" of "citizenship education" as it is now practiced. Citizenship education cannot succeed outside the real world of collective cultural and social processes. A new curriculum must be drawn from outside the schools and must focus on the restoration of collective civic values. Furthermore, such restoration must be lived. For example, students can participate in the lives of older citizens, to restore the connections between generations. Students can participate in environmental projects, to restore the connections between people and the land, and the concept of stewardship. The aim of such restoration projects is to build a new sense of place and community and to promote the democracy of expression.

The curriculum must emphasize the role of citizens in collective social processes and the responsibilities of full membership in our common endeavor: social life. The curriculum must account for and draw from current social formations. As we have suggested here, corporatism and professionalism contain potential bases for a new public culture of citizenship. Other potent social formations include the Green political parties of Western Europe, the Solidarity movement of Poland, and the mass movements in support of democratization in Eastern Europe and China. When citizenship education is re-embedded in cultural meaning, belief, and commitment, and in organized social practices, then citizenship education will become a public as well as an academic concern. Otherwise, it remains a backwater of administered social science in the corporatist era.

REFERENCES

Alilunas, L. J. (1949). Major controversies over "social studies" in American secondary education. *Harvard Educational Review, 19*(1), 1–15.

Allen, G. H. (1922). *The French revolution.* Philadelphia: George Barries.

Barth, J. L., & Shermis, S. S. (1970). Defining the social studies: An exploration of three traditions. *Social Education, 34,* 743–750.

Barth, J. L., & Shermis, S. S. (1980). Nineteenth century origins of the social studies movement: Understanding the continuity between older and contemporary civic and U.S. history textbooks. *Theory and Research in Social Education, 8*(3), 29–49.

Bellah, R., Madsen, R., Sullivan, W., Swidler, A., & Tipton, S. (1985). *Habits of the heart: Individualism and commitment in American life.* Berkeley: University of California Press.

Bledstein, B. J. (1976). *The culture of professionalism: The middle class and the development of higher education in America.* New York: W. W. Norton.

Bloom, A. (1987). *The closing of the American mind.* New York: Simon & Schuster.

Bowles, S., & Gintis, H. (1976). *Schooling in capitalist America: Educational reform and the contradictions of economic life.* New York: Basic Books.

Butts, R. F. (1977). Historical perspectives on civic education in the United States. In B. F. Brown (Ed.), *Education for responsible citizenship* (pp. 47–68). New York: McGraw-Hill.

Carroll, J. D., Broadnax, W. D., Contreras, G., Mann, T. E., Ornstein, N. J., & Stiehm, J. (1987). *We the people: A review of U.S. government and civics textbooks.* Washington: People for the American Way.

Cornbleth, C. (1985). Reconsidering social studies curriculum. *Theory and Research in Social Education, 13*(2), 31–45.

Dawson, R., Prewitt, K., & Dawson, M. (1977). *Political socialization.* Boston: Little, Brown.

Department of Health, Education and Welfare. (1976, September). *Education and citizenship* (Conference Report). Kansas City, MO: Office of Education.

Dunn, A. W., & Harris, H. M. (1919). *Citizenship in school and out.* New York: D. C. Heath.

Durkheim, E. (1977). *The evolution of educational thought* (Peter Collins, Trans.). London: Routledge and Kegan Paul. (Original work published 1938)

Fraser, D. M. (Ed.). (1969). *Social studies curriculum development* (39th yearbook). Washington, DC: National Committee for the Social Studies.

Hess, R. D., & Torney, J. V. (1967). *The development of political attitudes in children.* Chicago: Aldine.

Hyman, H. H. (1959). *Political socialization: A study in the psychology of political behavior.* Glencoe, IL: Free Press.

Janowitz, M. (1983). *The reconstitution of patriotism: Education for civic consciousness.* Chicago: University of Chicago Press.

Kettner, J. H. (1978). *The development of American citizenship: 1608–1870.* Chapel Hill: University of North Carolina Press.

Kliebard, H. M. (1986). *The struggle for the American curriculum, 1893–1958.* London: Routledge and Kegan Paul.

Lasch, C. (1984). *The minimal self: Psychic survival in troubled times.* New York: W. W. Norton.

Levi-Strauss, C. (1961). *A world on the wane.* New York: Criterion Books.

Lords, C. (1982). *Education and culture in the political thought of Aristotle.* Ithaca, NY: Cornell University Press.

Lybarger, M. B. (1987). Need as ideology: A look at the early social studies. In T. S. Popkewitz (Ed.), *The formation of the school subjects* (pp. 178–189). New York: Falmer Press.

Marshall, T. H. (1964). *Class, citizenship and social development*. New York: Doubleday.

Mauss, M. (1938). Une categorie de l'esprit humaine: La notion de personne, celle de moi. *Journal of the Royal Anthropological Institute, 68*, 59–93.

Merriam, C. E. (1931). *The making of citizens*. Chicago: University of Chicago Press.

Michener, J. A. (Ed.). (1939). *The future of the social studies*. Cambridge, MA: The National Council for the Social Studies.

Miller, P. (1965). *The life of the mind in America: From the Revolution to the Civil War*. New York: Harcourt, Brace and World.

Morgan, J. E. (Ed.). (1941). *The American citizens' handbook*. Washington, DC: National Council for the Social Studies.

National Education Association Commission on the Reorganization of Secondary Education. (1918). *Seven cardinal principles of secondary education*. Washington, DC: National Education Association.

National Education Association Committee on Social Studies of the Commission on the Reorganization of Secondary Education (1916). *The social studies in secondary education*. Washington, DC: National Education Association.

Newmann, F. M. (1977). Alternative approaches to citizenship education: A search for authenticity. In B. F. Brown (Ed.), *Education for responsible citizenship* (pp. 175–188). New York: McGraw-Hill.

Newmann, F. M., & Oliver, D. W. (1970). *Clarifying public controversy: An approach to teaching social studies*. Boston: Little, Brown.

Noble, D. D. (1990). *The militarization of education*. Unpublished doctoral dissertation, University of Rochester, Rochester, NY.

Noble, D. F. (1977). *America by design: Science, technology, and the rise of corporate capitalism*. New York: Knopf.

Oliner, P. V. (1983). Putting community into citizenship education: The need for prosociality. *Theory and Research in Education, 11*(2), 5–81.

Reinhold, M. (1984). *Classica Americana: The Greek and Roman heritage in the U.S.* Detroit: Wayne State University Press.

Roelofs, H. M. (1957). *The tension of citizenship: private man and public duty*. New York: Rinehart.

Rorabaugh, W. T. (1986). *The craft apprentice: From Franklin to the Machine Age*. New York: Oxford University Press.

Rosenberg, N. (1976). *Perspectives on technology*. Cambridge, England: Cambridge University Press.

Shaver, J. P., & Knight, R. S. (1986). Civics and government in citizenship education. In S. P. Wronski & D. H. Bragaw (Eds.), *Social studies and social sciences: A fifty year perspective* (pp. 71–84). Washington, DC: National Council for the Social Studies.

Smith, S. H. (1965). "Remarks on education: Illustrating the close connection between virtue and wisdom. To which is annexed a system of liberal education . . . " In F. Rudolph (Ed.), *Essays on education in the early republic* (pp. 167–223). Cambridge, MA: Harvard University Press. (Original work published 1798)

Torney, J. V., Oppenheim, A. N., & Farnen, R. F. (1975). *Civic education in ten countries*. New York: John Wiley.

Weinland, T. P. (1975). Social studies, history, and the 30s box. In A. Roberts (Ed.), *Educational innovation: Alternatives in curriculum and instruction* (pp. 106–116). Boston: Allyn & Bacon.

Wexler, P. (1987). *Social analysis of education: After the new sociology*. New York: Routledge and Kegan Paul.

7 The Social Psychological Perspective

Social Contexts, Processes, and Civil Ideologies

ALLAN BRANDHORST

Social psychology as a discipline has traditionally focused its attention on analysis of social behavior. Like sociology, the analytic perspective of social psychology incorporates a concern for patterns of organization in society; like psychology, social psychology is concerned with the study of individual behavior. This double focus is resolved by studying individual social behavior as a product of an interaction between environmentally present social influences and social influences mediated by attitudes and internalized norms. Social psychologists attend to the social context in which behavior is exhibited, and they look to past social influences on the actor which operate in the present as norms.

CITIZENSHIP DEFINED IN TERMS OF PROCESSES OF MIND

A social psychological perspective on citizenship is mainly concerned with the social influences on citizen action. That concern, however, incorporates both environmental influences on action and the internal processes through which past social experiences are activated as influences on action. Because of the concern with internal processes, social psychologists must construct theories of those processes. Over the years many theories of internal processes have been advanced. Each seems to reflect styles and patterns of thinking that were prevalent at the time of the theory's development.

Currently, information-processing approaches to cognitive theories

161

seem to be most popular among social psychologists, and in this chapter I will use such a framework to reflect upon citizenship. The framework synthesizes previous work by Fishbein and Ajzen (1975), in the domain of theory building, with the reflective conceptualizations of frames from the work of Goffman (1974) and the information-processing model of Goleman (1985), in order to accommodate processes by which the mind acquires information and transforms information into action.

The Fishbein and Ajzen (1975) model of the determinants of behavior proposes that two types of beliefs—normative beliefs and beliefs about consequences—act through attitudes and subjective norms to influence intentions. Intentions in turn determine behavior. Social psychological research demonstrates how the model applies to problems of citizenship behavior. Kahle and Beatty (1987), in a cognitive-dynamics-oriented study of Oregon's bottle-return bill, found that legally required behaviors influence attitudes toward the behavior, if subjective norms converge with the new position. Thus subjective norms (based on normative beliefs) and attitudes (based on beliefs about consequences) are determinants of behavior and are influenced by behavior.

The core element in information-processing theories is an information organizer labeled a *schema*. This is defined as an organized network of concepts that is stored in long-term memory. Schemata are hypothesized to function as vehicles for endowing perceptions with meaning. Thus the accumulated schemata in long-term memory are searched any time a perceptual event occurs. That search categorizes the perception in terms of relevant schemata, which are then activated. The conscious mind selects from activated schemata according to the momentary goals and purposes of the individual. The information networks that we have labeled schemata include some that represent beliefs about relationships in the real world. Scientific, quasiscientific, and mathematical knowledge is organized in the mind in the form of such schemata, and it can inform the individual about consequences of particular behaviors. The individual, however, makes choices about behavior based on the likeliness of the occurrence of those consequences. Thus, a smoker may possess schematically organized knowledge of the relationship between smoking and lung cancer, but continue to smoke anyway because she has discounted the consequences on the basis of probabilities that she would contract lung cancer.

Another kind of information network that we may consider a special form of schemata has been labeled a *frame* by Erving Goffman (1974). Whereas conventional schemata organize networks of generic information, frames operate in the episodic memory to organize memories of discrete events. Frames also organize perception. As Goffman describes it, individuals approach social contexts with the question, "What is going on here?" On the basis of cues in the environment, an individual calls up a frame, which circumscribes the appropriate behaviors, as well as describing a range of taboo behaviors. Cheering or booing at a funeral would be in bad taste, which is to say that these behaviors lie outside the range of appropriate behaviors for a funeral frame (at least for most American subculture groups). Frames may operate consciously or unconsciously, so that individuals can function within a frame, but be unable to explain their behavior.

Frames are critically important to an understanding of citizenship because they are the mechanisms through which social controls operate. The implication here is that social contexts control frames, and frames control the range of behavior that will be in evidence. There is also the possibility that generic schemata may also be embedded in frames, and thereby function under conditions of restricted access.

The centrality to citizenship of active involvement suggests that both frame theory and schema theory are necessary elements of a social psychological definition of citizenship. This perspective poses a number of issues for citizenship education. If frames and schemata filter our perceptions and can limit our behavior options, then is the electorate vulnerable when exposed to the media assaults of well-financed and psychologically sophisticated elites?

Social psychology can provide a useful perspective on citizenship, one that accommodates the views of other disciplines through the agency of information schemata and their influence on beliefs about consequences of behavior. Social psychology goes beyond the other social sciences, however, in providing a larger action context for considering the links between thought and behavior. In the following sections we will explore the concept of citizenship and relate it to the realities of influence that are being mapped by social psychology.

SOCIAL PSYCHOLOGY
AND THE IDEOLOGY OF CITIZENSHIP

Citizenship means different things to different Americans. During the Vietnam era, many Americans felt that it was their duty as citizens to oppose the war; others felt that it was their duty to obey the government and support the war. These differences arose out of very different beliefs about the proper relationship of a citizen to the larger society. In some cases the beliefs were normative, arising out of the social contexts in which individuals were living and working. In some areas where normative influences were strong, many citizens accepted the conventional wisdom that the war, once begun, ended the debate. By contrast, on many college campuses, with different normative influences, many citizens accepted the conventional wisdom that the war was illegal and required citizen opposition. In both cases individuals considered themselves good citizens.

In other cases, beliefs concerned consequences. Many individuals, including adolescent boys and their parents, could not anticipate any positive consequences of the war and, as the casualty figures rose, feared for their own and their sons' safety if drafted. Many other individuals, seeing in the Vietnam conflict an expansion of communism, feared the ultimate danger of an attack upon the United States and so supported the war out of a belief in negative consequences should the war be lost. In both cases these people considered themselves good citizens. In still other cases, some citizens ignored the war as best they could, neither opposing nor supporting it. These, too, considered themselves good citizens.

What does it mean to be a citizen? The question has no one answer, because in a complex, multicultural society such as the United States there are multiple groups, institutions, and ideologies, often contradictory, that compete for the allegiance of the individual. Although citizenship means a relationship between an individual and the larger society, that relationship can take many very different forms. Even the presumption that citizenship implies active participation in the political life of the larger society has been called into question by the proponents of revisionist theories of democracy (Dahl, 1961) and some social education theorists (Leming, 1989).

In an attempt to structure the debate about the nature of citizenship, it is useful to construct a model of the concept. Citizenship can be seen as a relationship based on beliefs that vary along three dimensions, or problems in the definition of citizenship. The first of these is the problem of the *scope of community*. In slightly different wording this problem concerns the identification of groups to whom moral consideration is to be accorded. This is the *moral parameters dimension*, a continuum ranging from parochialism on one end to cosmopolitanism on the other.

The second problem concerns *levels of active involvement*, that is, the determination of the level of community activity commensurate with citizenship. This *activity dimension* has active participation on one end and passive participation/nonparticipation on the other.

The third problem is somewhat more complex. Individuals vary with regard to their view of the *responsibilities of government* and the decision makers in government, and the nature of *citizens' responsibilities*. Some individuals see government as an economic institution, sometimes called a pork barrel, which is primarily in the business of dispensing benefits. Therefore it is the primary charge of the elected representatives of the people to provide constituent service, securing for their own constituents a maximum benefit package. Others see the government as primarily an agency for securing the well-being of the society as a collectivity, and to that end elected representatives are to formulate policy in the best interests of the society as a whole. This, then, is the *social integration dimension*, with its two extremes being the economic marketplace position and the social community position.

Moral Parameters Dimension

In 1958, E. C. Banfield reported a study of the ethos of life in "Montegrano" (a pseudonym), a small place in Southern Italy. Banfield coined the term *amoral familism* to describe the predominant conditions of association among Montegranesi, which were based on this belief: "Maximize the material, short-run advantage of the nuclear family; assume that all others will do likewise" (p. 83).

Amoral familism illustrates the most constrictive moral parameter for citizenship, because it extends moral consideration only to one's own nuclear family. At the other end of the continuum, one might find animal-rights activists, who oppose on ideological grounds the inhumane treatment of animals. For them, moral consideration extends beyond the parameters of the human race. In between the two extremes are a number of identifiable positions, including racists, sexists, nationalists, and social-class elitists. For example, the civil rights movement of the 1960s demonstrated that many white Americans place black Americans outside the parameters of moral consideration; the women's movement has illustrated that many Americans, men and women, do not fully extend the parameters of moral consideration to women; and, in the current international climate, many Americans display no sense of moral community with people in other nations. At the same time, many others have supported efforts at ending these divisions among groups of people and the community of nations.

The denial of moral consideration to any group, either legally or by individual intent or disregard, means in practice that individual citizen decisions systematically exclude the perspective of that group from consideration in the shaping of policy. In the aggregate, such practice can and does effectively alienate those groups from the society and reduces them from citizens to subjects.

The failure to accord moral consideration to others, either individually or by group, probably has its roots in the perceived "invisibility" of those others. The close linkage between empathy and moral consideration suggests that an understanding of the dynamic operation of empathy would throw light on the tendency to extend moral consideration. Several studies are pertinent here. Krebs (1975), for example, studied identification processes and their relationship to altruistic behavior. He found that subjects who were led to believe they were most similar to a player in a roulette game identified most with that player; those most empathic also exhibited the most altruism toward the player. Similar results were found by Coke, Batson, and McDavis (1978). In a study of 44 college students, those subjects who experienced the most empathic emotion also offered the most help to those with whom the empathic bond was established. In another study (Rapoport, 1988), the decision to contribute toward the public good was found to be dependent upon the perception of the collective good and altruism.

A final commentary relevant to the discussion of the moral parameters dimension results from research on moral norms. A study of 195 subjects' intentions regarding six kinds of medical transplant donations demonstrated that both attitudes toward the act and normative beliefs were predictors of intentions (Schwartz & Tessler, 1972). Normative beliefs, however, could be either personal or social. Personal normative beliefs were defined as norms with sanctions tied to the self-concept. In such cases, anticipation or actual violation of the norm results in guilt, self-deprecation, or loss of self-esteem (Schwartz, 1973). Social norms focus on the dispositions of significant other people toward certain behaviors. Sanctions for violations of social norms are linked to the experience or disapproval of others. Personal normative beliefs were equated with moral obligation and were much more predictive of intentions than were social normative beliefs. Elsewhere Schwartz (1968) presents evidence that the necessary conditions for the activation of moral norms include (1) an awareness that one's acts may have consequences for the welfare of others and (2) an acceptance of the responsibility for one's acts and their consequences.

The significance of this work for a social psychological perspective on citizenship lies first in the demonstration of the power of a personal sense of responsibility to impact on prosocial citizen behavior. It also shows that the failure to accept personal responsibility may obviate a personal sense of prosocial obligation, irrespective of the citizen's awareness of the consequences of actions for the welfare of others.

Activity Dimension

The activity dimension of beliefs about citizenship has two separate facets. One of these is specifically political in a narrow sense, described as the degree of involvement in the process of developing positions on issues, supporting candidates for office, influencing decisions of elected officials, and supporting or opposing established policy and/or laws. The other facet concerns the relationship of citizens to informal social institutions, such as fellow workers, family members, and the immediate community. In an unregimented society, although they are not considered political, these relationships are nonetheless reflective of the quality of citizenship on this dimension. While the discussion here will focus primarily on the narrow, political sense of citizenship, the reader is invited to consider the broader sense of citizenship as the discussion develops. (For a treatment of this aspect, see Oliner, 1983.)

American democratic ideology has featured the individual citizen, rationally considering political issues and then voting intelligently for candidates who matched the citizen's views on issues. This myth of the active citizen has its roots in the Jeffersonian ideal of the gentleman farmer and in the New England institution of the town meeting. Generations of American school children have been nurtured on this myth, for the expressed purpose of teaching them responsible citizenship.

Myth and reality, however, are often unacquainted, and the distance between them became apparent as public opinion research in the decades of the 1940s and 1950s revealed an electorate surprisingly uninformed and largely apathetic about politics and the issues of the day (see Dahl, 1961). Simon (1957) raised the additional problem that for many citizens the issues may be too complex, exceeding their capacity to appreciate the implications of various policy alternatives. This social reality of late-twentieth-century America posed a challenge for classical democratic theory, which assumed that representative government maintained the ideal of democratic ideology because the representatives faithfully reflected the views and positions of their constituents. Central to this thesis was the notion that the electorate had both the will and the ability to maintain an effective presence in the world of politics; and it was by their participation that the leadership was selected that faithfully represented the public will.

One response to this challenge to classical democratic theory was revisionist theory. It argued that, as long as there is competition among individuals and groups in the political elite, the essence of democracy is preserved, provided that citizens are afforded the opportunity to choose between alternative candidates for representative positions. Thus, open competition for political support by members of the political elite in the marketplace would lead to the selection of policy makers who would reflect the public will.

Alternative democratic theories thus legitimize both active and passive citizenship and thereby underline the importance of an active–passive dimension in the description of citizenship. According to revisionist theory, the politically passive are still citizens and not subjects, as long as institutional arrangements allow for re-entry to the political arena when individuals become dissatisfied with the operation of the system.

From this perspective the active–passive dimension of citizenship ranges from the unregistered, nonvoting citizen who obeys the laws and pays her taxes (passive citizenship) to the individual who actively campaigns for political office, shapes public policy directly, writes letters to her representatives, supports a political action committee, and/or devotes maximal attention to the study of policy (active citizenship). In between lie varying degrees of involvement, such as registered voter, voter in general elections, politically informed voter, voter in primary elections, campaign contributor, campaign worker, and so on.

Social Integration Dimension

The essence of humanness is the dynamic tension between the real and the ideal. While the demands of day-to-day existence pull the individual down, dreams of a more utopian existence free the spirit and inspire striving after an ideal. In its more noble moments, citizenship expresses a higher ideal and the pursuit of the utopian goal of community; in its more pedestrian moments, citizenship becomes the pursuit of hedonistic goals. That the citizenry is divided in terms of tendencies toward these two poles has been documented. Rasinski and Rosenbaum (1987), for example, in a study of citizen support for tax increases for education, found support for both self-interest and nonself-interest factors. The strongest and most consistent predictors of tax support among those most likely to be voters, however, were the nonself-interest factors.

At the birth of the American republic, the founders sought to institutionalize noble political instincts while accommodating the more base realities of political life. While recognizing that republican principles required either a direct or indirect responsibility of the officers of government to the public, the founders nevertheless hedged their bet by arranging for the election of senators indirectly through the agency of the state legislatures, and insulating them from public impulsiveness by granting them six-year terms. They further insulated the government by the creation of the Electoral College for the selection of the president. These measures were presumed necessary in order that the power of government be kept out of the hands of incompetents and demagogues. There was at the outset of the republic a keen awareness that unscrupulous politicians could use campaign promises of political payoffs to seduce the public into supporting their candidacies, and thereby divert the business of government from the general welfare to a focus on protecting special interests.

In our own time, the dynamic tension between politics as statesmanship and politics as an auction is formalized in such contradictory institutions as Common Cause on the one hand and, on the other, the political action committees sponsored by the AFL-CIO, NRA, AMA, NEA, ABA, NAM, and so on. The passage of the Gramm-Rudman-Hollings legislation to limit government spending very pointedly emphasizes the dangers in politics as an auction.

The debasement of politics does not occur in isolation from the citizenry, but is a direct response to the dominance of a particular view of the relationship of the citizen to the state. When, for most citizens, citizenship means participation for the purposes of maximizing one's own personal share of the spoils, then the political process has been reduced to a marketplace. When, for most citizens, citizenship means supporting the larger public interest, even if that interest runs counter to one's own personal short-run interest, then the political process can be conducted in accord with the principles of justice and community. Thus individuals' beliefs about the proper function of government and their relationship to it are of central importance to the definition of citizenship.

The social integration dimension of citizenship, ranging from the economic marketplace position to the social community position, shades gradually from one extreme to the other. Very few people act exclusively in accordance with the economic marketplace position, and very few come close to the selflessness of Mohandas Gandhi. Most people shift between the poles, in response to their personal interest in the issues of the times and the quality of leadership provided by statespeople and politicians.

Schemata, Frames, and the Three Dimensions of Citizenship

From the perspective of either schema or frame theory, information networks stored in memory may influence behavior. If behavior is to come under the control of schemata, however, those networks must have incorporated links between behavior and consequences. Thus, if a citizen possesses a schema linking a particular citizen behavior (e.g., voting) to some desired outcome, then the act of voting will be influenced by that information schema. If, however, the individual has had experiences in which the individual's behavior (e.g., voting) did not lead in any understandable way to anticipated outcomes, then the individual cannot construct reliable information networks to link that behavior to foreseeable consequences.

Let us suppose an individual has repeatedly voted for political candidates, with the intent of seeing particular policies implemented, but has repeatedly been disappointed in that the desired policies are not implemented. Experiences of this sort may reduce the likelihood of the individual voting on the basis of information networks centered on government policy. In the absence of adequate information networks on policy consequences, voting may come unduly under the influence of the personal appeal of the candidate, or the individual may vote for the candidate because of the candidate's political party affiliation. Alternatively, the individual may stop voting, or voting may come under the influence of normative beliefs (i.e., voting that is consistent with what others would expect one to do). Of course, in this latter case the frame that is activated would have a heavy influence on which others' expectations the voter would honor.

IMPACT OF THE PAST THREE DECADES ON AMERICAN CITIZENSHIP

A number of patterns or trends over the past three decades conceivably could be impacting on the practice of citizenship, in terms of active involvement, the according of moral consideration to others, and expectations of what elected officials are to do.

Active Versus Passive Involvement

Trends in political participation over the past 30 years consistently indicate reduced levels of political involvement, as evidenced in a steady decline in the percentage of eligible voters who vote. Possible explanations for this trend include decline in intensity of partisanship, perceived certainty of the outcome of elections due to the sophistication of polling, decline in interest in the campaign, declining sense of control (efficacy) over events, and declining sense of citizen duty (Hill & Luttbeg, 1983).

Intensity of partisanship of political participation, as an element in the determination of behavior, may be grounded in normative beliefs ("My family has always voted Democratic" or, "Everyone I know is a Republican"), or it may be grounded in beliefs about consequences ("If Democrats are elected they will raise my taxes"). The literature has steadily documented the decline of intensity of partisanship over the past three decades (Hill & Luttbeg, 1983). This may reflect a sense that there is no difference between the parties, diminishing the role of anticipated consequences in influencing behavior. Or, it may reflect a decline in family influence, rapid changes in social mobility, or the high rate at which Americans change communities, all of which would diminish the effects of normative beliefs on behavior.

Declining interest in campaigns due to media overkill may impact on voter behavior through the agency of beliefs about consequences. As citizens are exposed to more information than they can assimilate into their schemata, they may lose interest because of their declining understanding of issues. The growing emphasis on television as the medium for conducting political campaigns may be contributing to this trend, due to television's inadequacy in dealing in depth with complex issues (Brandhorst, 1988). Citizens may thus be left with a glut of political information that they cannot integrate into schemata. Interest in campaigns as an influence on voter turnout is instructive. While the decline in voter turnout has been steady for all groups at all levels of interest in the campaign, according to Hill and Luttbeg (1983), the decline in voting has been most precipitous for those with low interest—from 63 percent in 1964 to 35 percent in 1980. By contrast, voting turnout for those with high interest in the campaign has only declined from 88 percent in 1964 to 79 percent in 1980.

Declining sense of control over events as an influence on citizen behavior is grounded in beliefs about consequences. When the individual can see no connection between voting behavior and the consequences of that vote (the preferred candidate was elected, but the hoped-for policies were ignored), the linkage between voting behavior and policy outcomes in the individual's information network is eroded. Due to a lack of basis for beliefs about consequences in the network containing policy information, those schemata have a diminished influence on the voter's attitude toward the candidates. Unless a candidate with an established personal appeal (e.g., a Ronald Reagan) is available, no particular schemata will be activated to influence behavior, and probability of voting may decline.

Declining sense of control (percentage of citizens feeling alienation and powerlessness) has likewise been documented (Hill & Luttbeg,

1983). From 29 percent of respondents agreeing that they felt alienated and powerless in 1966, the figures rose to 60 percent in 1980. Some of that alienation may be attributable to the Iranian hostage crisis, as the figure was down to 56 percent by 1982. Nevertheless, the level of alienation and powerlessness far exceeds the 1966 level and presumably influences voter turnout and other forms of participatory citizenship.

Scope of Moral Consideration

The second dimension of citizenship, the scope of community or moral consideration, has evidently changed markedly as well during the past three decades. Whereas active citizen participation has showed signs of decline, the according of moral consideration to others has apparently expanded in a formal sense. Perhaps the single biggest change in the social fabric of American life during the past two decades has been the dismantling of the formal structure of segregration. Twenty years ago many black Americans in the South were effectively barred from voting by the system. Today more than a dozen major cities in the United States—including Los Angeles, Oakland, Philadelphia, Atlanta, and Detroit—have black mayors. The significance of this change for citizenship, among both whites and blacks, is that white citizens are increasingly willing to vote for black candidates for public office, demonstrated most recently by the degree of white support for a black candidate for mayor of New York. This would appear to be solid evidence that the beliefs of many white Americans about black Americans have changed.

The change in beliefs may be centered in beliefs about consequences. Practically every identifiably different ethnic group to join the mainstream of America was initially suspect. As long ago as the 1830s and 1840s, the tide of immigration from Ireland and Germany aroused fears among the established population of the time: The Irish were Catholic and would bring the power of the papacy into American life; the Germans spoke a different language and had different customs, which would pervert traditional American values. And so it was with each succeeding wave of immigrants.

The pronounced difference in the case of black Americans is that, while they have been in America for centuries, they were walled off by legal and de facto racial segregation. This effectively prevented mainstream America from becoming familiar with black America. In typically American fashion, that which was culturally unfamiliar was feared. Many Americans feared that integration of the races would lead to the corruption of American values; in more extreme cases, white America feared for its physical safety if black Americans were not kept apart by segregation.

As white and black America have mixed and each has become familiar with the other, white American beliefs about negative consequences of association with black Americans have diminished. What discrimination exists today is increasingly based on social class rather than race. This suggests that the belief structures or information schemata that incorporate black Americans make distinctions among different classes of black Americans. Of course, discrimination will not have disappeared until those information schemata only note skin color as an attribute of an individual person, rather than as an organizing principle. Only when black Americans are considered to be Americans who happen to be black will the potential for according full moral consideration, regardless of race, be realized.

Alternatively, the changes in beliefs about the latitude of community may be centered in normative beliefs. The institution of segregation created an environment that encouraged racially disparaging remarks, since one can always talk about people who aren't present. Such conversation influences behavior, because it fosters normative beliefs concerning black Americans. Irrespective of the personal beliefs of an individual concerning black Americans, the perception that others disapproved of association became a powerful influence on behavior.

Several changes in the past three decades can be directly implicated in the changes of beliefs concerning black Americans as a group. These include integration in schools and the workplace and the inclusion of black Americans in casting for television programming. Integration in schools and the workplace has afforded both black and white Americans the opportunity to appraise each others' strengths and weaknesses firsthand, and to come to know members of the other race on a personal basis. But, perhaps more important, it has reduced the opportunity for the bigot to disparage openly members of the other race, white or black. The impact on normative beliefs has been to legitimize, as influences on behavior, beliefs about what black or white Americans would think of racist comments, and to diminish the weight and legitimacy of normative beliefs grounded in bigotry.

Certainly such change is frame focused, so that white and black Americans in their family settings may still reinforce bigoted normative beliefs; but, even that frame may be changing, as black Americans are increasingly portrayed on television as multidimensional, real middle-class people (e.g., the "Cosby Show"). The entry of realistic, human portrayals of black Americans into the living rooms of white America has the potential to change forever the place of black Americans, as a group, in the frames that organize normative beliefs and channel their influence on behavior.

While patterns of citizenship beliefs have changed with regard to the dismantling of barriers to moral consideration of black Americans, a different pattern may be moving in the opposite direction. Americans may be becoming more class conscious, so that middle-class citizens increasingly withhold the accordance of moral consideration to lower-class Americans. This pattern is manifested in legislation that is clearly discriminatory on a class basis, and it indicates an increasing willingness of middle-class Americans to disregard the interests of the poor in their support of candidates and policies. This growing class consciousness cuts across races, so that many middle-class citizens, both white and black, support class-discriminatory policies. There is now a large and growing black middle class in mainstream America, and it is middle class first and black second. While this can be considered a success story, the failure is that the black lower class is cut off in the ghettos, stripped of role models of successful blacks (who have moved to the suburbs), and increasingly forgotten by both white and black America. As the people of poverty become invisible to mainstream America, they are, by default, no longer accorded moral consideration in the political life of the nation.

Role of Elected Officials

The third dimension of beliefs about citizenship is that of the proper role of elected representatives, and the relationship between the representatives and their constituents. The trend throughout American history has been toward a more pronounced expectation that elected representatives should concern themselves primarily with constituent service. In the past two decades, this trend has become formalized with the increased organization of special-interest groups and the proliferation of political action committees, or PAC's (Sabato, 1983). The increasing visibility of PAC's in one sense legitimizes them and makes the economic-marketplace view of politics a more pronounced normative influence. As more and more Americans are perceived to be pursuing their vested political interests through PAC's, the normative belief that "it's okay because everyone is doing it" overbalances public-interest citizenship as a normative influence on behavior. Once the political-spoils mentality has taken over the public consciousness, the belief in negative personal consequences of public-interest citizenship is reinforced, and a snowball effect ensues.

The increasing visibility of PAC's over the past decade parallels the increases in the number of PAC's and the amount of money they spend to influence Congress and the president. Between 1976 and 1983, the number of lobbyists registered with Congress nearly doubled, from 3,420 to 6,500; and between 1974 and 1984, the number of PAC's increased from 608 to 3,803 (Cormier, 1985). The money contributed by PAC's to congressional candidates, as a percentage of total campaign contributions, doubled between 1972 and 1982, from 14 percent to 28 percent (Cormier, 1985). The widespread increase in the use of media, particularly television, in conducting political campaigns has raised the costs of campaigning astronomically; as a result, the politician who does not accept PAC support and PAC influence does not return to Washington.

A glance back at the past three decades, then, reveals a gradual change in the electorate toward more passive citizenship, as evidenced by declining voter turnout and increasing feelings of alienation. These changes are probably manifestations of changes in the dynamics of beliefs about consequences of behavior. Those changes in turn are probably centered in the subjective probability that electoral behavior will lead to anticipated consequences; or they may be centered in the disorganization of policy schemata.

The parameters of community have changed, so that Americans seem less inclined to dismiss others from moral consideration on the basis of racial group identity; however, they may be more inclined to do so on the basis of social class. This shift may reflect a change in normative beliefs, so that it is now unacceptable in most social frames to express disparaging sentiments toward racial and ethnic groups. Over time, this change in social communication patterns has altered the way in which race is organized in schemata, with race becoming an attribute of individuals rather than individuals being exemplars of races. Along the way it has become increasingly acceptable to condescend toward lower-class people, and over time this has restructured social class as an element in schemata.

Americans are increasingly being subjected to pressures to treat the political arena as a marketplace where policy makers and policies can be bought and sold. This change probably operates through changes in both beliefs about consequences and normative beliefs. When everyone else is perceived as playing a competitive game, one either competes or one loses. This is obviously a belief about consequences, but it also reflects an enhanced valuation of a competitive rather than a cooperative frame. These trends, then, provide a foundation for projecting the direction of change in the 1990s.

CRITICAL ISSUES IN THE 1990s

Political Schemata

To understand critical issues in the 1990s it is necessary to understand political schemata as they are organized in the minds of Americans. The broadest organizational factor in considering individual differences in the schemata of the electorate is the distinction between schematics and aschematics. Individuals who have a well-elaborated structure in a domain (e.g., politics) would be labeled *schematics*; those with poorly elaborated or nonexistent structures in a domain are labeled *aschematics* (Markus, 1977).

Another crucial factor in understanding political schemata is the reality of multiple schemata for thinking about politics. Four major types of schemata dominate the political thought of Americans on the threshold of the 1990s. These are partisanship (Republican, Democrat, etc.), ideology (liberal, conservative, etc.), class (white collar, blue collar, etc.), and race/ethnicity (Hispanic, Asian, etc.) (Hamill & Lodge, 1986). In the previous section, evidence was cited to support the contention that racial schemata have declined in use but class schemata may be increasingly important. Declines in party identification suggest a decay of partisan schemata.

Cognitive algebraic theory suggests that people will use those schemata which have high probabilities of producing anticipated consequences in shaping their action (Fishbein & Ajzen, 1975). This would infer that the more highly developed the schema the more likely that it will dominate action. Ideological schemata are most closely identified with policy issues; thus, an understanding of the basis of the development of ideological schemata should throw some light on the prospects for citizen decision making on the basis of policy issues. Certainly active citizenship implies voting on the basis of informed decision making, and in democratic theory decision making centers on policy issues rather than the personality of candidates.

Some recent research has thrown light on the kinds of influences associated with the development of ideological schemata. A study by Hamill, Blake, Finkel, and Lodge (1984) found that cognitive ability, posited on the basis of education, vocabulary, and abstract ability, was highly related to ideological sophistication; and, to a marginal degree, that political experience, media usage, and political participation are related to ideological sophistication. The close relationship between ideological sophistication and cognitive ability suggests that the development of active citizen participation in decisions concerning policy choice is dependent on citizenship education and that political experience is no substitute for education in the development of ideological schemata and policy decision-making ability.

How, then, does the ideological aschematic participate? It has been speculated that, lacking ideological sophistication, citizens fall back on class and race schemata (Hamill, Lodge, & Blake, 1985). The obvious consequences for community in a politics based on race and/or class needs no discussion; yet this is the most ominous problem of citizenship in the present, given the dynamics of information dissemination in the late 1980s.

Television and the Political Process

The relationship of the citizen to the state in the United States began to change dramatically with the Kennedy–Nixon debates of 1960. During the ensuing 30 years the business of politics has been transformed by the media experts, so that today any candidate for political office on the national level must finance an expensive media campaign and plot campaign strategy to capitalize on the six o'clock news. Patterson (1980) observes that, in the 1976 presidential election campaign, 60 percent of news coverage was concerned with the "game" aspects of the campaign—focusing on who was winning, rather than on the issues and policy positions related to them. The presidential election of 1988 illustrates the ultimate refinement of the art of media politics, with the substantive issues effectively obscured, their place taken by sound bites selected for their emotional impact.

The intrusion of television into the political process was an inevitable outcome of changes in the American people. For many years newspaper circulation has not increased at the same rate as the population. In 1985, the *World Almanac* reported that less than 75 percent of U.S. homes received newspapers. When those data are combined with the newspaper-reading habits of Americans, it would appear that nearly half of those eligible to vote in elections cannot or do not get information about political choices from newspapers. Of course, the alternative source is television: 98 percent of U.S. homes had television in 1984 (*World Almanac*, 1985). Television viewing increased by an average of 22 percent between 1965 and 1981 (*Information Please Almanac*, 1983). America is wedded to television, and the politicians are naturally going to use whatever medium reaches the most people.

The transformation of the political process at the hands of the media industry is problematic because of the constraints the visual media place on the dissemination of information. It is probably not a meaningless observation that the attention to politics in the media shows little causal relationship to ideological sophistication (Hamill & Lodge, 1986). Television as a source of political information is inadequate for developing ideological schemata, because the expectation for constantly changing visual and auditory images on the part of the television viewers precludes serious, in-depth development of the information structures necessary for ideological schemata development. On the other hand, the impressionistic information from which race and class schemata can be constructed are well adapted to the television medium.

The argument here is not that television is inadequate as an information source on politics for all citizens. For citizens with well-developed ideological schemata, quite conceivably impressionistic information can be quickly processed to generate appropriate affective responses (Lau, 1986). This affective response in turn would influence the intention to act. What is problematic for citizenship is the inadequacy of television-based information for citizens with undeveloped ideological schemata. Rather than building sophisticated ideological schemata, television tends to erode them. If such deterioration is allowed to continue on a mass scale, it is reasonable to anticipate a further decline in participation and an increase in alienation, unless demagogues emerge to capitalize on the vulnerability of the electorate to appeals to their race and class schemata. In the latter case it should be anticipated that the scope-of-community dimension would certainly show a decline, with citizens excluding one another from moral consideration on the basis of race and class. The lessons of history should not be lost on Americans. A mere half-century ago the holocaust in Germany resulted from just such a psychodynamic.

One other problem of television for citizenship concerns the manipulation of schemata by television. The individual's readiness to use a schema is determined by a variety of factors, including expectations, goals, values, needs, and frequency of use (Higgins & King, 1981). Campaign media experts know at least as much as the social psychologists about the effective cueing of desired schemata. Thus, to an increasing extent, the American public may become victims of manipulation by the media experts.

The final problem posed by television for the practice of citizenship has already been alluded to. The cost of campaigning increasingly makes candidates dependent upon PAC's for campaign financing, with the effect of skewing citizenship toward politics as an economic marketplace. As there is no reason to believe that the costs of campaigning will go down, so there is no reason to believe that pressures on individual citizens to use political activity to protect their personal rather than the community interests will diminish. If developments continue on their present course, we may be headed into a future of decidedly uncivil politics.

AN AGENDA FOR CITIZENSHIP DEVELOPMENT

An agenda for the development of citizenship in the United States must address the three dimensions of citizenship that were discussed earlier in this chapter. Thus, the following recommendations are made:

1. The means for increasing active participation based on ideological sophistication must be developed,
2. The means for expanding the range of citizens accorded moral consideration must be identified and developed,
3. The means for reducing the pressure on citizens to accept the norms of politics as marketplace must be found.

Some of these agenda items can be addressed by traditional formal education programs; some require more experiential learning; and some require programs for the development of thinking.

Increasing Active Participation

Active participation can mean voting, or it can mean active involvement in political campaigns to help elect someone else. Learning how to vote intelligently on the basis of policy alternatives requires the development of ideological schemata. Future citizens need to acquire and understand political terminology, so they can link concepts into networks of meanings that enable them to understand the implications of political messages they receive via television. Educational programs designed to carry out this goal probably should include the analysis of videotapes used to transmit political messages in previous elections, so that the learners become more accustomed to reflecting on the particular influence techniques used by media experts. This is very similar to recommendations for teaching critical thinking, but with the difference that this instruction would be context specific. By focusing on the particular kind of content about which citizens need to think critically, and by exploring it in the frame in which citizens normally are confronted with the need for critical thinking, normative beliefs about constructive critical thinking concerning political messages can be reinforced.

Such a program runs the risk of generating political cynicism, unless it is handled carefully. Used as a basis for considering the impact of advocated policies on different groups, the tapes might sensitize future citizens to the full range of human costs behind any policy, thereby encouraging the building of support for normative beliefs relevant to a broad range of classes and groups.

These educational programs, however, cannot begin with the analysis of videotapes of political messages and policy statements. A foundation of information must first be developed and integrated into schemata that represent in some approximate fashion the way the real socioeconomic world works. Understanding of economic interdependence should precede analysis of policy alternatives, and a solid foundation in geography should precede attempts to develop the schemata for economic interdependence.

The method for developing these schemata should follow the basic principles for the development of thinking processes, so that the verbal/symbolic contents of schemata are linked in turn to visual/spatial representations of real-world phenomena. Brandhorst's (1984) simile model of thinking-process development is one of several incorporating these basic principles (also see Holley & Dansereau, 1984).

Active participation beyond voting requires more than information. Citizens generally develop participation skills in small quasi- or nonpolitical social groups. The range of social skills that underlies successful participation skills is generally acquired more easily in informal groups (Rathjen & Foreyt, 1980). The need for participation skills is underlined by some of the current research. For example, a study of energy conservation behavior concluded that the most effective influence processes are those that emphasize vivid, concrete, and highly personalized information (Costanzo, Archer, Aronson, & Pettigrew, 1986). The setting (frame) in which information is received seems to be as important as the way in which information is processed. In short, people are much more subject to influence from people they know, in face-to-face contact, than they are to media appeals. Efforts to equip future citizens better for small-group participation via training in social skills will enhance their capacity to develop alternatives to television political advertising as their sources of information and influence. Current efforts to foster cooperative learning in the schools are a natural context for social-skills training.

Expanding the Scope of Moral Consideration

Americans have always been a basically justice-oriented people. The denial of moral consideration to others in the political process may be more a function of the invisibility of the victim than the pursuit of purely selfish interest. The key to expanding the scope of moral consideration in the political process lies in putting a human face on poverty. Visual media dramas that depict the human costs of poverty in a classroom context can force future citizens to face the true costs of public policies. The challenge to teachers is to construct curricula that juxtapose policy issues with dramatic portrayals of the victims of those policies. By conducting these kinds of educational efforts in a classroom, the teacher can control the normative beliefs that are attached to schemata and prevent the development of a cynical frame. Recent research in social psychology suggests that many people resolve social dilemmas on empathic, moral, and group-egoistic grounds. It remains for teachers to tap the natural inclination toward justice latent in their students.

Countering the Pursuit of Narrow Self-interest

The cornerstone of this problem for citizenship is the growth of PAC's and their dominance of campaign financing. The study of social psychology as a discipline, with a focus on advertising, media impact, and propaganda techniques, might serve as an immunization to neutralize their effects. As adolescents become sensitive to the way that they can be manipulated, the competence motive may generate a reaction against such techniques. If public susceptibility to media advertising were reduced, the dependence of candidates on PAC money would be reduced, thereby freeing them from PAC control.

Working to reduce the effective power of PAC's, however, is only half of the problem. The other half lies in developing positive norms toward the society as a community, through the fostering of altruistic and group-egoistic motives. A recent study by Kramer and Brewer (1984) is informative here. In it, individuals were found to be more likely to exercise personal restraint in their use of an endangered common resource when a superordinate group identity was made salient. It is possible that individuals with a superordinate identity are willing to compensate for the selfish and destructive acts of others, as long as they are not alone in so doing. Creating such a superordinate identity was long one of the cornerstones of the study of history in the schools. Heroic literature in the curriculum has traditionally served this purpose in the United States, and it continues to do so in most nations of the world today. Such heroic literature does not have to emphasize wars, but can center on the heroic struggle of humankind against many kinds of adversity.

From this perspective, social studies programs in elementary schools best serve the cause of community when they mythologize great acts of citizenship, courage, and sacrifice in the past, thereby generating empathic identification with the community. By thus creating positive norms toward the community, a basis for public-spirited citizen action is created.

Social psychology has much to offer the study of citizenship. As some of the promising lines of inquiry in the area of information processing theory are explored, social psychology should shed much more light on the problems of insuring a fuller capacity for participation to all Americans.

REFERENCES

Banfield, E. C. (1958). *The moral basis of a backward society*. New York: Free Press.

Brandhorst, A. R. (1984). *The simile model of thinking skill development: Theory and practice*. Washington, DC: National Council for the Social Studies Convention. (ERIC Document Reproduction Service No. ED 251 347)

Brandhorst, A. R. (1988). An information processing model for the design of instruction on foreign policy issues. *Social Science Record, 25*(2), 42–45.

Coke, J. S., Batson, C. D., & McDavis, K. (1978). Empathic mediation of helping: A two stage model. *Journal of Personality and Social Psychology, 36*, 752–766.

Cormier, F. (1985). Lobbying the lawmakers. In R. O. Zeleny (Ed.), *The 1985 world book yearbook* (pp. 145–157). Chicago: World Book.

Costanzo, M., Archer, D., Aronson, E., & Pettigrew, T. (1986). Energy conservation behavior: The difficult path from information to action. *American Psychologist, 41*, 521–528.

Dahl, R. A. (1961). *Who governs?* New Haven, CT: Yale University Press.

Fishbein, M., & Ajzen, I. (1975). *Beliefs, attitudes, intentions and behaviors: An introduction to theory and research*. Reading, MA: Addison-Wesley.

Goffman, E. (1974). *Frame analysis*. Cambridge: Harvard University Press.

Goleman, D. (1985). *Vital lies, simple truths: The psychology of self-deception*. New York: Simon & Schuster.

Hamill, R., Blake, R., Finkel, S., & Lodge, M. (1984). *A cognitive model of ideological sophistication and attitude constraint*. Paper presented at the annual meeting of the American Political Science Association, Washington, DC.

Hamill, R., & Lodge, M. (1986). Cognitive consequences of political sophistication. In R. R. Lau & D. O. Sears (Eds.), *Political cognition* (pp. 69–93). Hillsdale, NJ: Lawrence Erlbaum.

Hamill, R., Lodge, M., & Blake, F. (1985). *The breadth, depth, and utility of political schemas*. Paper presented at the annual meeting of the Midwest Political Science Association, Chicago.

Higgins, E. T., & King, G. (1981). Accessibility of social constructs: Information processing consequences of individual and contextual variability. In N.

Cantor & J. F. Kihlstrom (Eds.), *Personality, cognition, and social interaction* (pp. 69–122). Hillsdale, NJ: Lawrence Erlbaum.

Hill, D. B., & Luttbeg, N. R. (1983). *Trends in American electoral behavior* (2nd ed.). Itaska, IL: F. E. Peacock.

Holley, C. D., & Dansereau, D. F. (Eds.). (1984). *Spatial learning strategies: Techniques, applications, and related issues.* Orlando, FL: Academic Press.

Information please almanac. (1983). New York: A. & W.

Kahle, L. R., & Beatty, S. E. (1987). Cognitive consequences of legislating post purchase behavior: Growing up with the bottle bill. *Journal of Applied Social Psychology, 17,* 828–843.

Kramer, R. M., & Brewer, M. B. (1984). Effects of group identity on resource use in a simulated commons dilemma. *Journal of Personality and Social Psychology, 46,* 1044–1057.

Krebs, D. (1975). Empathy and altruism. *Journal of Personality and Social Psychology, 32,* 1134–1146.

Lau, R. (1986). Political schemata, candidate evaluations, and voting behavior. In R. Lau & D. Sears (Eds.), *Political cognition* (pp. 94–109). Hillsdale, NJ: Lawrence Erlbaum.

Leming, J. (1989). The two cultures of social studies education. *Social Education, 53,* 404–408.

Markus, H. (1977). Self-schemata and processing information about the self. *Journal of Personality and Social Psychology, 35,* 63–78.

Oliner, P. (1983). Putting community into citizenship education: The need for prosociality. *Theory and Research in Social Education, 11*(2), 65–81.

Patterson, T. (1980). *The mass media election.* New York: Praeger.

Rapoport, A. (1988). Provision of step-level public goods: Effects of inequality of resources. *Journal of Personality and Social Psychology, 54,* 432–440.

Rasinski, K. A., & Rosenbaum, S. (1987). Predicting citizen support of tax increases for education: A comparison of two social psychological perspectives. *Journal of Applied Social Psychology, 17,* 990–1006.

Rathjen, D. P., & Foreyt, J. (Eds.). (1980). *Social competence: Interventions for children and adults.* New York: Pergamon.

Sabato, L. (1983). Parties, PACs, and independent groups. In T. E. Mann & N. J. Ornstein (Eds.), *The American elections of 1982* (pp. 72–110). Washington, DC: American Enterprise Institute for Public Policy Research.

Schwartz, S. H. (1968). Words, deeds and the perception of consequences and responsibilities in action situations. *Journal of Personality and Social Psychology, 10,* 232–242.

Schwartz, S. H. (1973). Normative explanations of helping behavior: A critique, proposal and empirical test. *Journal of Experimental Social Psychology, 9,* 349–364.

Schwartz, S. H., & Tessler, R. C. (1972). A test of a model for reducing measured attitude–behavior discrepancies. *Journal of Personality and Social Psychology, 24,* 225–236.

Simon, H. A. (1957). *Models of man: Social and rational.* New York: John Wiley.

World Almanac. (1985). New York: Author.

8 The Anthropological Perspective

Anthropological Insights for Civic Education

JOHN H. CHILCOTT

TRIBAL SOCIETIES AND NATION STATES: AN EVOLUTIONARY PERSPECTIVE

Anthropology is unique among the social sciences in that its holistic, naturalistic study of the human condition provides a broad-based perspective on reality. The traditional comparative analysis of anthropology, wherein a similar social phenomenon or social process is examined across cultures, provides an objective description or "mirror" with which one can better understand one's own culture. There is much to be learned by comparing a tribal society with that of an industrial society such as the United States, with regard to the social phenomena of the citizenries and the social processes of citizenship education.

Basis for Membership

To begin with, the basis for membership in a tribal society is kinship. One is related to other members of the society, and often great care is exercised in specifically delineating these kinship relationships. With each kinship relationship there are prescribed behaviors that dictate the social relationships, and following behavioral prescriptions constitutes good citizenship within the tribal group. To become a citizen of a tribal society, an outsider must either marry into the group or be provided with a "fictive kin," much in the same manner that we in our society incorporate a good friend as a member of the family by referring to them as "Aunt Mary" or "Uncle Bill" to our children. In the tribal world, kinship and citizenship are equated.

With the rise of agricultural nation–states and, more recently, modern industrial states, kinship was replaced with other mechanisms of social integration. The state created a legal code for determining citizenship among the large number of diverse social units incorporated within the nation's boundaries, as well as to regulate commerce. In these nations one could lose one's citizenship by committing crimes against the state and, in some instances, crimes that disrupted commerce. Groups of people who were considered inferior were often not allowed citizenship status, as was the case with Afro-Americans, Native Americans, and women in the United States, until relatively recently. These qualitative differences in defining citizenship between tribal societies and nation-states suggest, as well, qualitative differences in citizenship education within the two types of societies.

Citizenship Education

Since there are no formal schools in tribal societies, the major responsibility for citizenship education lies with the extended family, although this does not mean that other nonfamily members of the society are not also included. One feature of citizenship education in a tribal society is that there is general consensus within the tribe as to what constitutes a good citizen. Thus, a Hopi mother living in a traditional village in northern Arizona can admonish her misbehaving child with the adage, "That is not Hopi!" Everyone in the village knows what being a "good Hopi" signifies. With this consensus, all members of the village can participate in the citizenship socialization of the children, even though they might not be close kin. The village as a whole reinforces the attempts of the family to produce a good citizen.

Not only are all members of the tribal society participants in citizenship education, but the total enculturation process is involved, including storytelling, observation of exemplars, and, later, participation in ceremonies as a youth. This multidimensional socialization process, with a central focus on citizenship, can provide considerable conformity to a society that uses customary law as a means of social control.

With the rise of large nation-states, which incorporated into their societies nonkin, outsiders, and conquered peoples, the school, with its specialists in citizenship education, became a major mechanism for political socialization. In the Inca empire, for example, the children of the nobility of the conquered city-states were sent to Cuzco to be educated in the Inca language (Quechua), religion, and government. The Soviet Union has applied the same principle today through creating schools that teach Russian language, communist ideology and government, and modern technology to the millions of "conquered" nationalities and tribal peoples within the boundaries of the Soviet Union. In these totalitarian states, teaching citizenship is made easier by securing a consensus regarding the expectations for citizenship education, at least among the ruling elite and the bureaucrats.

CITIZENSHIP AND CITIZENSHIP EDUCATION IN THE UNITED STATES

By contrast, political socialization in the United States is characterized by a lack of consensus as to its goals. (The exception to this might be the citizenship classes that are conducted for new immigrants who wish to pass an examination to qualify for citizenship.) This author reached this conclusion after examining the "artifacts" of citizenship education in a local social studies school resource center. These included social studies periodicals, monographs, textbooks, catalogues, and curriculum guides. (These are listed separately at the end of the bibliography.) Some examples that illustrate this lack of consensus, drawn from my sampling, follow:

> We may disagree about exactly how to do it, who is responsible for it, or how to assess it. Yet few readers would seriously question that citizenship education still lies somewhere at the core of social studies. ["Civic Intelligence," 1985, p. 670]

> Despite widespread agreement as to its centrality and importance to social studies, however, there is little agreement about the meaning of citizenship, the nature of the citizen role, or the major focus of citizenship education efforts. [Morrisett, 1982, p. 119]

Citizenship Defined

It was interesting to note, in my artifact analysis, that the words *citizen* and *citizenship* were not included in any of the glossaries of the textbooks I reviewed. From this one might conclude that there is no standard definition of *citizen* or *citizenship* that is acceptable to teachers. One might also conclude that each teacher would define *good citizen* in a personal, idiosyncratic fashion. When one compares this with the standardized Hopi definition, one can begin to understand why there is no agreement as to the goals and content of citizenship education among social studies educators.

The textbook publishers, for their part, appear to have made a decision as to the appropriate content of citizenship instruction, as an analysis of the contents of the textbooks turned up such common topics as the presidency; the U.S. Constitution; the Bill of Rights; federal, state and local government; the court system; and free enterprise.

School curriculum guides, even though they differ from one school to another, may also provide a good source for what is considered proper content for citizenship education:

> During the eighth grade the social studies program will strive to lay the basic foundation of effective citizenship in American democracy through the study of the development and implementation of our system of government. The documents, institutions, and ideals of our society will be examined as they have changed to meet the needs of our citizens in the interdependent world of today. ["Curriculum Guide," 1985, p. 1]

This statement would suggest that one of the reasons that citizenship education is lacking in consensus is that, in a rapidly changing society such as ours, the role of the citizen is likewise changing. In the tribal world the role of citizen was based on tradition, rather than change and a future orientation.

Brown (1977) suggests that, since modern states are pluralistic, it is understandable that there is no agreement on goals and methods in citizenship education. An anthropologist might disagree, as it would appear that the major function of the state schools would be to develop some level of agreement among the pluralistic factions as to the type of political institutions and political behaviors that are best for the majority of the population. Therefore the need is to provide a degree of conformity that could incorporate the society's many social and political units. In a developing nation these oftentimes include a common national language, the development of an allegiance to the state rather than the local tribe or village, a legal code that legitimizes actions taken toward integration of these local social units into a common political institution, and an army to enforce the legal code.

With the exception of Native Americans, ethnic plurality in the United States is a result of immigration rather than conquest. As a consequence, the integrating forces that serve as common bonding for the cultural and political segments of society consist of English as a common language, a pride in being an American, the U.S. Constitution, patriotic symbols and culture heroes, and a common belief in equality and "American" democracy.

Global Citizenship Education

When I examined the documents on citizenship in the global community, the matter of goals and methods became even more confusing. It would appear that at one time the social studies programs in the

United States emphasized a global conflict between world communism and capitalism. More recently it seems that this focus has been replaced with the notion of interdependence, or what the anthropologist refers to as a "world paradigm." This is especially true with reference to peace, economic, and environmental issues, such as the growing economic inequality, world hunger, pollution, the proliferation of nuclear weapons, and the use of the world's oceans (Brown, 1977; Patrick & Remy, 1986).

Other statements on global education were very vague on its operationalization:

> To prepare students to be humane, rational citizens, in a global context, that is our mission as social studies teachers. [Hepburn, 1983, p. vii]

> Think globally while acting locally. [Parker & Jorlinmek, 1984, p. 1]

> [To prepare] citizens who can capitalize on the world's resources and accumulated wisdom in making cooperative attacks on shared problems of people everywhere. [Parker & Jorlinmek, 1984, p. 2]

One of the questions on the Gallup Citizenship Test (Brown, 1977, p. 215) was particularly intriguing: "Where is Angola?" How would the person who constructed this test item explain how it measured the understanding of global citizenship?

This evolutionary and comparative approach to understanding citizenship education in the United States would suggest that current definitions of citizenship are obscure when compared to the understanding of most tribal definitions. The lack of consensus as to what constitutes "good citizenship" at the national and international levels may be one of the major problems facing educators in a pluralistic society.

FIVE ANTHROPOLOGICAL THEORIES OF CULTURE

Over the course of its history, the discipline of anthropology has devised several perspectives on examining culture. The following five anthropological perspectives were deemed useful by the author in examining citizenship education in the United States. Other anthropologists may have selected other perspectives or used only a single perspective.

Citizenship Education from a Functionalist Perspective

A common perspective often used by sociologists and anthropologists in analyzing societies is that of functionalism. A functionalist perspective on the form, function, and meaning of citizenship education in the United States would have to conclude, as did Malinowski (1922), that it is amorphous, except perhaps for the content of the social studies textbooks. The variety of definitions of citizenship is shown in the following examples:

> Defined by the 14th Amendment to the Constitution. [Parker & Jorlinmek, 1984, p. 6]

> Social studies includes the teaching of political skills, syndetic skills, social causation, negotiation, leadership, and ways to overcome the shortcomings of society. [Brown, 1977, pp. 37–45]

> The rights, duties, and responsibilities of citizenship. [Patrick & Remy, 1986, p. 5]

> Citizenship skills include how to influence people and how to make decisions. [Social Studies School Service, 1986, p. 7]

> All the courses in the school should be considered as part of citizenship education: English, Mathematics, Science, Humanities, and Social Studies. [Parker & Jorlinmek, 1984, p. 7]

The form of citizenship education also varies, from formal courses such as American government and history to a "process approach" in the development of a democratic classroom. In a similar fashion, the function of citizenship education is highly variable:

> To teach the ideals of American democracy. [Post & Johnson, 1983, p. 8]

> To develop patriotic loyal citizens. [Patrick & Remy, 1986, p. 7]

> The democratic citizen is an informed person, skilled in the processes of a free society, who is committed to democratic values and is able, and feels obliged, to participate in social, political, and economic processes. [Parker & Jorlinmek, 1984, p. 7]

The meaning of citizenship education in the United States appears to be related to the ideology that, if the U.S. style of participatory democracy is to survive, it requires an educated citizenry, in terms of literacy; knowledge of U.S. history and government; and a value orientation based on equality, altruism, and citizen responsibility. To what degree are these goals being taught by the schools? In a tribal society, if the goals of socialization are not reached, then the society does not survive as constituted. Unfortunately there are no ethnographic studies of social studies classrooms that focus on citizenship education with an eye toward assessing success with either the process or goals of the pro-

gram. Such a study could also describe any covert function of citizenship education, or what educators sometimes refer to as the "hidden
curriculum." Some authors suggest that citizenship education is in fact
dysfunctional. Spring (1976), for example, describes the school as a
"sorting machine" that classifies youth into adult social categories.
McDermott (1974) describes the school as a mechanism for achieving
failure. Further study is needed to determine if these allegations are
true of citizenship education.

Citizenship Education
from a Structural/Functionalist Perspective

The following question appeared on the Gallup Citizenship Test
(Brown, 1977): "Who was the Democratic candidate for President in
1972?" The question that needs asking here is, what is the purpose
(function) of this question? What is the concept of citizenship education
being tested here?

Using a structural/functionalist perspective (Radcliffe-Brown, 1952)
of citizenship education, the anthropologist would investigate the degree
to which the citizenship education program contributes to student and
school governance. One document that I reviewed suggests that the best
way to teach citizenship is through a democratic classroom and school.
Although Horace Mann at one time objected to political discussions in
the school, describing them as dangerous (Butts, 1977), they have now
become rather common in social studies classrooms. Are there also
political discussions in science, English, language, math, and vocational
education classes? Kluckhohn (1949) has described the school curriculum as a formal English garden, each course separated by a high hedge
from the other courses. To what degree is the citizenship education
program structured into the whole curriculum and the operation of the
school? To what degree is it structured into the reality of politics in the
United States?

Citizenship Education
from a Structuralist Perspective

This question appeared on the Gallup Citizenship Test (Brown,
1977): "Does a person who cannot read or write have a right to vote?" If
this item is taken literally, it would suggest that citizenship education
should be a part of the total curriculum, included in learning to read and
write. To what degree is literacy a component of the ritual of voting?

An anthropologist using a structuralist perspective of citizenship
education (see Levi-Strauss, 1966) would examine the myth that citizen-

ship education produces good citizens; that, if students participate successfully or appropriately in the rituals performed on them by the high priests (social studies teachers), they will ultimately become good citizens. There appears to be great faith in this myth on the part of the writers of most social studies documents. By examining this myth through the perspective of a structuralist, one could conclude that society is structured into good and bad citizens, based on the criteria suggested in the citizenship program. Further, failures in society could be attributed to bad citizens, just as tribal members might blame adversity on the dissatisfaction of their ancestors with the rituals performed in their honor. Good citizens and, apparently, good social studies teachers believe in the myth that, if the "bad citizens" (people who do not vote) would behave properly, then the abuses of big government could be eliminated. Is this any more of a myth than that displeased spirits of the ancestors cause adversity? In this sense "voting" can be viewed as ritual behavior that results in eliminating the "evil" within the society.

It is not necessary to dispel this myth, as myths provide important symbols to society, upon which individuals base their behavior. The myth of citizenship education is necessary for social studies educators to continue their efforts on behalf of the state. However, a structuralist analysis of the myths is propagated in a citizenship education program can be instrumental in raising the consciousness level of the social studies teacher. For example, consider this question, which appeared on the Gallup Citizenship Test (Brown, 1977): "Describe the contributions of George Wallace as a world figure." One might ask, Are George Wallace's contributions to the nation and the world a myth? If his contributions to society represent a benefit, what were the bad features of society which his contributions surmounted? This sort of questioning is important to creating informed citizens.

Citizenship Education
from a Cultural/Ecological Perspective

An anthropologist using a cultural/ecological approach (see Netting, 1977) would be interested in how citizenship education is used to solve societal problems, in order for the society to survive. One feature of this approach would be an analysis of the use of power. In tribal societies, who has what power and on what basis, and how is it rationalized among the population so as to sustain itself? In most cases, tribal power accrues to an individual with a charismatic personality or a particular skill that proves useful to the group during a period of crisis, such as disease, warfare, or a family quarrel. The Hawaiian chief possessed his power through "mana," an ethereal substance inherited from his ancestors and sustained through offerings of food to his gods. Both the Inca ruler and the French king convinced the people that he was the sun god.

In the United States and in the global community, who has what power and on what basis, how is that power sustained, and how does it contribute to our survival? How does the global community solve the problem of distribution of scarce resources? Within the social studies textbooks I examined were explanations of the power of the president, the power of Congress, and the power of the Supreme Court, but there was no discussion of individual and institutional power in any of the documents analyzed. This does not mean that there are no citizenship education documents existing that address this topic, but those in the sample did not. As recommended in one, "Citizenship education needs to be expanded beyond government and economics" (Brown, 1977, p. 214).

Consider this question from the Gallup Citizenship Test (Brown, 1977): "Who is the Chief Justice of the Supreme Court?" Using a cultural/ecological perspective, the question would be reconstituted to raise such questions as, "Why can this person be classified as a 'powerful person'?" "On what basis?" and "What is the ideology associated with the Chief Justice of the Supreme Court that sustains that individual's power?"

Citizenship Education from a Symbolic/Interactionist Perspective

Using a symbolic/interactionist approach (see Turner, 1967) to the study of citizenship education, the anthropologist would be interested in the manner in which the symbols of citizenship are interpreted by the teachers and students. Symbols such as the American flag, the U.S. Constitution, and the White House would be interpreted in terms of three analytical frameworks: an exegetic frame (emic) supplied by the participants in the classroom, an operational frame that describes the use of the symbol in the classroom, and a positional frame that focuses on the relationship of the symbol to other symbols within the school system.

CONCLUSION

In this chapter I provide several ways to look at citizenship education, based upon five anthropological theories of culture. These are extremely conjectural and may in some instances be value laden, but they are an attempt to determine if anthropology has anything to contribute to citizenship education. This chapter suggests that the cultural diversity within a pluralistic society creates an amorphous condition for citizenship education, but that the continuous attempts to reduce the vagueness produces a form of dynamism that has high survival value in a rapidly changing society. The chapter also suggests that social studies educators need to move from the myth to the reality of citizenship education, through more naturalistic research. As an individual moves from membership in a tribal society to membership in a modern state and a global community, that individual's relationship to the state is altered dramatically. Citizenship education needs to take this new relationship into account.

This relationship between citizen and state requires a well-defined listing of behavioral descriptors of good citizenship, whether they be defined by a legal code or by customary law. The behavior of good citizens is often defined in terms of ideals (the ideal culture) rather than in terms of reality (the real culture). Members of certain ethnic and/or lower-class groups might react differently to a highly idealized citizenship program.

If the school as an agent of the government has assumed the major responsibility for political socialization, then the school should be a locale where citizenship behavior can be enacted. Some schools provide such opportunities as role playing, simulation, mock trials, school newspapers, elections, letters to the local newspapers, appearances on local TV stations, debates, and protest activities, in an attempt to encourage future political participation.

It has also been suggested that, from the point of view of an anthropologist, another major problem of U.S. citizenship education in the school and in society is the undefined role of the nonparticipant. In tribal society, all the people participate to some degree in the affairs of the family and society. In the U.S., a participatory democracy, are nonparticipants good citizens? Such a question requires not only speculation on what constitutes good citizenship, but further research as to whether or not nonparticipation is affecting the survival of the nation. It challenges the very premise of citizenship in a participatory democracy.

REFERENCES

Butts, R. F. (1977). Historical perspectives on civic education in the United States. In B. F. Brown (Ed.), *Education for responsible citizenship* (pp. 47–68). New York: McGraw-Hill.

Kluckhohn, C. (1949). *Mirror for man.* New York: Whittlesey House.

Levi-Strauss, C. (1966). *The savage mind.* Chicago: University of Chicago Press.

Malinowski, B. (1922). *Argonauts of the Western Pacific.* London: Routledge and Kegan.

McDermott, R. P. (1974). Achieving school failure: An anthropological approach to illiteracy and social stratification. In G. D. Spindler (Ed.), *Education and cultural process* (pp. 82–113). New York: Holt, Rinehart and Winston.

Netting, R. (1977). *Cultural ecology.* Menlo Park, CA: Benjamin-Cummings.

Radcliffe-Brown, A. R. (1952). *Structure and function in primitive society.* Glencoe, IL: Free Press.

Spring, J. (1976). *The sorting machine.* New York: McKay.

Turner, V. W. (1967). *The forest of symbols.* Ithaca: Cornell University Press.

SOURCES USED AS DATA FOR THE "ARTIFACT" ANALYSIS

Brown, F. B. (1977). *Education for responsible citizenship.* New York: McGraw-Hill.

Civic intelligence: A provocative approach to citizenship education. (1985). *Social Education, 49,* 670.

Curriculum guide for American government and history: Grade 8. (1985). Tucson: Orange Grove Junior High School.

Hepburn, M. A. (Ed.) (1983). *Democratic education in schools and classrooms* (National Council for the Social Studies Bulletin No. 70). Washington, DC: NCSS.

Morrisett, I. (Ed.). (1982). *Social studies in the 1980's.* Alexandria, VA: Association for Supervision and Curriculum Development.

Parker, W., & Jarolimek, J. (1984). *Citizenship and the critical role of the social studies* (National Council for the Social Studies Bulletin No. 72). Boulder, CO: Social Science Education Consortium.

Patrick, J., & Remy, R. (1986). *Civics for Americans* (2nd ed.). New York: Scott, Foresman.

Post, A., & Johnson, W. (1983). *The young American citizen.* Boston, MA: Sadlier-Oxford.

Rakes, T. A., DeCaprio, A., & Randolph, J. (1985). *Citizens today* (rev. ed.). New York: Steck-Vaughan.

Social Studies School Service. (1986). *Catalog.* Culver City, CA: Author.

Stacy, D. (1985). *Arizona: Government and citizenship.* Phoenix: Arizona State Department of Education.

Suter, C., & Croddy, M. (1984). *The crime question: Rights and responsibilities of citizens.* Los Angeles, CA: Constitutional Rights Foundation.

9 The Philosophical Perspective

The Role of Philosophy in the Education of Democratic Citizens

H. MICHAEL HARTOONIAN

> Why should there not be a patient confidence in the ultimate justice of the people? Is there any better or equal hope in the world? Is there any greater wisdom?
>
> > —Abraham Lincoln
> > First Inaugural Address
> > March 4, 1861

Lincoln's confidence in the people and in their ability to administer civic justice with some degree of wisdom suggests an interesting tension between the public and private lives of individuals. Exploring this tension is at the heart of any study of education for citizenship. Such a study is also driven by a philosophical framework that might suggest such questions as

- Who should be a citizen? Why?
- Who should rule? Why?
- What must I give up in order to become a member of the community?
- Must my personal identity be tied to my society?
- As a citizen, what obligations and rights do I have?
- Can there be justice for all? How?
- Is happiness a function of service to others?

DEFINITIONAL ISSUES:
PHILOSOPHY AND EDUCATION

Philosophy in its broadest sense means the pursuit of wisdom. For our purposes here, wisdom may be defined as an organic application of information, knowledge, and imagination to human dilemmas, desires, and dreams. Wisdom ties us to our cultural heritage and gives us the ability to find and build the moral framework upon which human life is defined and within which meaning resides. The patterns of life, constructed upon this framework, are manifested in the motivating concepts of our culture—concepts such as justice, love, courage, and beauty. Further, wisdom helps us destroy those areas of ignorance most dangerous to human life and spirit, such as arrogance, certainty, and loneliness.

The reflective process of intellectual growth that helps us discover and overcome our own ignorance is called education (Dewey, 1916), and within the democratic conception of society the purpose of education is, above all, the development of the enlightened citizen (Barth & Shermis, 1980; Hartoonian & Laughlin, 1989; Hunt & Metcalf, 1968; Shaver, 1980a, b). Thus, the citizen of a free republic must be educated in the art of reflective or philosophical thought.

CITIZENSHIP DEFINED
THROUGH LOVE, CRITICISM, AND MEANING

The argument is advanced here that the essence of philosophy and citizenship is found in the habit of love, the knowledge and practice of criticism, and the search for meaning. The knowledge, skills, and dispositions that are necessary for holding the office of citizen are found in these fundamental themes of philosophy. The citizenry are further seen as constituting the fourth branch of the government, along with the legislative, executive, and judicial branches. The quality of the first three branches of government is dependent upon the quality of the fourth, and that quality is defined in the attributes of love, criticism, and meaning.

To begin, then, we must understand that love, criticism, and meaning are parts of the same whole. Each of the three ideas defines itself in terms of the others. The notion is not unlike the trilogy advanced by Plato in regard to the concept of justice. In the dialogue between Meno and Socrates (e.g., Jowett, 1937), Socrates defines justice in terms of temperance and courage. He asserts that an understanding of justice is possible only within the context of temperance and courage; that to be just is to be courageous and temperate; that to be courageous is to be just and temperate; and so on. The defining qualities of one value are held within the other values. This notion of defining one value in terms of other values holds for the qualities of citizenship as well as for the elements developed within the discipline of philosophy (see any edition of Aristotle's *Nicomachean Ethics* and Plato's *Republic*, and their other works). If we address the three themes of love, criticism, and meaning as an inclusive set that defines the necessary attributes of citizenship, we can better understand the significant concepts and issues that tie together philosophy and citizenship. It should be understood that, in the following discussion, philosophy is seen as a human creation, tied to the contexts of time, place, will, and chance.

The Habit of Love

Let us begin our journey into philosophy and citizenship through the theme of love. Montesquieu, writing in *Spirit of Laws* (1977), stated, "A government is like everything else; to preserve it, we must love it" (p. 31). Within Western thought, the ancient Greeks provided us with language that exercised great influence on the modes of expression and discourse associated with the concept of love. The Greeks had many words for love, which relates to its importance in Greek life. From friendship (*philia*) to passion (*eros*) to high affection (*agape*), the Greeks—from Heraclitus in the sixth century B.C. to Empedocles in the fifth century B.C.—established love as *the* physical principle (unifying agent) of the universe. Heraclitus believed that there were two forces in nature—*repulsion* and *attraction*—and he suggested that love (*harmonia*) results from the tension of opposites. Empedocles held that similar phenomena attracted, and the result of this process of attraction is also love. The notion of the same and other—of Greek and Barbarian, of the one and the many—is still at the center of the political/economic debate and manifests itself in questions of equity and justice. It was also at the center of Plato's arguments on human discourse, namely, the problem of opposition between the singular and the "infinite" dyad, and of their reconciliation and unity. Love was the agent of true discourse, and the function of unification was its definition. The role of love, if we can think of the concept as playing a role, is one of unifying the parts from the reconciliation of singular and dyad, referring to the concept of "many in one" (*E Pluribus Unum*). Love is necessary in keeping the union a union.

Within the concept of love, an important attribute (of citizenship) is loyalty. The understanding of loyalty as an attribute of love can be traced back to Deuteronomy (6:5; King James version): "You shall love your God with all your heart." Israel is to have one loyalty—one love or unifying force. In Leviticus (19:18) this idea is extended to one's neighbor: "Thou shalt love thy neighbor as thyself." (Also see Matthew 22:37–40 and Luke 10:27–28.) The individual was to be loyal and love God, her own soul, and her neighbors.

The concept of love and its application to the state or country (other citizens) and even the land has been made explicit over time.

> It is also true that the victorious man's conduct is often guided by the *love* of his friends and of his country and that he will, if necessary, lay down his life in their behalf.
> —Aristotle, *Nicomachean Ethics* (p. 121)

> These are the times that try men's souls. The summer soldier and the sunshine patriot will, in this crisis, shrink from the service of their country; but he that stands it now deserves the *love* and thanks of men and women.
> —Thomas Paine, *Crisis* (1777, p. 23)

> That land is a commodity is the basic concept of ecology, but that land is to be *loved* and respected is an extension of ethics.
> —Aldo Leopold, *Sand County Almanac* (1966, p. xix)

While love and loyalty to one's soul, one's self, one's neighbors, and one's environment are necessary attributes of the good citizen, it is also the case that the whole business of civic loyalty must be viewed with skepticism, particularly by the democratic citizen. Great injustices can be perpetrated in the name of love. So, if citizens are to pursue justice and truth, to say nothing of friendship, our second theme in the necessary attributes of enlightened citizenship—criticism—must be invoked.

The Knowledge and Practice of Criticism

Criticism, within the context of citizenship, yields a comprehensive understanding of reality. It presupposes a philosophical world view that lends direction and predisposes methodology in the pursuit of certain goals and relationships between the individual (or family) and the state. Criticism is concerned with judgments about self, education, existence, values, and thinking itself. Civic criticism, by definition, means *clear* communication among citizens; that is, criticism is only possible when citizens respect standards of clarity, truth, and human dignity. Empathic listening is as important as the right of free speech. But criticism goes beyond clarity to embrace the concept of courage. This concept was expressed quite succinctly by Henry Giroux (1984):

> The notion of being able to think critically on the basis of informed judgement, and to develop a respect for democratic forms of self- and social-impowerment represent the basis for organizing schools around the principle of critical literacy and civic courage. In other words, schools should be seen as institutions that prepare people for democracy. They should promote the acquisition of a critical culture and social practices that allow students and others to view society with an analytical eye. [p. 190]

Civic criticism carries at least three interrelated behaviors. First, the citizen must value, observe, and absorb the social culture of the state or society so as to bring in a more complete picture or a more true impression of the situation. (We should note the contradictory nature of the phrase *true impression*.) This calls for the ability to take in information, impressions, and arguments, and conceptualize the setting within a temporal and spatial context, complete with explicit as well as subtle issues, promises, and problems. Next, the citizen must be able to react to the setting; that is, he must be a countervailing force, or at least, an asker of questions. These questions should probe the consciences of self and others as part of the search for the good society. Finally, the citizen must judge.

Judgments must be made of policy, political leaders, and self. It is particularly important that the citizen of the republic develop a critical view of the political economy, even though it is extremely difficult. As Pierre Bayle (1697) noted, however,

> most men decide to accept one notion rather than another because of certain superficial and extraneous traits which they consider to be more in conformity with truth than with falsehood and which are easily discernible; whereas solid and essential reasons which reveal truth are difficult to come by. Hence, since men are prone to follow the easier course, they almost always take the side on which these superficial traits are apparent. [p. 376]

It is this proneness for superficiality that is dangerous to the republic, and it is why criticisms, even of personal behavior, are so vital to the health of the state. But people will lovingly criticize only those institutions, ideas, and people in which they find personal meaning.

The Search for Meaning

Meaning is achieved through engagement. Engagement means being intensively involved with others in common activities, commonly perceived as good for self as well as for others so engaged. Meaning may be at the heart of happiness as well as the heart of citizenship. Meaning and citizenship are linked as well as limited in two significant ways. One has to do with settings of time and place, and the other with rhetoric. Conceptual limitations are defined by place and time, or, in terms of receiving meaning from the utterances of others, by convention and circumstance. Paraphrasing Habermas, Cherryholmes (1985) suggests that meaning resides in what the speaker is engaged in, and what the hearer is counting on. To be meaningful, communication must rest on truthfulness and comprehensibility, but these elements of rhetoric will only "work" within a homogeneous context where norms and expectations are shared. I could even add discipline and logic to rhetoric, to obtain a more complete notion of discourse, and still fall short of a definition of meaning that ties together love and criticism. Meaning in this more complete sense addresses not only the context of discourse but discloses those human visions or theories of social systems that illuminate as well as disguise and conceal the ethical acts of people. Meaning cuts through to the moral bone of society, baring the collective nerve and exposing such questions as, Who rules? Why? What rules should we follow? Why should we obey them? Will obeying rules lead me to the good life?

Any discussions about the relationship between rules and the good life are usually stated in the sequence of "rules, then virtue" (character). That is, rules cause a person to be good, and virtue follows rules. The belief is that the house of virtue is entered through the door of rules, as the temple of reason is entered through the courtyard of habit. Meaning, however, is brought to life when we first focus upon virtue, and let virtue help create good rules. Rules and virtue do work together, but "good" rules will simply follow from virtue. The philosophical questions at issue, then, are, What is the nature of virtue? Can virtue be taught? And, what is the relationship between virtue and meaning, virtue and education, and virtue and the concept of citizen? In defense of the new U.S. Constitution, James Madison in 1788 stated,

> I go on this great republican principle, that the people will have virtue and intelligence to select men of virtue and wisdom. Is there no virtue among us? To suppose that any form of government will secure liberty or happiness without any virtue in the people is an absurd idea. [p. 42]

VIRTUE, THE REPUBLIC,
AND THE OFFICE OF CITIZEN

The notion of "the people" as a reservoir of virtue, as opposed to virtue being vested in a monarch or the aristocracy, is a radical political concept. Yet at our nation's birth it was an idea supported in the writings of men as politically different as Hamilton in *The Federalist Papers* and Jefferson in the Declaration of Independence. Using the writings of Locke, Montesquieu, Hume, and even Machiavelli, the writers of our constitution constructed an experiment to see whether or not people were capable of establishing and running a good government. The American republic thus manifested a radical change in traditional ideas about good government, human character, and civic virtue. Primacy was placed upon the importance of the individual, so that the source of virtue was in the American *citizenry*—all of them. It was this reservoir of virtue that would guide people to build the good society.

From the classical periods of Western civilization through the Enlightenment, the conception of virtue that held center stage claimed that the highest goals of politics—goals such as freedom and empire—will ultimately encourage ambition and a vulgar prestige. Virtue in the pursuit of power, empire, or even freedom turns ultimately to vice, because virtue, in the classical view, cannot be a means to an end, it is an end in itself. Virtues such as courage, temperance, and justice are important in and of themselves; as such, they give life its purposes. Thus, while these virtues may help promote safety and prosperity in a society, they are esteemed in the classical sense as good in their own right, and not necessarily useful in the pursuit of safety, prosperity, or liberty. But, to the founders and the authors of *The Federalist Papers*, virtue was seen as an instrument or a means to life, liberty, and the pursuit of (public) happiness. Thus the founders transformed the classical tradition, seeing virtue as a way to build a better society, with emphasis upon individual dignity, liberty, and integrity. This change, from ends to means, paved the way for Americans to conceptualize virtue as the underpinning for both the economic and civic worlds of the citizen.

It should be made clear that property, prosperity, and the attitudes needed to succeed in the economic world were seen as part of the American system of virtue. American virtue expresses itself in an "adventurous entrepreneurship" that distinguishes our commercial character. On the other hand, it should also be emphasized that "happiness" as used in the Declaration of Independence was perceived as *public* happiness, that is, the ability and willingness to participate in the public life of the community. This was much more than economic participation.

This source of happiness was defined as giving of oneself and one's resources for the betterment of the community.

Since the acquisition of virtue had been seen as a function of who rules—who had power and legitimacy—the important discussion at the end of the eighteenth century centered on the question of how virtue was to be reflected in the people. In the classical view, the aristocracy rules because, through education, they have the greatest potential for virtue and therefore the clearest title to participate in government. The aristocracy does not serve the people in the sense of obeying the people, but rather serves to guide them toward a better way of life. On the other hand, the American view of "who rules" is a function of the majority voice, and allowing the majority of the people a significant voice in government calls for popular or public education. Requiring rulers to gain the consent of the governed is a mighty bulwark against tyranny, if and only if the people understand the role of virtue in public life.

The founding generation addressed the question of securing life, liberty, and public happiness in two ways. First of all, they developed a system of checks and balances to place one person's ambition against another's. As it was put in *The Federalist Papers*, "What is government itself but the greatest of all reflections on human nature? This policy of supplying by opposite and rival interests, the defect of better motives, might be traced through the whole system of human affairs" (Fairfield, 1981, p. 87).

Second, they addressed the condition of securing individual rights through education. In fact, the founders were extremely uneasy about the feebleness of civic education in the new order. Jefferson, particularly, argued long and eloquently that education for citizenship was the first responsibility of the republic and particularly of the states. To this end, he effectively proposed educational reforms for the State of Virginia as well as for the whole republic. Washington wanted a national university for the training of political leaders, and even the Bill of Rights, appended to the U.S. Constitution, was viewed as a way for future generations to educate citizens into civic responsibilities (virtue). Not only would the tenth amendment give states the responsibility for education, but the Bill of Rights itself was seen as a curriculum that the citizen could study, reflect upon, and use as a passageway to civic participation. The citizen, through education, would go beyond self-serving private action and protection, to manifest public or civic virtue, which, in reality, is the only true protection for private liberty.

Together, then, the dual concepts of public education and checks on ambition were to serve the republic in the development of civic conscientiousness (virtue), that is, a self-critical, self-righting ability coupled with an enlightened sense of statehood or enlightened nationalism. These ideas of civic well-being function, of course, only in those settings where individuals can feel some self-worth as contributors to their families and communities.

The premise upon which our republic is built, then, is the belief that virtue, law (rules), and education work together as a total system. Individuals will be virtuous if they are educated so they might construct good laws within a setting of civility, discipline, and love, and within a conception of the public good. It is within this context that the centrality of virtue and meaning to public education is made explicit. The school, along with the family, helps to develop the good citizen, who develops good law, which defines the good community, which provides for civic education. In a real sense, law sanctions virtue, and the enlightened citizen continually defines and redefines the interaction of these two notions. This endeavor on the part of the citizen demands criticism, love, and meaning—the philosophical perspective.

PHILOSOPHY AND CITIZENSHIP EDUCATION

Taken together, the office of democratic citizen and the discipline of philosophy suggest a pedagogical structure for citizenship education. This structure is built upon discourse (including rhetoric) and discipline (including logic and ethics). At one level, discourse reaches from one generation to the next; in fact, it may represent the moral thread that ties the culture together over time. This discourse takes place in those public and just spaces or settings where people can discuss stories about moral lessons, or the virtues of a heroic people. These stories provide a perspective for judging contemporary acts. They tell of duties and privileges and of one's place in society. They tell how changes in the social structure can be made and that a person is equal to her actions. Most of all, stories help in the search for virtue and create the criteria for social and personal judgments. Without these criteria for judgment, human empathy would be destroyed and with it the human community. Without judgment, public beauty and the courage to do good would disappear.

At a second level, discourse helps us defend ourselves against the popular culture. This discourse (rhetoric) arms the citizen with the tools of reflection and helps us understand what is expected of us within the public office of citizen. This is not unlike John Dewey's (1916) statement, "Philosophy is thinking what the known demands of us—what responsive attitude it exacts. It is an idea of what is possible, not a record of accomplished fact" (p. 326). While discourse includes attention to reason or the use of disciplined thinking, its main function is to provide a structure for us to act knowingly, voluntarily, and with high principle. What this suggests, again, is that philosophy is a theory of education, and education is, at its best, a search for wisdom. That is, with criticism, meaning, and love, a sensitive and graceful search can enhance both the citizen and the community in which a civic craft is practiced. To practice our civic craft in the pursuit of the common good may also be the area of greatest reward or (public) happiness. As Marcus Aurelius (1964) said, "Thou wilt do what is right, not because it is proper, but because thereby thou givest thyself pleasure" (p. 61).

CRITICAL ISSUES IN PHILOSOPHY AND CITIZENSHIP EDUCATION

While there is wide agreement among educators that the major goal of the public schools in general (Dewey, 1960), and of the social studies curriculum specifically, is the development of the enlightened citizen through participation grounded in reflective thought, according to Shaver (1980a; also see Butts, 1988; Newmann, 1988), there is little in the way of reflective or philosophical teaching in our schools, and there are very few philosophy courses. However, Shaver also suggests two ways in which to bring philosophy into the school program. One is just to offer a philosophy course in the school curriculum. The second is through "teaching philosophically." While more will be said about separate courses later in this chapter, it is suggested here that a more positive impact could be made on the educational goal of citizenship if we could address "philosophical teaching" in social studies, language arts, science, and the humanities.

Manicas (1978), for example, suggests that philosophical teachers would

- Challenge and seek justification of beliefs which may be cherished, never articulated, or never consciously addressed;
- Be wary of the pretense of facts and try to determine frames of reference, points of departure, and problems of orientation;
- Be wary of all definitions and assume that the subject matter and its key concepts are equivocal, contestable, and open;
- Try to identify values and commitments;
- Ask as many questions as possible;
- Avoid multiple-choice and true/false testing as much as possible.

These "philosophical behaviors," however, are quite different from the actual classroom behaviors reported on by Shaver, Davis, and Helburn in 1978. Their research suggests that

- The textbook is the dominant instructional tool.
- There is little attention given to the study of societal (controversial) issues.
- The dominant instructional mode continues to be large-group, teacher-controlled recitation and lecture, based primarily on the textbook.
- The students are expected to know information.
- Inquiry teaching is rare.
- Teachers tend not only to rely on, but to believe in, the textbook as the source of information.
- A major goal of science, mathematics, and social studies teachers is the socialization of students, that is, getting them ready for the next grade level.
- There is also a citizenship component, involving the advocacy of values and a commitment to inculcating them [by] teaching facts in U.S. history, not because the details will necessarily be remembered and used, but hopefully to create for each new generation an aura of American greatness.

While the foregoing certainly does not describe all classrooms, it would seem that, despite the historical link between philosophy and citizenship education, there is little reflective or philosophical teaching in our school programs. This may be due to the way in which teachers practice self-censorship because of real or imagined community pressures to maintain order and give students information which they can then use on standardized tests. It may also be due to the modeling that teachers receive at the university during their own "training." The model of the academician as one who gives out information is hardly appropriate for philosophical teaching, whether in the elementary, secondary, or postsecondary school. Yet, this is the main method of teaching used in our institutions of higher learning.

Thus, the central issues of philosophy and citizenship can be stated in two questions: Why is there a disconnection between our stated purpose for education and our attending educational practices? And, given the school's two responsibilities of developing intellectual liberation and commitment to the continuity of core values, to what degree can philosophy address both?

RECOMMENDATIONS

Given the close theoretical relationship between philosophy and education (despite school practices), and given that the central purpose of education in a democratic republic is the development of enlightened citizens, the following recommendations for the improvement of civic literacy are tied to a vision of the comprehensive improvement of school.

Affirming the Centrality of Citizenship

To begin, we should affirm the centrality of citizenship as the major goal of public schools. To accomplish this, much more attention must be given to the study of the humanities and, within the humanities, the study of philosophy (including rhetoric, logic, and ethics). Attention should be given to reading and discussing some of the philosophical classics, but consideration should also be given to more contemporary works. It would be interesting and intellectually challenging to develop a reading list of great and not-quite-so-great books that could be used with students and colleagues. Perhaps a reading list could be started from the references at the end of this chapter.

Moving Away from Scientific Positivism

In today's world, science—or what might be better described as positivism and not science at all—presents us with the currently dominant way of thinking about the world. Within the popular literature and mass media, there seem to be three common beliefs that would suggest a need for less emphasis upon a positivist perspective for citizenship education. First of all, there seems to be a belief that the world is so corrupt that the ethical behavior of one person is insignificant to the social settings in which we live. Second is the belief that the individual is so powerless in the face of large corporations and bureaucracies that social/political impotency, and with it moral impotency, is inevitable. Finally, individuals seem to accept little personal responsibility for social ills. All of these attitudes are extremely dangerous to the survival of self and society. Underlying this malaise is, perhaps, the implicit and fallacious belief that technological advances make it unnecessary to be concerned with philosophical issues. After all, the ultimate origin of truth, in this belief, is in what is observable and quantifiable; that is, if you cannot measure it, it does not exist. Citizens permit "scientific" gains to act as a substitute for the vigilance, discipline, and hard work necessary for ethical development; a scientific "pill" can, for example, remove an ethical question regarding behavior and its consequences.

Why has this attitude developed; what are its antecedents? In large measure this attitude rests on our reliance on logical empiricism and its nineteenth-century parent, positivism. While it is difficult to define, positivism is an assumption about the world and reality based upon "objective observations." Its genesis can be traced back at least to August Comte, who insisted that theory can be freed from the imaginary powers of the human mind and based upon the nature of things and the laws that govern them. This notion represents a major paradigm shift from classical ideas about theory, which held that people could free themselves from the "objective" world, thereby providing an orientation for ethical action, that is, a search for truth and justice. Positivist theory views itself as "value free," and it presents a set of methodological techniques devoid of ethics, goals, and historical roots. In the Western intellectual tradition, this separation of ethics and knowledge has not always been the major orientation of meaning and thought. In the classical assumptions of Plato, the two were seen as inseparable. With the decline and fall of classical knowledge during the medieval period, ethics and knowledge were separated, with ethics and values seen as more important than knowledge. With the Enlightenment, the division continued, first with no assumption of primacy of either values or factual knowledge, and later with the ascendancy of observable data over values and ethics—positivism.

Under positivism's central assumptions of objectivity and empirical verification, facts became self-subsistent and questions about the creation of knowledge were buried under the weight of "value-free" notions of epistemology. Further, knowledge, information, or data taken from philosophy, ethics, religion, history, or other "nonscientific" frameworks were not acceptable—this kind of knowledge was and is considered irrelevant.

But it is not only the nature of positivism that is at issue, but its pervasiveness in human consciousness. It is the fundamental paradigm of our time. In fact, some people will even forsake the power and beauty of a nonpositivist epistemology (i.e., philosophy or religion) in order to be counted with the popular epistemology of positivism (i.e., science or, better, scientism). This is done without realizing that each has its place in our search for meaning and that to try to put all knowledge into one category—to suggest that there is only one paradigm—is folly. This certainty and arrogance are dangerous. This paradigm teaches us to approach problems in isolation, instead of comprehending the world as a holistic network of interconnected components, ideas, and phenomena.

It cuts away philosophy from the "important" elements of the cultural heritage, and this "cutting" is done in the name of objectivity. It is the paradigm of positivism that replaces questions of "what should be" with questions of "what is," thus relegating ethics to the category of "uselessness." It argues that social organizations such as bureaucracies are independent of human beings. It tells people that they are only passive pawns in a game of social chess. It dissolves meaning and criticism by failing to make room for historical experiences or social memory. Positivism denies the essence of love by neutralizing hope and rejecting the future.

Practicing Ethical Reasoning

In addition to the pervasive "consciousness of positivism," the philosophical perspective is also eroded by notions of certainty that come from the fringe areas on both ends of the political spectrum. Certainty is almost always antithetical to philosophical and ethical literacy. This does not mean that ethics are relative. Ethics must always make reference to moral principles. Ethics are those things like "codes of ethics," which are specific to certain professions, societies, or human transactions. Morals, on the other hand, are general in the sense that they are the criteria by which we judge human motivation, behavior, and consequences. Morals are absolute, but they are difficult to delineate because of complicated contextual extensions in all moral decision making. If, for example, you knew where an individual was hiding from a Gestapo-type gang who you knew wanted to kill this individual, would you lie to protect her life? While it is clear, as stated in one set of moral principles (the Ten Commandments of Judeo–Christian heritage) that you should not lie or kill, you can readily see that, within the context of the Gestapo story, an appeal to a simple list of moral principles—any list of moral principles—would be insufficient in making the *moral* decision.

Thus, morality can never be relegated to a listing of moral principles, for morality is ultimately manifested in what people think and do. Our moral principles can be demonstrated in such simple terms as telling the truth, caring for others, doing justice, and so forth. The manifestation of moral principles in the behavior and thought of people, however, is primarily a function of our ethical reasoning abilities or what might be called the practice of making moral decisions. This is, in essence, the center of both educational philosophical purpose—ethical reasoning practiced within a just setting (the classroom).

But, what is it that the individual needs to practice and learn relative to "literacy as philosophical perspective?" Certainly, students need to learn what people who study philosophy have said about ethical decision making. They also need to attend to the concepts of intent (motive), behavior, and consequences. All three of these items must be considered if we expect ethical literacy. Intent is perhaps the most difficult to understand and discuss. For example, an individual may behave in an admirable way, and said behavior might even have positive consequences. But what of intent?

For example, consider this scenario: You see an elderly woman with a large purse attempting to cross the street. Let us say that you intend to steal the purse as you escort (help) her to the other side of the street. Halfway across the street, however, you spot a police officer and you change your mind about the theft and proceed to escort the woman across. She thanks you and you both go on your separate ways. The consequences turn out to be okay, and the behavior seems to be quite ethical, but what about your intent? Ethical literacy is more than stumbling into a good ending; further, it is at its base a personal or individual phenomenon. We cannot delegate ethical decisions, nor should we attempt to. This is particularly true of the citizen. We erode our effectiveness as citizens through noninvolvement. Try as we may, decisions about voting or about economic and social issues will demand our direct attention. This means that individuals must take the time and make the effort to learn how to become "better" decision makers and philosophers. This can be done not only through practice, but also through the study of decisions that other individuals have made throughout time and the *reasoning processes* that they have used, which we all can use as models.

If we focus on the goal of ethical reasoning, then philosophy will be placed higher on the educational agenda, and our school programs will have to explore the dynamics between social/personal principles and the facts of the so-called "real world." That is, a dialogue will be needed between the ideals of society and reality, between social theory and gross facts. For the ideal and real to be in sparking communication, educators must get beyond naïve realism (Chandler, 1987), or the belief in certainty and one truth. They must get beyond multiple rationalism, or the belief in no truth or in complete relativism. They must arrive at an understanding of construct validity (Cherryholmes, 1985), or the belief that, if we study social theory (principles) as well as the empirical settings in questions, and try to move ourselves and society toward those principles, we may bring more meaning and justice into the lives of citizens of the republic.

Barbara Tuchman (1978) articulates this situation when she writes about fourteenth-century Europe. The parallels to our contemporary world cannot be missed by the reader, but the important idea is the discrepancy between principles and practice. From our vantagepoint today, educators should see the relevancy of this dynamic to citizenship education.

> Chivalry, the dominant political idea of the ruling class, left as great a gap between ideal and practice as religion. The ideal was a vision of order maintained by the warrior class and formulated in the image of the Round Table, nature's perfect shape. King Arthur's knights adventured for the right against dragons, enchanters, and wicked men, establishing order in a wild world. So their living counterparts were supported, in theory, to serve as defenders of the Faith, upholders of justice, champions of the oppressed. In practice, they were themselves the oppressors, and by the 14th Century the violence and lawlessness of men of the sword had become a major agency of disorder. When the gap between ideal and real becomes too wide, the system breaks down. Legend and story have always reflected this.

Is the gap between ideals and practice too wide today? Where do we find and develop our social principles? How can we bring more congruency between the social theories of the United States and the facts of everyday life?

These questions should be addressed by students and educators. All of us can develop social theory statements based upon our understanding—historical and contemporary—of such documents as the Declaration of Independence, the Preamble to the U.S. Constitution, Martin Luther King Jr.'s "I have a dream" speech, and so forth. Students can also assess current social/personal circumstances and develop policy statements that can help bring social theory and practice closer. This type of general pedagogical strategy can also help students become better at constructing personal and public policies, as well as focus on the future and on the ethical health of the republic. It can place before them the opportunity to confront the meaning of Proverbs 29:18:

"Where there is no vision the people perish."

In its original Aramaic or Northwest Semitic language context (Anderson, 1957) and even in the Greek translation, the word *vision* meant virtue, so this proverb can read, "Where there is no *virtue* the people perish." Metaphorically, we might understand the importance of virtue and ethics to social, economic, political, and legal systems by envisioning an iceberg. The ice above the waterline can represent our visible social and cultural institutions, while the ice below the water is analogous to our philosophical and ethical systems. The constellation of values within the latter keeps the social institutions buoyed up. While invisible to the passing ship, the quantity of ice below the water is larger than that which we see above. It is also the case that the visible ice on top of the water cannot exist without the invisible below. In a similar vein, our social, economic, political, and legal systems are visible and viable only so long as the "foundation" values are functioning.

Using Education to Cultivate Virtue

Every society and culture has its operational philosophical systems. The issue is never the existence of values, but the nature of those values. Do they illuminate the best of human hope, faith, courage, integrity, and compassion, or do they deny the universality of the human spirit? Such a denial, of course, separates and belittles the different and the unique among us. It skews power and resources into the hands of the few and the very few. Such a denial also betrays the future and ignores the past by failing to cherish human beings and their accumulated wisdom. Within the context of a democratic republic, education, by definition, means the movement toward this wisdom (virtue/vision).

To enhance our discussion and help move educational content and practice toward virtue, we might ask,

1. What is virtue?
2. Can virtue be taught?
3. What is the nature of good and evil?
4. What knowledge is of most worth?
5. When may the individual justly heed a "higher" law than that of the state of which he or she is a citizen?
6. Who/what do I love?
7. How can I achieve happiness and freedom?
8. What obligations do I have to my parents (past); to my children (future)?
9. What obligations do I have to my community?
10. What is a good person? A good society?
11. How can education help a person become better?
12. Can a political, economic, legal, or social system have a conscience?
13. How can social institutions become more ethical?
14. What social theories do I hold?
15. What facts about our society and the world support my social theories? How do I know?

Students might address questions like these through readings and discussions, and by writing about their own ideas, giving attention to motives, behaviors, and consequences of their actions and thoughts.

Developing a New Curriculum

In addition to the emphasis placed on the kinds of questions just listed, my final recommendation is that we consider developing new courses, as well as units within existing courses. It would be useful to develop such courses in the context of how they would help students understand philosophy in a more direct way, that is, in a way that will focus on those contemporary issues that help raise persistent philosophical questions and outline the philosophical perspective. Consider, for example, the following high school courses and some attending questions:

Aesthetics, Environment, and Architecture
* What is the proper relationship between the "house" in which we live and the demands upon the environment?
* Between lifestyle and resources?
* Between individual and social needs?
* Between individual and social costs?

Law and Conscience
* Can the law work without voluntary compliance to that law?
* Is law the antithesis of ethics?
* Is being at war the natural state of humankind?

Society and Science
* How can the paradigm of science be used to study political, economic, and social systems?
* What role should the humanities play in the study of society and science?
* How should public policy on scientific issues be made?

Ethics and Technology
* What is the relationship between tools and world view?
* How can technology lead one person or a whole society to the good life?
* To what degree is social (and human) evaluation driven by technology (tools)?

Given our present temporal location, it would seem that some creative curriculum activities in these directions might be fruitful in the developmental process of helping students become enlightened citizens. These kinds of courses might also help us address the basic obligation of schools in a democratic republic—that of freeing individuals from irrational constraints on their behavior and thoughts, while at the same time promoting continuity of our core values.

In addition to courses such as the foregoing, there are several ongoing issues or questions that modern citizens of a democratic republic should address. These can be used by teachers at any grade level as they prepare lessons about citizenship. They offer an intellectual crucible out of which can emerge better citizenship instruction. There are seven questions discussed here, but the list itself should not be considered as final. It is suggested that the process of working through these questions will help establish the necessary conditions of mind for one to assume the office of citizen in a democratic republic.

1. *What is the proper relationship between the constitution of the state (nation) and the character of its citizens?*

It seems to be the case that the office of citizen is unnatural to the character of the individual. The person is fundamentally a private being, content with family and friends but uncomfortable in the more public role of citizen. Nature seems to have crafted us for the private life, yet civic responsibility demands public involvement. Even more basic is the notion that there must be in all citizens an understanding that our government or constitution is implemented through the character of each of us. In a real sense, civic education is unnatural, for it addresses the public side of life and the realization that private character and public virtue are linked in ways that are mutually interactive. That is, the ability to develop privately (to become the good person) is always tied to the group (the building of the good society). Good citizens understand this relationship and work to overcome the unnatural attitude of being public persons. They come to the realization that happiness is always defined within a civic or public framework. From Pericles to Marcus Aurelius, from Thomas Jefferson to John F. Kennedy, from Eleanor Roosevelt to Mother Teresa, there is agreement that service to your city, state, or nation is not only the right or even the good thing to do, but the joyful thing to do.

2. *What is the proper relationship between self-interest and public interest?*

The state exists because the people give their authority to it. The state also exists to give the people justice. Thus, the state is made legitimate because of the people, and people experience justice because of the state. This exchange occurs when people become involved in their government and raise certain questions about that involvement, such as

How can I give my ideas and authority to the state?
How can I be assured that the state is doing justice to its citizens?

These questions form the basis for civic responsibility. They address how an individual sanctions his government (i.e., through voting, circulating petitions, working for candidates, running for office, and so forth) and judges the quality of laws and legislation passed and implemented in society, always keeping in mind the direct relationships between self-interest and public interest.

3. *What is the relationship between forms of government and social/ economic class? Will a large impoverished mass and a small elite generally produce oligarchy? Does greater equalization of wealth favor democratic rule?*

The ancient Aristotelian idea that there is a relationship between a society's distribution of wealth and its form of government keeps returning. [See, for example, *A Vision for America's Future: An Agenda for the 1990's* (Children's Defense Fund, 1989).] Perhaps the most important knowledge for the citizen is of how economics and politics work together in forming public policies. There is a symbiotic relationship between capitalism and democracy, and citizens must understand the balance that is established between personal (economic) freedom and public (political) law. The individual plays various roles within the personal and public domains of society and must care for the home as well as for the community, supporting each so that both are strong and healthy. Ignorance and poverty of even the few diminish the well-being of the many. Ignorance and poverty of the many destroy democracy and capitalism. The citizen's role, then, is to take Aristotle seriously, for, whether we like it or not, wealth, power, and knowledge, which are all interrelated, must be earned and shared by all citizens. This is the beginning of social justice.

4. *What is the relationship between education and democratic citizenship?*

Since every society is established with some vision of the good or virtuous life, every community must provide a procedure for citizens to find their way to rightful behavior and rational principles. What is clear in the writings of virtually every Western philosopher from Aristotle to Jefferson is the argument that education is necessary for the office of citizen. What is less clear is the content of that education. Aristotle did recommend the educational goal of reasoning, and Jefferson argued for a common education for all citizens paid for by the state. He also suggested that the curriculum include the study of history. Over the past 50 years, more attention has been given to the issue of content (Hartoonian & Laughlin, 1989), and it does seem that the following knowledge areas appear necessary for citizenship education in a democratic republic: the study of the cultural heritage; the study of the political, economic, and legal systems; the study of rational and ethical decision making; and some sort of civic involvement with the community. What is most agreed upon is the idea that, within our republic, literacy and freedom are inseparable.

5. *What is the relationship between the health of our social institutions and the well-being of our citizens?*

The fragility of democratic institutions is now a concern for citizens. The realization that families, schools, the judicial system, Congress, business, and even the presidency are ethically weak and in many ways malfunctioning has caused citizens to understand, even if only dimly, that their personal well-being is directly tied to the health of our social institutions. This means, of course, that we need to make greater investments of time, energy, money, and knowledge in our infrastructure and our institutions. It is becoming a truism that our democratic republic and our capitalistic economic system cannot exist without a healthy community. That is, all citizens must understand that their own self-interest is tied to the health of the total society. Self-interest properly understood means that I'd better care for the community or my own interest will never be realized.

6. *What is the relationship between the historical myths of separation and the inclusive reality of the twenty-first century?*

The diversity, cultural pluralism, and multiculturalism of the modern nation are realities for the citizen today. Customs, laws, and social practices that have separated people in the past will have to be altered, for the facts simply call for the inclusion of all people into the community, into political involvement, and into the economic system. The demographic changes taking place in the United States are so profound that the question of how we define our "inclusive reality" may be the most serious issue confronting us today.

7. *What is the proper relationship between natural law and positive law?*

Laws and "natural" principles suggest a tension that is necessary to the maintenance of justice in any society. Citizens must understand this tension and how to use it in the governing process. Natural principles represent the laws of Nature, or God's law. These are the laws that Jefferson referred to in the Declaration of Independence; they are the "higher laws" to which civil rights leaders made reference when breaking "humanity's" laws. There is always a need for a higher reference, because all laws and governments are based upon an ethical and/or religious system that helps keep people from causing too much mischief. On the other hand, people can do even greater mischief in the name of the church (e.g., Ireland, Iran) or the flag (e.g., colonialization, imperialism), particularly when they believe they are doing God's work or the work of the country. What citizens of a democratic republic must be able to do is balance the higher references with legislation, keeping in mind the dynamic nature of all law and the realization that governments and people have the potential for both good and evil.

CONCLUSION

Young people today are truly concerned with concepts such as good and evil, relationships with self and with others, their future and the future of society. The exploration of the foregoing questions, issues, and courses provide a point of entry into important areas of citizenship education. Perhaps the concern is even more fundamental in that it is only when we add the synoptic disciplines like philosophy to our investigations that we can search for wisdom. Beyond this, the study of philosophy also serves to establish or give students a significant part of those data necessary for the intellectual discussion of public issues. Philosophy can also help us stop fragmenting our intellectual and cultural resources. When we fail to use these resources, our investigations soon fall into the quicksand of simple answers or nonanswers to complex problems. In truth, can issues like peace, birth control, environmental pollution, genetic engineering, and space exploration be intellectually discussed without reference to philosophy? Can we even begin to address these issues without a careful study of the tension between the public and private lives of the citizen? It is my belief that we cannot, and that philosophy is not only a desirable element of these debates, but a crucial one.

REFERENCES

Anderson, B. W. (1957). *Understanding the Old Testament*. Englewood Cliffs, NJ: Prentice Hall.

Aristotle. (1987). *The Nicomachean ethics* (J. E. C. Weldon, Trans.). Buffalo, NY: Prometheus Books.

Barth, J. L., & Shermis, S. S. (1980). Social studies goals: The historical perspective. *Journal of Research and Development in Education, 13*(2), 111.

Bayle, P. (1965). *Historical and critical dictionary: Selections* (R. H. Popkin, Trans.). Indianapolis: Bobbs-Merrill.

Bellah, R. N., Masden, R., Sullivan, W. M., Swidler, A., & Tipton, S. (1986). *Habits of the heart: Individualism and commitment in American life*. New York: Harper & Row.

Bragaw, D. H., & Hartoonian, H. M. (1988). Social studies: The study of people in society. In R. S. Brant (Ed.), *Content of the curriculum* (pp. 9–29). Alexandria, VA: Association for Supervision and Curriculum Development.

Butts, R. F. (1988, October). *Democratic values: What the schools should teach*. Paper presented at the Citizenship for the 21st Century Conference, sponsored by the Foundation for Teaching Economics and the Constitutional Rights Foundation, Washington, DC.

Chandler, M. (1987). The Othello effect. *Human Development, 30*(3), 137–159.

Cherryholmes, C. (1985). *What does meaning mean? And what to do about it in curriculum and in instruction?* Unpublished manuscript. Michigan State University, East Lansing, MI.

Children's Defense Fund. (1989). *A vision for America's future: An agenda for the 1990's*. Washington DC: Author.

Dewey, J. (1916). *Democracy and education*. New York: Macmillan.

Dewey, J. (1960). *Theory of the moral life*. New York: Holt, Rinehart, & Winston.

Empedocles. (1981). *The extant fragments* (M. R. Wright, Ed.). New Haven: Yale University Press.

Fairfield, R. P. (Ed.). (1981). *The Federalist Papers* (Nos. 1, 2, 6, 10, 14, 23, 35, 37, 51, 52, 55, 57, and 63). Baltimore: Johns Hopkins University Press.

Friedman, M. (1962). *Capitalism and freedom*. Chicago: University of Chicago Press.

Giroux, H. G. (1984). Public philosophy and the crisis in education. *Harvard Educational Review, 54*(2), 186–194.

Gross, R. E. (1977). The status of social studies in the public schools of the United States: Facts and impressions of a national survey. *Social Education, 41*(3), 194–200.

Hartoonian, H. M., & Laughlin, M. A. (1989). Designing a scope and sequence. *Social Education, 53*(6), 388–398.

Heraclitus. (1987). *Fragments* (T. M. Robinson, Trans.). Toronto: University of Toronto Press.

Hunt, M. P., & Metcalf, L. E. (1968). *Teaching high school social studies: Problems in reflective thinking and social understanding* (2nd ed.). New York: Harper & Row.

Jowett, B. (Ed.) (1937). *The dialogues of Plato.* New York: Random House.

Kent, E. A. (Ed.). (1970). *Law and philosophy: Readings in legal philosophy.* Englewood Cliffs, NJ: Prentice-Hall.

Ketcham, R. (1987). *Individualism and public life: A modern dilemma.* New York: Basil Blackwell.

Leopold, A. (1966). *Sand County almanac.* New York: Ballantine Books.

Lipman, M. (1980). *Mark.* Upper Montclair, NJ: Montclair State College, Institute for the Advancement of Philosophy for Children.

MacIntyre, A. (1984). *After virtue* (2nd ed.). Notre Dame, IN: University of Notre Dame Press.

Madison, J. (1976). *The Federalist.* Washington, DC: R. B. Luce. (Original work published 1788)

Manicas, P. (1978). The social studies, philosophy, and politics. *The Social Studies, 178*(6), 244–248.

Marcus Aurelius. (1964). *Meditations* (M. Staniforth, Trans.). Harmondsworth, England: Penguin Books.

Montesquieu. (1977). *Spirit of laws* (D. W. Carrithers, Ed.). Berkeley: University of California Press. (Original work published 1748)

Newmann, F. M. (1988). *Higher order thinking in high school social studies: An analysis of classrooms, teachers, students, and leadership.* Madison, WI: University of Wisconsin, National Center on Effective Secondary Schools.

Paine, T. (1973). *Common sense and the crisis.* Garden City, NY: Anchor Books. (Original work published 1777)

Palmer, R. R. (1959). *The age of the democratic revolution: A political Europe and America, 1760–1800.* Princeton, NJ: Princeton University Press.

Plato. (1955). *Republic.* (F. M. Cornford, Trans.). London: Oxford University Press.

Sennett, R. (1978). *The fall of public man.* New York: Vintage Books.

Shaver, J. P. (1980a). The teaching of philosophy in social studies. *Viewpoints in Teaching and Learning, 56*(4), 32–40.

Shaver, J. P. (1980b). Toward the 21st century: Social studies goals for decision making and research skills. *Journal of Research and Development in Education, 13*(2), 36–46.

Shaver, J. P., Davis, O. L. Jr., & Helburn, S. W. (1978). *An interpretive report on the status of pre-collegiate social studies education based on three NSF-funded studies.* Washington, DC: National Science Foundation.

Smith, A. (1937). *An inquiry into the nature and causes of the wealth of nations.* New York: Random House. (Original work published 1776)

Sophocles. (1973). *Antigone* (W. Arrowsmith, Ed. & Trans.). London: Oxford University Press.

Tuchman, B. W. (1978). *A distant mirror: The calamitous 14th century.* New York: Ballantine.

Young, P., & Myers, J. T. (Eds.). (1967). *Philosophic problems and education.* New York: Lippincott.

Zevin, J. (1978). Thinking critically, thinking philosophically. *The Social Studies, 178*(6), 69.

10 The International Perspective

American Citizenship in an Interdependent World

ANDREW F. SMITH

Educating for citizenship is a central mission of the school curriculum. Traditionally, citizenship education has been conceptualized as the study of governmental institutions at the local, state, and national levels and the relationship of the individual citizen to those institutions (Remy, n.d.). Likewise, most states and school districts maintain requirements to promote understanding of other nations and cultures (American Forum for Global Education, 1989a).

Since World War II, the division between traditional civic education and the responsibility to teach about the world and other cultures has blurred. International events and trends have influenced the United States, the needs of American citizens have altered, and American schools have reacted to these new needs. For instance, as the Cold War became entrenched, the schools required teachers to sign loyalty oaths, mandated courses in anticommunism, and installed courses on free enterprise. As independence movements spread throughout Asia, Africa, and Latin America, area-studies courses became a part of the required curriculum. As Sputnik soared into space, American schools improved mathematics and sciences courses and Project Social Studies was launched to improve the academic content of history, geography, government, and social science courses.

Today, global economic, political, ecological, technological, and cultural interconnections have increased among the world's nations and cultures, creating an emerging global system. Simultaneously, global issues (e.g., energy fluctuations, population migrations, international trade, national security) are fast weaving a fabric of planetary interconnections that affect the lives of individual Americans on a daily basis. Likewise, Americans make decisions and judgments and take actions that affect this global society (Anderson, 1979). Citizenship education now requires the development of competencies that take into account the new rights and responsibilities of citizens in this global age.

DIVERGENT PERSPECTIVES
ABOUT THE WORLD AND AMERICAN EDUCATION

Defining these competencies requires an understanding of the world and how it operates. Different substantive conceptualizations have alternative implications for citizenship education. While there are many substantive formulations about the world, the most significant conceptual points related to the international dimension of citizenship education have revolved around a limited number of bipolar dimensions, including nationalism and globalism, Eurocentrism and the non–Western world, optimism and pessimism, and cultural transmission and cultural change.

Nationalism and Globalism

Nationalists believe that the nation–state is the major international actor and will continue to be for the foreseeable future. Citizenship is a legal creation of the nation–state, and citizenship education should mainly teach American history and government. This approach prepares citizens for membership in a particular society. Nationalists believe that the most important values to be taught in the schools are patriotic love of one's country and commitment to the nation's leadership responsibilities in the world (Cunningham, n.d.; Finn & Bauer, 1986; Schlafly, 1986). While patriotism is not incompatible with an international consciousness, many nationalists do believe that current educational efforts deny moral absolutes, are skewed toward the left-wing political positions, and promote one-worldism. They believe that educators ought to be paid by the public to perform citizenship education, not to undermine the American political system.

Globalists believe that all human beings have responsibilities for, and loyalties to, the human species; hence, nation–states have proven to be a major stumbling block for solving the problems of humankind. In this view, the schools need to shed their traditional nationalistic tendencies and dramatically increase courses on world history, geography, the study of other cultures, and the study of global issues and topics. Some support the call for a world citizenship that supercedes national citizenship. Others believe that it is possible to maintain multiple loyalties

(Anderson, 1979; Alliance for Education in Global and International Studies, n.d.).

Eurocentrism and the Non–Western World

The American educational system has been criticized as being Eurocentric, to the detriment of the study of other cultures, values, and languages. The study of European history, literature, and languages has dominated the curriculum. Those supporting a Eurocentric position maintain that Western culture and values are the basis for our government and lifestyle and that everyone should be socialized into this national culture (Ravitch, 1989).

Those who favor including the study of the non–Western world argue that the world encompasses many different cultures and languages and that the different value systems inherent within these cultures should be as respected and honored in the schools as are the traditional Western cultures and values. Each culture is unique and merits respect in its own right. Each culture forms part of a global cultural bank and gives a vivid reminder of the diversity of the human experience. The curriculum, then, should include the study of cultures other than the dominant one, including the study of minority groups at home and non–Western cultures abroad, to help students understand others, thereby gaining better insight into their own culture.

According to many critics, those supporting the study of the non–Western world are cultural relativists, whose "value-free" approach intentionally avoids making judgments about other cultures for fear of being ethnocentric. This leaves students with the mistaken impression that there are no universal values. Stan Wronski (1987) responded that cultural relativism is just another way of referring to the fact that cultures differ from one another in their beliefs and customs. This differs from the term *moral equivalence*, which denotes the belief that there are no moral absolutes.

Optimism and Pessimism

While optimism and pessimism have consistently been a part of the American ethos, the schools traditionally reinforced the spirit of optimism: America and the world were becoming better places, and the future would be even better than it is today. During the early 1960s, this began to change. First, the creation of nuclear weapons, combined with strategic ballistic missiles, made it possible to end the world with the flick of a switch. Second, several studies of the late 1960s and early

1970s predicted that population growth would outstrip available food production and other necessary resources, producing mass starvation and violent conflict before the end of the century (Meadows, 1972). Third, scientists in the 1980s warned of dire and irreversible consequences of environmental degradation, global warming, and the depletion of the ozone layer.

The optimists countered that the world was safer because of nuclear weapons, that the studies were inaccurate, and that the crises presented by these reports were solvable (London, 1984; Simon & Kahn, 1984). It was a major mistake to infuse pessimism into the curriculum, which might produce a self-fulfilling prophecy. In this view, new materials and elective courses needed to be developed to excite students to want to take part in solving these problems (Newitt, 1983).

Cultural Transmission and Cultural Change

Many groups supporting specific perspectives on the preceding three dimensions developed curriculum materials and lobbied schools to enlist them in supporting their particular positions. Many critics strongly disagreed with this politicization of the American public education system and charged schools with propagandizing students to particular solutions. These issues raised questions regarding the purpose and function of American education: Was the function of the schools to transmit cultural values or promote cultural change?

Many believe that the major function of the school is to transmit cultural information and values and are more inclined to encourage the teaching of basic skills and essential knowledge about the heritage of our nation and other Western values. They maintain that the schools are not performing this function adequately and that international topics simply detract from the schools' meeting noncontroversial, agreed-upon tasks.

Progressive educators believe that students will be confronted with problems throughout their lives and that the most important function of the schools is to help students learn the skills of problem solving, conflict resolution, and political participation. Educators supporting this position emphasize the inclusion of controversial issues and case studies, and they encourage students to become politically involved in these topics.

As discussed in the next section, most "global" educators fall somewhere between the two extremes, believing that the curriculum should include both nationalistic and global components, European and non–

Western cultures and values, and healthy doses of optimism and pessimism. Likewise, they would maintain that the schools should both transmit cultural heritage and prepare students to become problem solvers. Merging these polarized positions has been a difficult task requiring extensive consideration of the conceptualization of the global dimensions of citizenship education and the implementation of programs in the schools.

EMERGENCE OF GLOBAL EDUCATION

The reconceptualization of citizenship in a global age has led to the creation of the field of global education (Smith, 1989). Colleges and universities, academic associations and educational organizations, and local school districts and nonprofit community organizations launched hundreds of projects and programs (American Forum for Global Education, 1989b). Curriculum writers developed thousands of supplemental materials and several "global" textbooks (American Forum for Global Education, 1990; Social Studies School Service, 1990). Colleges and universities conducted teacher education programs with international dimensions. National education organizations issued publications and sponsored conferences. National commissions and studies reported on the state of international competence of American youth and made recommendations on how international studies programs should be implemented in the nation's schools (Coalition for the Advancement of Foreign Languages and International Studies, 1989; National Governors' Association, 1989). In addition, dozens of textbook reviews, doctoral dissertations, research investigations, and evaluation studies have been added to the effort (Rentel & Errante, 1989). International schools are now a part of many school districts (Lonzetta, 1988). Many states have created state commissions, legislated mandates, offered guidelines, and launched projects and programs that include global and international studies components (American Forum, 1989a).

CONCEPTUALIZATION OF GLOBAL EDUCATION

Global education is broadly concerned with the knowledge, skills, and values that American citizens need in order to function effectively in an interdependent world. Rationales, frameworks, and lists of goals and objectives abound, which define specifically what is meant by global education (Kniep, 1985). Global education differs from the traditional conceptualization of citizenship education on the significant dimensions of content, skills, and values.

Content

The core of global education includes content from geography and world history, world literature, foreign languages, area studies, and many other disciplines. However, does the international dimension of citizenship education include all of this content? While most educators respond that it is important for American citizens to have a general knowledge about these subjects, much content of the traditional world history, geography, area-studies, and global issues courses, as important as they are in their own right, are not central to citizenship education.

The major issue that has plagued global education is how this massive amount of data is to be organized and what priorities are to be set. Traditionally, the organizing concepts in the geography and world history courses were chronology and description. Global educators have offered two paradigms designed to help organize the school curriculum: global perspectives, concepts, and comprehensive approaches.

Concepts. Hanvey (1976), in "An Attainable Global Perspective," presented five organizing concepts:

1. Perspective consciousness,
2. State-of-the-planet awareness,
3. Cross-cultural awareness,
4. Knowledge of global dynamics,
5. Awareness of human choices.

While these "perspectives" have provided heuristic interest, they are so remote from the existing curriculum that their application has been of limited use.

During the 1970s, concepts such as conflict, interdependence, communication, and change were offered as organizing tools for content (King, Branson, & Condon, 1976). The advantage of these broad concepts was their applicability to the entire curriculum. Elementary school programs could deal with conflict, as could secondary school programs. These concepts could easily be applied to disciplines other than social studies. The specific content that educators used to help students understand the concept was less important than the concept itself.

As important as concepts are, they have not been clearly defined, and they have frequently overlapped in scope. No attempt has been made to map these global concepts or to explore the relationships among those offered for inclusion in the curriculum. No criteria have been offered for judging which concepts should be included. Little research has been conducted to suggest where these concepts would best fit in the curriculum, nor has a definitive list of concepts been developed.

Comprehensive Approaches.   During the 1980s, more comprehensive attempts have been offered to pull together a wide range of global content. Building on the work of the arts and humanities, Kniep (1986) has offered a broader organization of global education content, into four major domains: human values and cultures, global systems (economic, ecological, and technological), global issues and problems, and global history. These domains are an attempt to systematize global education and move it out of the realm of a fuzzy, unclear, sometimes contradictory and often unconnected collection of facts, goals, objectives, concepts, and special-interest groups pleading for a particular area, topic, or global issue. Despite progress, still better approaches are needed, particularly those related to the nonsocial studies part of the multidisciplinary content of global education.

Skills

As the content of global education differs from traditional content of citizenship education, so does the application of skills. For the term *skill*, global educators have had at least three overlapping meanings: basic skills, critical thinking skills, and participatory or policy-making skills.

Some attention has been given to basic skills (Lamy, 1987), which include reading, writing, and computation. The rationale for addressing these skills in global education programs is both pedagogical and pragmatic. From a pedagogical standpoint, skills should not be taught in isolation from content. Students have to read about something and compute about something. Skills are interrelated and grounded in thinking. If the content is significant, research shows that skill development is greatly improved (Branson, 1978). With this in mind, curriculum units have been developed that combine global education substance with instruction in reading, writing, and computing.

From a pragmatic standpoint, much of the time that students spend in elementary school is focused directly upon reading, writing, and computation. By focusing upon skills that elementary school teachers are required to teach, global educators have a better chance of getting their objectives incorporated into the school curriculum.

Global educators have expanded the three-item list of basic skills to include listening, speaking and discussion, computer literacy, television viewing, observation, bargaining or conflict resolution, and problem solving or decision making, as well as library or research skills (Anderson, 1987; Lamy, 1987). Few of these new skills have been clearly defined, nor have their applications differed greatly from other approaches that have used them.

The traditional conceptualization of citizenship education has been extended to include the development of skills in making decisions and participating in public affairs (Butts, 1988). The thinking skills identified in the global education literature are judgment making, analysis, evaluation, comparison, inquiry, creative thinking, consequential thinking, and cost/benefit analysis (Anderson, 1987; Becker, 1979; Gillespie & Patrick, 1975; Kerr, 1987; Lamy, 1987). The Study Commission on Global Education (Kerr, 1987) noted policy-making skills as particularly important for global education. According to the report, students need to be actively involved in considering issues that cut across disciplinary boundaries, in order to attain a larger view of problems and their alternative solutions. Issues seldom fall neatly into traditional school subjects, but instead involve aspects of a variety of subjects and require integrating ideas and methods from a variety of disciplines.

The skills of analytical thinking are taught with the aim of encouraging people to understand themselves and their world. These skills are essential if citizens are to be effective actors in the local, national, and global context. These are the tools that enable them to unravel the complexities and find the connections.

Values and Attitudes

Perhaps the most difficult issues faced by global educators have been related to values and attitudes. The global education field is broadly based and includes individuals of different political and ideological perspectives. While these difficult issues are not unique to the field of global education, problems related to values and attitudes surface periodically.

Many global educators state that their major goal is not to teach specific content about the world but to teach values and attitudes that will help students with future problems. Unfortunately, throughout the global education literature, there has been almost no attempt to define either *attitude* or *value*. There are but few attempts to link global education with the growing academic literature on values and attitudes, or with the affective domain. Like the term *skill*, these terms have been used loosely and inconsistently, even by the same author, and often overlap with *skill*. For example, the following terms and phrases, generally considered attitudes, have been offered as global skills (both negative and positive): egocentric perception; ethnocentric perception; stereotypic perception; empathy; and constructive attitudes toward diversity, change, ambiguity, and conflict (B. Winston & C. Anderson, cited in Bragaw, Loew, & Wooster, 1983, pp. 4–5).

Many topics related to global education are inherently controversial; as such, global educators have the responsibility to present balanced views on controversial issues. The role of global education is not to propagandize students, but to help prepare them to make decisions on those issues that they will likely confront during their lifetimes.

IMPLEMENTATION ISSUES

Global educators have approached implementation issues pragmatically: Whatever works with a particular teacher, school, or school district has been encouraged. Some global educators have created a required course; others have established social studies elective courses. Most schools, however, do not have the capability to create a new global education course within an already overcrowded social studies curriculum. Even if it were possible, a single course would be unlikely to accomplish the goals and objectives inherent within global education. Many have attempted to resolve this problem by maintaining that global education should be infused into all courses in the curriculum, and not just a few social studies courses.

Conceptually, many global issues are related to topics normally covered in nonsocial studies courses. For instance, the science curriculum includes issues related to the environment, ecology, nuclear physics, and migratory pollution (Staley, 1987). Foreign language courses discuss at least the specific culture and history of the language area; oftentimes the study of a language helps students understand culture and communication (Bragaw et al., 1983; Conner, 1981; Geno, 1981). Mathematics problems could easily include statistical problems related to population growth rates, currency exchange rates, or other global content (Schwartz, 1989). Cultural understanding can be achieved through the study of the literature, music, and art forms of other peoples.

Because of its multidisciplinary nature, serious problems in vocabulary, definition, and conceptualization of global education have emerged. As those from still other disciplines begin to make their contributions, we can expect additional models.

Further, most observers agree that educational systems vary greatly regarding their capability to prepare students for national citizenship in a global age. Most teachers have had little preparation in non–Western history or geography, and even fewer have had any academic preparation on the range of global issues now pressing for inclusion into the curriculum. Several surveys over the years have maintained that textbooks are factually inaccurate, full of stereotypes, and conceptually unsophisticated. Those opposed to the inclusion of this international dimension are genuinely concerned with the ability of educators to teach effectively and accurately about these complex and difficult topics. As the schools are confronting so many other crises, it seems unlikely to some that they could effectively add another dimension. Besides, the expense of developing such programs would be exorbitant.

Those in favor of including an international dimension within the schools maintain that the nation's well-being may rest upon the success of this effort. For instance, the 1989 National Governors' Association report argues that, without an adequate preparation of citizens in foreign languages, world history, and world geography, states will be unable to remain economically competitive. Therefore, they maintain, it is worth the cost of retraining teachers and preparing better texts and supplementary materials.

CONCLUSIONS AND RECOMMENDATIONS

Unlike traditional citizenship education programs, the emerging field of global education has been fraught with controversy. These tensions have been based upon divergent views about the world and about the role of education. As there are many different views about the world, so have there been different views of what American citizens need to know to function effectively in a global age. Likewise, there are many different views as to the purposes of public education, its current capabilities, and what its priorities should be. Each of these perspectives has influenced the content, skills, values, and attitudes inherent within citizenship education programs. This analysis suggests several recommendations for overcoming the disarray confronting the international component of citizenship education.

1. *Global educators need to work more closely with others concerned with citizenship education.*

With perhaps the important exception of issues related to substance or content, many issues faced by global educators confront other approaches to citizenship education. The lack of communication and cooperation among professionals concerned with citizenship education is a major stumbling block to future progress. The artificial boundary between global education and citizenship education was created by differences in academic preparation, professional associations, and funding sources. Many global educators have a background (or at least a strong interest) in international studies; other citizenship educators have background in law, American government, and American history. Citizenship educators belong to different professional associations, and this can make communication difficult. Having different funding sources for global education and other citizenship education programs has also often put them at odds with each other. It is now time to overcome these differences among those interested in citizenship education.

2. *Global education needs to explore further its multidisciplinary and interdisciplinary aspects.*

Social studies has been the traditional common home for global and citizenship education. Global education has now outgrown the social studies curriculum, so it is important to continue the exploration into other areas. It is also important to begin to create interdisciplinary programs among traditionally isolated courses of study and to examine their implications for citizenship education. Can citizenship education become a fundamental part of the foreign language, mathematics, or science classroom?

3. *Agreement needs to be reached on the content of the international dimension of citizenship education.*

Global educators cannot continue to assume that all the content that global educators promote can or should be a part of citizenship education. It is incumbent upon global educators to help determine what is important for all students to be able to do, and what values should be promoted. Citizenship educators have a responsibility to answer the following types of questions: What are the priorities? What should be known and understood by all students? What should be known by students who will continue their studies in college and graduate school? With the limited time available in the curriculum, what should be emphasized? Failure to address these issues will only continue to lead to additional confusion.

4. *Immediate attention should be given to articulating skills and values for citizenship education.*

Citizenship educators need to tie their efforts more closely with other efforts concerned with skills and values. In addition, skills and values need to be tied more closely to curriculum content. A much clearer definition of values and improved approaches to controversial issues are crucial priorities for future work.

5. *It is essential that we develop a systematic approach to citizenship education that includes a global perspective.*

Citizenship educators cannot continue to change the social studies or other parts of the curriculum on a piecemeal basis. The curriculum revision must be developed comprehensively. As there is no national authority requiring a particular curriculum, it is necessary for the professionals in citizenship education to make an attempt at a systematic K–12 curriculum.

REFERENCES

Alliance for Education in Global and International Studies. (n.d.). *Goals and values.* Mimeographed paper. New York: Author.

The American Forum for Global Education. (1989a). *Global, international and foreign language education: 1988–89 state profiles.* New York: Author.

The American Forum for Global Education. (1989b). *The new global yellow pages* (3rd ed.). New York: Author.

The American Forum for Global Education. (1990). *The new global resource book* (2nd ed.). New York: Author.

Anderson, L. (1979). *Schooling and citizenship in a global age: An exploration of the meaning and significance of global education.* Bloomington, IN: Social Studies Development Center.

Anderson, L. (1987). Education with a global perspective: Avenues for change. In W. Kniep (Ed.), *Next steps in global education: A handbook for curriculum development* (pp. 137–146). New York: Global Perspectives in Education.

Becker, J. (Ed.). (1979). *Schooling for a global age.* New York: McGraw-Hill.

Bragaw, D., Loew, H., & Wooster, J. (Eds.). (1983). Moving toward a global perspective: Social studies and second languages [Special issue]. *Intercom, 104.*

Branson, M. (1978). *Infusing law-related and humanities content and skills into the elementary language arts curriculum.* Paper presented to a symposium of the American Bar Association.

Butts, R. (1988). *The morality of democratic citizenship: Goals for civic education in the republic's third century.* Calabasas, CA: Center for Civic Education.

Coalition for the Advancement of Foreign Languages and International Studies. (1989). *International competence: A key to America's future.* Washington, DC: Author.

Conner, M. (1981). *A global approach to foreign language education.* Skokie, IL: National Textbook Co.

Cunningham, G. L. (n.d.). *Blowing the whistle on "global education."* Mimeographed paper. Denver, CO: U.S. Department of Education Region VIII.

Finn, C. E., & Bauer, G. (1986, May). Globaloney. In *American Spectator.*

Geno, T. H. (Ed.) (1981). *Foreign language and international studies: Toward cooperation and integration.* Middlebury, VT: Northeast Conference on the Teaching of Foreign Languages.

Gillespie, J., & Patrick, J. (1975). *Comparing political experiences.* Washington, DC: American Political Science Association.

Hanvey, R. (1976). *An attainable global perspective.* Occasional Paper. New York: Global Perspectives in Education.

Kerr, C. (1987). *The United States prepares for its future: Global perspectives in education.* Report of the Study Commission on Global Education. New York: Global Perspectives in Education.

King, D. C., Branson, M. S., & Condon, L. E. (1976). Education for a world in change: A working handbook for global perspectives [Special issue]. *Intercom, 84*(5).

Kniep, W. (1985). *A critical review of the short history of global education: Preparing for new opportunities.* Occasional Paper. New York: Global Perspectives in Education.

Kniep, W. (1986). Defining a global education by its content. *Social Education, 50,* 437–446.

Kniep, W. (Ed.). (1987). *Next steps in global education.* New York: Global Perspectives in Education.

Lamy, S. (1987). Basic skills for a world in transition. In W. Kniep (Ed.), *Next steps in global education: A handbook for curriculum development* (pp. 133–135). New York: Global Perspectives in Education.

London, H. (1984). *Why are they lying to our children?* New York: Stein & Day.

Lonzetta, M. (1988). International high schools. *ACCESS, 77-78,* 5–10.

Meadows, D. (1972). *The limits of growth.* New York: Universe Book.

National Governers' Association. (1989). *America in transition—The international frontier: A report of the task force on international education.* Washington, DC: Author.

Newitt, J. (1983). *The treatment of limits-to-growth issues in U.S. high school textbooks.* Indianapolis, IN: Hudson Institute.

Ravitch, D. (1989). *International studies in the California framework.* Paper prepared for the U.S. Department of Education; published in an abbreviated form in *ACCESS, 86–87*, 2–7.

Remy, R. (n.d.). *Handbook of basic citizenship competencies.* Alexandria, VA: Association for Supervision and Curriculum Development.

Rentel, K., & Errante, A. (Eds.). (1989). *The global classroom: An annotated bibliography for elementary and secondary teachers.* Vol. 2. Minneapolis, MN: University of Minnesota.

Schlafly, P. (1986). What is wrong with global education? *St. Louis Globe Democrat*, March 6.

Schwartz, R. (1989). *Mathematics and global survival.* Needham, MA: Ginn Press.

Simon, J., & Kahn, H. (Eds.). (1984). *The resourceful earth, a response to Global 2000.* New York: Basil Blackwell.

Smith, A. (1989). *Pre-collegiate global and international education: A brief history.* Paper prepared for the U.S. Department of Education; published in an abbreviated form in *ACCESS, 86–87*, 8–15.

Social Studies School Service. (1990). *Global education catalog.* Culver City, CA: Author.

Staley, F. (1987). Reforming the Science Curriculum with a Global Perspective. In W. Kniep (Ed.), *Next steps in global education* (pp. 159–171). New York: Global Perspectives in Education.

Wronski, S. (1987). Global education: In bounds or out? *Social Education, 51*, 242–249.

About the Editors
and the Contributors

Ronald A. Banaszak is Vice President, Educational Programs, for the Foundation for Teaching Economics. Previously Dr. Banaszak was a junior and senior high school teacher in Chicago, and Assistant Professor at the University of the Pacific. He is a frequent presenter at national educational conferences and the author of articles and books, including *Teaching Economics: Content and Strategies*. He has also authored the scripts for nine videos and written numerous economics lessons and units. Recently he has been working on a new approach to civics education that will include an integrated study of the political, legal, economic and social systems.

Allan Brandhorst is Associate Professor of Education at the University of North Carolina–Chapel Hill, where he teaches social studies methods courses and doctoral seminars on research in curriculum and instruction. Previously he was on the faculty of the University of South Carolina–Columbia. Dr. Brandhorst received his M.Ed. and Ph.D. degrees from the University of Missouri–Columbia. He has broad experience in cross-cultural education, having taught geography in Ethiopian secondary schools, and government courses on the secondary school level in the former Trust Territory of the Pacific Islands. His research interests center on the application of social psychology to the problems of citizenship education.

John H. Chilcott was educated at Harvard University, University of Colorado, and University of Oregon. He has been a secondary school teacher, principal, and a college administrator. He was the founding editor of the *Anthropology and Education Quarterly*, a former associate editor of the *American Education Research Journal*, and is co-editor of *Readings in the Socio-Cultural Foundations of Education*. He also has directed several National Science Foundation Summer Institutes in Anthropology for teachers. Currently, he is Professor of Anthropology

Emeritus, University of Arizona, and an Associate at Associates in Anthropology, a private consulting firm.

Thomas L. Dynneson (Editor) is Professor of Education at The University of Texas of the Permian Basin, located in Odessa, Texas. He has written in the areas of anthropology education, social studies curriculum, and citizenship education. Dr. Dynneson is currently serving as chief researcher and Director of The Citizenship Education Development Study Project, along with Professor Gross and Professor James A. Nickel. This project has published several research reports through The Center for Educational Research at Stanford (CERAS), and is currently working toward the publication of additional studies on the status of citizenship education in American schools and society. Dr. Dynneson holds a Ph.D. degree from the University of Colorado. He has been a visiting scholar in the School of Education at Stanford University.

Richard E. Gross (Editor) is Professor of Education at Stanford University and is a past president of the National Council for the Social Studies. He has written and edited numerous books and articles in the fields of citizenship education, history didactics, teacher education, social studies curriculum and instruction, and on American government, United States and world history. He has taught at the secondary and university levels in Wisconsin, Florida, and California. He has served as an educational consultant in many states, as well as overseas; has been a guest professor in Wales, Germany, and Australia; and has lectured in several other countries. In addition to the Citizenship Education Development Study Project, his current research includes an analysis of the treatment of the United States in Chinese textbooks. He received his Master's degree from the University of Wisconsin and his doctorate from Stanford University.

Raymond R. Grosshans is Assistant Professor of Industrial Technologies at the Rochester Institute of Technologies, National Technical Institute for the Deaf. He is a doctoral student at the Graduate School of Education and Human Development, at the University of Rochester, New York. His research focus is the social and historical analysis of apprenticeship.

H. Michael Hartoonian is Supervisor of Social Studies Education for the State of Wisconsin, Department of Public Instruction, and Adjunct Professor, Department of Curriculum and Instruction, University of Wisconsin–Madison. His chapter is based upon a paper prepared for delivery at the October 6, 1988 conference, "Citizenship for the 21st

Century: A National Conference on the Future of Civic Education," Washington, D.C. The author wishes to thank Ronald A. Banaszak, William T. Callahan, Jr., James S. Leming, Fred M. Newmann, John R. Palmer, James Shaver, and the Foundation for Teaching Economics for reactions to this manuscript and support in its development.

Nicholas Helburn was educated at the University of Chicago, Montana State University, and the University of Wisconsin. He has been a Professor of Geography at Montana State and the University of Colorado. At Montana State, he worked with both preservice and in-service teachers, with special emphasis on conservation. At the University of Colorado, he served as the first director of the ERIC Clearinghouse for Social Science/Social Studies Education. He also directed the High School Geography Project, financed by the National Science Foundation, from 1964 to 1970. Currently, he is Professor Emeritus at the University of Colorado and remains active in curriculum development and teacher training.

Kerry J. Kennedy is an Australian educator who completed his doctoral work at Stanford University. He has a special interest in history education with an emphasis on students' understanding of historical concepts. He has researched and written broadly in the area of general curriculum issues, and most recently has focused attention on policy studies in relation to the curriculum. He has held appointments at a number of Australian institutions of higher education and was Assistant Director of the Australian government's Curriculum Development Centre. He has served as Assistant Secretary, International Participation Branch, in the Department of Employment, Education and Training, in Canberra. Currently, Dr. Kennedy is Professor of Education at the University College of Southern Queensland, Toowoomba, Australia.

Byoung-Uk Kim is Assistant Professor of Education in the School of Education at Chonnam National University, Kwangju, Korea. He is a doctoral student at the Graduate School of Education and Human Development at the University of Rochester, New York. His research interests are curriculum and the sociology of education.

Andrew F. Smith is currently President of The American Forum for Global Education, a non-profit educational organization dedicated to helping American youth prepare for American citizenship in a global age. Prior to this, he was a classroom teacher and administrator in San Bernardino, California; Supervisor of Teacher Education, University of California–Riverside; Executive Director of the California Council for

Social Studies; and Director of the Center for Teaching International Relations, at the University of Denver. He has written numerous articles on global and international education for educational and professional journals. Dr. Smith serves on several Boards of Directors of educational organizations, including the Alliance for Education in Global and International Studies, the International Exchange Association, the International Development Conference, and as the secretary of the North American Division for the International Network on Global Education. He has delivered over 1,000 papers and presentations at state and national conferences, and has consulted with more than 100 school districts, colleges and universities.

Philip Wexler is Dean of the Graduate School of Education and Human Development, and Professor of Education and Sociology, at the University of Rochester, New York. His books include *The Sociology of Education: Beyond Equality, Critical Social Psychology,* and *Social Analysis of Education: After the New Sociology.* He is the current editor of the journal, *Sociology of Education.*

Robert B. Woyach is a member of the Senior Faculty of The Ohio State University's Mershon Center. He also holds an appointment as Adjunct Assistant Professor in the Department of Political Science at Ohio State. Since 1982 Dr. Woyach has directed several curriculum and staff development projects aimed at infusing international dimensions into the social studies curricula of elementary and secondary schools. He has written and edited eight volumes of curriculum materials, including a five-volume series entitled *Bringing a Global Perspective to Basic Social Studies Courses.* His most recent publications include *National Security and World History* and *Approaches to World Studies: A Handbook for Curriculum Planners.* Dr. Woyach's current efforts center on his interest in civic leadership. He is working on a book entitled *Preparing for Leadership: A Young Adult's Guide to Leadership Skills in a Global Age.* He received a Ph.D. in Political Science from The Ohio State University in 1981. He also holds a Master's degree in International Relations from Yale University.

Qiao Hong Zhang is a graduate of the Nan Chang Teachers College of Jiang Xi Province, People's Republic of China. She is a doctoral student at the Graduate School of Education and Human Development at the University of Rochester, New York. Her research focuses on education and the professions.

Index